FINDING YOUR
MEXICAN
ANCESTORS

Other titles in the Finding Your Ancestors series:

Finding Your Irish Ancestors
Your Swedish Roots
Finding Your African American Ancestors
Finding Your German Ancestors

FINDING YOUR
MEXICAN
ANCESTORS

A BEGINNER'S GUIDE

GEORGE R. RYSKAMP, J.D., AG
PEGGY H. RYSKAMP

ancestry publishing

Library of Congress Cataloging-in-Publication Data

Ryskamp, George R.
 Finding your Mexican ancestors : a beginner's guide / George Ryskamp,
Peggy Ryskamp.
 p. cm.
Includes bibliographical references and indexes.
ISBN 1-59331-307-1 (alk. paper)
1. Mexico—Genealogy—Handbooks, manuals, etc. 2. Mexican Americans—
Genealogy—Handbooks, manuals, etc. I. Ryskamp, Peggy. II. Title.

CS102.R97 2006
929'.10720896872073—dc22

2006035483

Published by
Ancestry Publishing, a division of The Generations Network, Inc.
360 West 4800 North
Provo, Utah 84604
www.ancestry.com

First Printing 2007
10 9 8 7 6 5 4 3 2 1

ISBN-13: 978-1-59331-307-4
ISBN-10: 1-59331-307-1

Printed in the United States of America

TABLE OF CONTENTS

INTRODUCTION

The study of family history and genealogy is nothing more than a study of people—unique individuals, each with distinctive looks, personalities, and circumstances, who shared their lives with other equally unique members in a family unit. This book deals exclusively with how to do genealogy and family history for Mexican American families. Through reading these pages and following the guidelines provided therein, you can become the historian of your own family, tracing the individuals within it as completely and accurately as possible. You will learn what records exist for your Mexican American heritage, and how they can be located and used to trace your family lines and rich, distinctive history. You will find records that give not only names and important dates and places, but an understanding of the time and events that shaped the lives of your ancestors.

Today nearly 20 million people in the United States trace their roots to Mexico.[1] Their ancestors came here in one of four different migration periods. The first large wave of Mexican immigrants came during the Spanish colonial period, which began with the Conquest of the Aztecs in 1519 and ended in 1821. By 1821 the total number of Mexicans living in what is now the United States numbered approximately forty thousand. During the Mexican national period, ending in Texas in 1836 and in Arizona, New Mexico, and California in 1848, that number doubled so that by 1848, when the Mexican War ended, there were eighty thousand Mexican immigrants living within the current U.S. borders.

The second large migration period covered the last half of the nineteenth century and ended in 1910 with the beginning of the Mexican Revolution. During this period, migration was more gradual and families often crossed the border and returned several times. Between 1850 and 1880 about 55,000 Mexicans came to the United States to work mainly in agriculture and mining, while from 1880 to 1890, jobs were more likely in light industry and the railroad. By the time of the 1910 U.S. Federal Census, the Mexican population in this country was estimated at 367,000.

A third migratory period occurred as a result of the difficult conditions during and following the Mexican Revolution. Nearly 1 million Mexicans poured across the border into the United States in search of security and economic stability, bringing the total Mexican population in the United States, according to the 1930 U.S. census, to 1,422,000. The window of this migratory period lasted until the beginning of the Great Depression in 1930. During the time from 1910 to 1930, approximately 8 percent of all Mexicans crossed the border into the United States, while another 10 percent died from the war and its impacts. The population in Mexico dropped from 15.2 million in 1910 to 14.3 million in 1921, in spite of a continuously high birthrate.[2]

Since the end of World War II, particularly as economic conditions in the United States grew stronger while those in Mexico generally did not, significant numbers of Mexican nationals have continued to cross over and settle not only in the states bordering Mexico, but in nearly every state in the Union. Many of these individuals still speak Spanish and know about relatives living in their ancestral hometowns in Mexico. The number of Mexican nationals estimated in the United States in the year 2000 was about 7.8 million people, and its numbers are swelling literally every day.

The search for Mexican ancestors—no matter who they were or when they came to the United States—will involve many common components, such as the use of Catholic Church records. Other record sources, however, will be of primary value to those whose ancestors came at a certain time period. For example, border crossing records are most helpful to those with ancestors who immigrated between 1906 and 1929. Those with ancestry in the United States during the Spanish colonial period or in the early 1900s will do research in United States records that in many ways will resemble that of any Anglo-American doing genealogical research, although their chances of success will be greatly improved by the quality of Catholic Church records and other Spanish-language materials. Ultimately, however, descendants of all these groups will find themselves working in the excellent records of Mexico. As you continue to read this book, watch for records that relate to your specific ancestors and when they arrived in the United States.

The single most important message for the Mexican American researcher is that possibilities for success are excellent. To help you find that success, this book will concentrate on two central themes: connecting with Mexico, or finding the ancestral hometown of your immigrant ancestor(s); and learning about, finding, and using the many excellent records available for Mexican research, whether across the border or in the United States.

In the 12 March 2005 issue of the MyFamily Weekly *newsletter, Belinda Rose (Torres) Corre wrote, "This is a photo of my grandparents and their twelve children! It was taken in 1925. My dad, Guadalupe O. Torres, is the youngest of the twelve kids and is standing in front of his dad, Adrian Torres."*

At any level of genealogy and family history research, remembering some basic guidelines will prove helpful. One of these is to always *work from the known to the unknown*. In other words, begin your research using facts you already know, like the birth date (or closely approximated birth date) and birth place of a grandmother. Look for the actual documentation of that birth in either civil registration or parish records (as will be explained in detail later in the book). That birth record will give you the names of your grandmother's parents and possibly even her grandparents, moving your family lines back in time.

Another guideline is to *work in complete families*. Some beginning researchers may decide to concentrate on learning about a certain family member, wanting only to

This Brownsville, Texas, border crossing manifest has a subsequent note concerning the death of the immigrant.

find information pertaining to that one person. But many times the clues that will most efficiently move research along will be found in the records of sibling births or marriages. As you work with entire family lines you will ultimately find information on that one person you are perhaps most interested in, but in the process you have a much better picture of the family as a whole, and the places and circumstances of their lives.

In learning about your Mexican American family, remember to look beyond simply names, places, and events. Look for clues about, and document, the full story of your ancestors. One long-time researcher of Mexican American descent realized, as the story of her family's settling in the United States emerged, that for years she had heard others tell or remember these events as the story of victims: victims of exploitation and of discrimination, by both Anglo-Americans and Mexicans. Now, after her years of researching her Mexican American family history and working with many others doing the same, she sees things differently. The story that *does* come forward to her is that of exuberant, colorful, and dynamic people raising good families who have been successful in life, claiming a place in their society while at the same time transmitting to their descendants a rich Mexican American culture.

Some beginning Mexican American researchers—hearing others talk about "instant family history" success stories on the Internet and expecting the same—may find their first research experiences disappointing. In the vast Internet databases so many people rely on today you won't find many Mexican names, especially for those born after 1900. Why? Simply stated, because not many Mexicans in the past have searched out their family lines. This will change as more Mexican American researchers like you become involved in family history and contribute their findings. Any initial disappointment you might feel in an Internet search should disappear as you explore original records and discover the hundreds of thousands of rolls of microfilms available from Mexico.

In a sense, the growing number of Mexican Americans becoming involved in family history are pioneers in their own right, crossing boundaries of time to uncover the past. As you become more deeply involved in the excitement of discovering your ancestry, take advantage of the many opportunities that will come your way to share what you know with other Mexican Americans doing the same. Exchanging ideas and information, and networking with the growing number of Mexican Americans and other Hispanics doing genealogy, will not only aid you in your research, but will bring lasting friendships within that large and dynamic community. In addition, you will be able to share your findings with the many thousands of genealogists of other ethnic backgrounds searching their family histories. The common bond of tracing family lines transcends ethnic or cultural differences, and you will find the experiences you share amazingly similar, even if the record sources are different.

Success awaits you! The pages of chapter 1, "Getting Started: Home, Family, and Internet Searches," will guide you in the first steps of the adventure of finding your ancestors. Later chapters will give you detailed steps and background information to guide you even farther and to enrich the paths you follow.

NOTES

1. See <www.census.gov/main/www/cen2000.html>.
2. Campbell, Gibson and Kay Jung, "Historical Census Statistics on Population Totals By Race, 1790 to 1990, and By Hispanic Origin, 1970 to 1990, For The United States, Regions, Divisions, and States" (September 2002), U.S. Census Bureau <www.census.gov/population/www/documentation/twps0056.html>.

GETTING STARTED
HOME, FAMILY, AND INTERNET SEARCHES

While at first the idea of researching your family lines may seem overwhelming, the best thing to do is simply *start*. And the best place to start is at home—your own home as well as the homes of your parents, siblings, aunts and uncles, and other family members. Although it may seem more exciting to go straight to researching in outside sources, you will ultimately save yourself time if you first learn all that is already known about your family. (This is sometimes called a "preliminary survey.") Do this with two goals in mind—to learn as much as possible about your family, and to determine your immigrant ancestor's birth place and approximate date of birth in Mexico.

THE HOME SEARCH

Some beginning researchers have found it helpful to take a box and set it in a place in the house where they will see it often, such as the kitchen. With this as a reminder, they then begin filling it with photographs and documents and other important family papers, like those listed in the "Things to Look for in a Home Search" sidebar later in this chapter (see also figure 1-1). Some of the possibilities that will give you information about your family are discussed below.

Vital Records

A vital record is a government or church document recording a major event such as a birth or baptism, marriage, or death. While usually made at the time of the event, they may also be copies made several years later. Since vital records are frequently used as a source of proof (for example, school districts require a birth certificate to prove a child's age when entering a school system), most family members should

---

WHERE TO BEGIN

- Look in your home, and the homes of other family members, for important family papers.
- Talk to other family members.
- Search the Internet
- Check for other printed sources, such as biographies.

Figure 1-1: The first step to take in your research is to gather the documents, items, and photos you already have. This photo shows the family of Alberto and Petra Chapa. Photo courtesy of Mimi Lozano.

have little trouble finding these, at least for more current generations. Vital records from any country are extremely valuable documents as they give the exact date and location of the event and names of the parties involved. Check the place name carefully. Unlike some other forms of documentation that may only give the country or state of the event ("Mexico" or "Sonora"), a vital record, especially from Mexico, may list the actual town of residence. (See figure 1-2.)

Old Photographs

Nothing else conveys the immediate, concrete impression of a person like a photograph. Pictures of deceased family members from several generations past are especially compelling, and their details—the clothes, hair styles, men's facial hair (or the lack of it), stance, and surrounding objects—give us a glimpse into the lives of the people they've captured.

The photograph itself may reveal valuable information. Check for a studio name and/or location on the edge of the picture, as well as any dates, descriptions, or names on the back. These details could prove extremely helpful in pinpointing specific times and places (and are a reminder of the importance of labeling and dating our own family photos).

Immigration and Naturalization Papers

The legal process of crossing a border from one country to another and becoming a citizen of that new country produces paperwork. While more about immigration and naturalization records will be discussed in chapter 8, "Searching for Your Mexican Surnames," common documents from the immigration process include passports or visas, applications for citizenship, and certificates of naturalization, any or all of which could turn up in a home search (see figure 1-3).

A "green card," or migrant work permit, is another document to watch for. The process of issuing "green cards" began in the 1940s when Mexican nationals living in the United States needed to have a residence permit. The cards can give important personal information as well as details about the person's entry into the United States. For many years, migrant workers coming into the southwestern United States needed to obtain a work permit at the border before they could be hired.

EL SEÑOR PRESBITERO DON J. DEL REFUGIO QUEVEDO,

CURA AUXILIAR DE LA PARROQUIA DE SAN JOSE DE CALVI

LLO, AGS.,

C E R T I F I C A :

QUE EN EL LIBRO NUMERO TREINTA Y UNO DE BAUTIS-

MOS DE HIJOS LEGITIMOS QUE OBRA EN ESTE ARCHIVO PA- -

RROQUIAL, A LA FOJA NUMERO CIENTO NOVENTA Y NUEVE, --

frente, Y MARCADA CON EL NUMERO MIL CIENTO DIECIOCHO

SE ENCUENTRA UNA PARTIDA QUE DICE LITERALMENTE:

"En la Parroquia de Calvillo, á veintinueve de
julio de mil ochocientos noventa y cuatro: Yo el --
Presbítero Pedro Rivera de licentia parrochi, bauticé
solemnemente y puse los santos óleos y sagrado crisma
á un niño nacido en Tepezalilla el día dieciocho a --
las diez de la mañana á quien puse por nombre J. JESUS,
hijo legítimo de Secundino López y Eugenia Serna, abue
los paternos Toribio y Francisca Velasco, abuelos maternos Antonio y Telésfora de Loera, padrinos Gerardo
Ruiz y Ma. Jesús López, á quines advertí su obliga- --
ción y parentesco espiritual. Y para constancia lo fir
mé con el Señor Cura.- Firmados: Dr. Manuel Muñoz.- Pe
dro Rivera.- Rúbricas.-Al márgen: 1118.- Tepezalilla.-
J. Jesús.- P. R.".- - - - - - - - - - - - - - - - -

PARA LOS FINES QUE PUEDAN CONVENIR AL INTERESADO

SE EXTIENDE EL PRESENTE.

PARROQUIA DE SAN JOSE DE CALVILLO, DIOCESIS DE A-

GUASCALIENTES, A SIETE DE MARZO DE MIL NOVECIENTOS +)-

TREINTA Y NUEVE.

Figure 1-2: Vital records, like this baptismal certificate from the parish of San Jose de Calvillo, can help you find where your anceestors lived, and can often be found in your home or in the home of a relative.

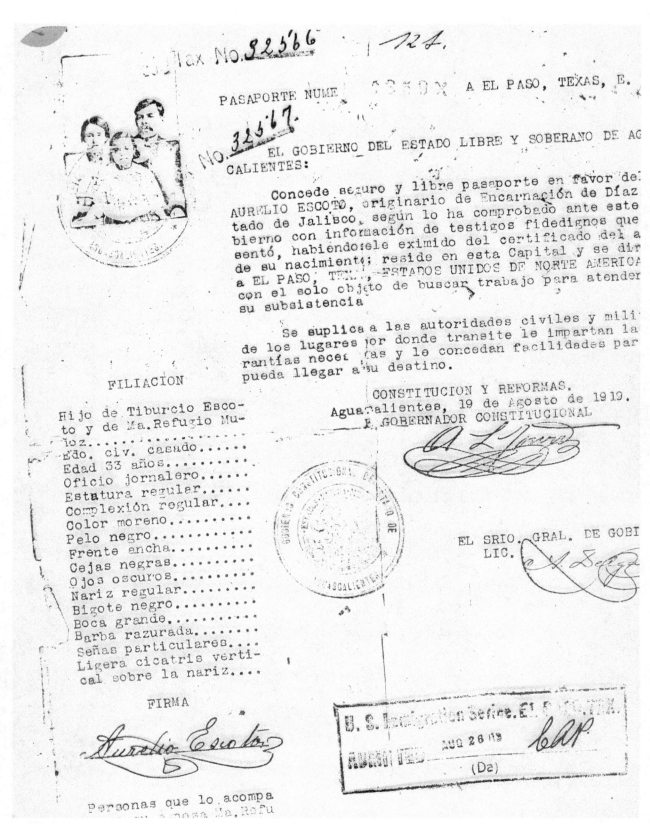

Figure 1-3: A passport like this is another example of a record you might find in a home search.

Invitations or Announcements

Invitations and announcements aren't generally thought of as genealogical documents, but like vital records they give the date of the event and names of the parties involved. Along with the common wedding and birth announcements, many Mexican Catholics share the tradition of sending formal printed invitations to both baptisms and first communions. A *quinceñera* may also be a time for sending printed invitations. Although today we commonly think of only joyful occasions in connection with announcements, in the past—especially before the common use of the telephone—announcements were sometimes used to inform family members of a death. You can often recognize these by the black border on the envelope (see figure 1-4). Memorial cards about the deceased may have also been distributed at funerals.

Old Letters

In a generation increasingly dependent on electronic communication and the telephone, it's easy to forget the importance letters once played as the only means of sharing information and feelings. While not everybody who lived in the past had the education or natural inclination to easily write letters, it would still be a good idea to check your own home and question other family members to see if any exist. Even a few short lines written by a long-deceased family member could be a treasure for your family. As you read these letters, look particularly for place names, even those connected to people who may not be related. These could prove helpful in finding where the family came from in Mexico.

Legal Documents

If family members owned land, made a will, or died while their children were young, documents from the legal processes related to these should exist (see figure 1-5). The monetary value of these transactions doesn't matter—the purchase or sale of even the smallest of houses or properties should have produced legal documents. Since these papers showed a right of ownership to property, or contract rights, they usually would have been carefully preserved by some family member.

Military Records

Did your ancestor live during the time period in which a war was fought? He may have preserved a record of his service that will tell when, where, and under whom he served.

Figure 1-4: Memorial cards were distributed at funerals, and also mailed to relatives far away.

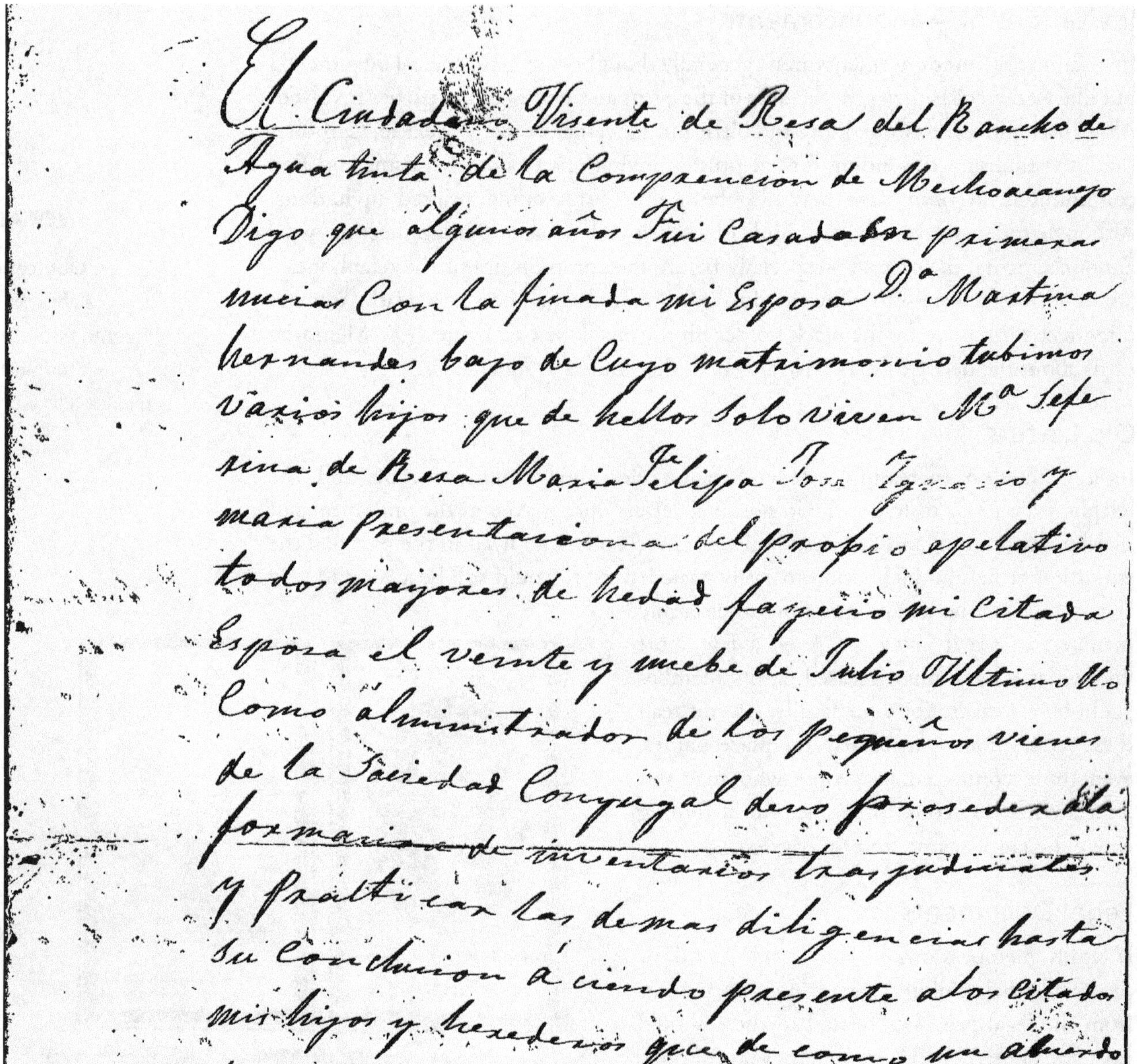
El Ciudadano Visente de Resa del Rancho de
Agua tinta de la Comprencion de Mechoacanejo
Digo que algunos años Fui Casado por primeras
nucias Con la finada mi Esposa Dª Martina
hernandes bajo de Cuyo matrimonio tubimos
varios hijos que de hellos solo viven Mª Sefe
rina de Resa Maria Felipa Jose Ygnacio y
maria Presentacion a del propio apelativo
todos mayores de hedad fallecio mi Citada
Esposa el veinte y nuebe de Julio Ultimo y
Como alministrador de los pequeños vienes
de la Sociedad Conyugal devo prosedera la
formacion de inventarios traxjudiciales
y practicar las demas diligencias hasta
su Conclusion a ciendo presente a los Citados
mis hijos y herederos que de comun acuerdo
devemos nombrar peritos abaluadores para
la particion de los pequeños bienes como lo
ago por el mismo interes que tengo y nombro
para avaluadores a los Ciudadanos Doma
cio Chaires y Praxedis hermanos, y para testi
gos los P.

Figure 1-5: This guardianship paper is an example of a legal document. Such documents often provide more information about children, property, and other aspects of your ancestor's life that were governed by the law.

Newspaper Clippings

We typically think of newspaper clippings as relating only to people with social status or wealth, but even if your ancestors lived relatively simple lives, their names may have been recorded in the newspaper, especially in small towns. For example, many towns would record the names of all the graduating students each year, or participants in a school, social, or civic event. Obituaries are an excellent source of information because they summarize the life of the deceased, nearly always giving the date of birth and family information (and occasionally the birth place).

Even if a search of your family's homes reveals nothing, consider reading through old hometown newspapers on microfilm. (These may be obtained through interlibrary loan by checking with your local library.) Whether or not you find an actual entry for a family member, you will come away with a better understanding of the place and time period in which your ancestor lived.

School and Occupation Records

Did your ancestor work on the railroads or in a factory? Did he go to school in Mexico or the United States? Work records, identification cards, report cards, or other types of records could help identify where and when your ancestor participated in these activities. They might also lead to other record sources you could search.

TALK TO FAMILY MEMBERS

The important family papers you have gathered will undoubtedly start filling your thoughts with ideas for further research. Perhaps going through this chapter has made you aware of records you could order, such as copies of birth or marriage records, or a certificate of naturalization. Another natural response is an eagerness to see what documents, photographs, or information other family members might have.

Talking with family members, especially those who are older, is an invaluable way to learn more about your family. Many times the simple act of showing an interest in another person's past can trigger their memories, and help them remember details they had previously forgotten, or thought were unimportant.

While a lot can be learned through casual conversation, it's wise to realize it will undoubtedly take more than spontaneous visits with family members to recreate your family's history or answer all your questions. Take time to think through the things you would like to know. Your ideas might range from specific questions about family relationships to details such as a certain person's looks, or what type of clothing he or she wore and how it was made and cared for, or the food people cooked and how it was preserved. All of these questions will give you a feeling for life in a certain time period, and the daily lives of your ancestors.

Have some way to record what is being said as you talk with family members. Advances in technology have given us amazing new possibilities for recording and preserving the past, with options that didn't exist only a few years ago. Perhaps, if the idea of this makes you uncomfortable, a younger family member could help you.

Remember, however, that even if you are talking into an "old fashioned" tape recorder or simply jotting down notes of what was said, you will be able to remember and preserve the conversation better if you have some type of record of it.

Every person's perspective of a time period or a certain event will be unique, based on their experience. If possible, get observations from several family members about the same event, whether it be a wedding, a sudden death, or a war. Talking to more than one person will give you a better perception of what actually took place, and its impact. Be aware as you talk that while you have the perspective time has brought, these topics may be highly emotional and perhaps controversial for the subject of your interview. Be careful how you phrase your questions, and sensitive to the other person's feelings.

It's a wise idea to keep these conversations from growing too long. Several short, enjoyable experiences together will leave you both looking forward to the next time.

INTERNET SEARCHES

The process of learning more about your family through home sources and talking with family members can continue for a lifetime. However, as you learn more you will undoubtedly sense a natural desire to find out what others beyond your family might know. Again, technology is influencing genealogy, and we see the Internet becoming an increasingly important means of finding and sharing information. Because of its constantly-changing nature, this book makes no attempt to describe each genealogical database for Mexican American researchers on the Internet. Instead, a broad overview of some of the major genealogical databases is discussed from a Hispanic researcher's viewpoint. (See appendix F. "Internet Sites for Mexican Genealogy," for a listing of more specific Mexican American Internet sites.)

FamilySearch.org

The database FamilySearch.org contains literally millions of names from Mexico, a result of work done by members of The Church of Jesus Christ of Latter-day Saints in extracting data from microfilms of Mexican Catholic parish records. These names can be found primarily in two collections, the International Genealogical Index (IGI) and the Mexican Vital Records Collection. Most of these names date from before about 1885, stemming from the one hundred year privacy rules observed by those doing the extracting in the 1980s.

After entering the website address <www.familysearch.org>, click the "Search" tab, and then the "Search For Your Ancestors" option. Go to the list of options on the left and select "All Resources," then type the name you wish to search for and the date range, if you know one (be generous with this). You will then see a list of potential matches drawn from each database. Those from the IGI will be arranged alphabetically by Mexican states.

Although there are some Mexican names in the other databases called Ancestral File and Pedigree Resource File they are considerably fewer, since these are collections of work submitted by those doing their own research. In the future, as more Mexican Americans become involved in doing their family history and submit the work they have done, these databases will grow larger and become more helpful to other researchers of Mexican ancestry.

Ancestry.com

Ancestry.com contains the largest collection of genealogical data in the world, though little of it currently comes from Mexico (for example, the list of country possibilities does not include Mexico and you will need to type in the field "All Countries" instead). That situation is changing, however, and in 2007, Ancestry.com has plans to release a site devoted to Hispanic research. Ancestry.com is a subscription site.

Other Genealogy Websites

Ancestry.com, while the largest basic genealogy website, is not the only one. Don't forget others such as HeritageQuest Online <www.heritagequestonline.com> and Genealogy.com, both of which also have a digitalized version of the United States Census, newspaper collections, and other materials. Like Ancestry.com, these are subscription sites. Rootsweb and the worldwide Genweb projects provide a myriad of local genealogical materials, accessed at <www.rootsweb.com>. As a suggestion, look under the county name of the state in which you are searching. Information about Mexico can be found on the Mexico Genweb page found at <www.rootsweb. com~mexwgw/>.

Mexican American Websites

A growing number of websites have been created specifically to help Mexican American and other Hispanic researchers. While they vary in content and emphasis, their main focus is to help other researchers by sharing information and ideas and by creating large databases. Lists of these sites can be found at Cyndi's List <www.cyndislist. com/hispanic.htm>. Another method is to go to Google <www.google.com> and clicking "more" on the task bar. Then go to "Directory," and click successively the words "Society," "Genealogy," "By Region," "North America," and finally "Mexico." For a list of sites dedicated to Mexican genealogy, see appendix F. "Internet Sites for Mexican Genealogy."

WHAT NEXT?

In a sense, the concept of a home search is never finished. As you continue to gather information, however, you will reach a point when it's time to consult outside sources. Select one immigrant from among your ancestors and ask yourself if you know the following:

- What is the *nombre* and *apellido* of this person?
- Approximately when was he/she born?
- Where in Mexico was he/she born?

VOCABULARY

Nombre—name.

Apellido—surname.

If you know this information, go now to chapter 2, "Finding and Working with Mexican Records," and learn how to find Mexican records. (You may later want to come back and explore this person's immigration experience.)

If you do not yet know the answers to these questions, go to chapter 9 to learn about searching for Mexican Americans in United States records.

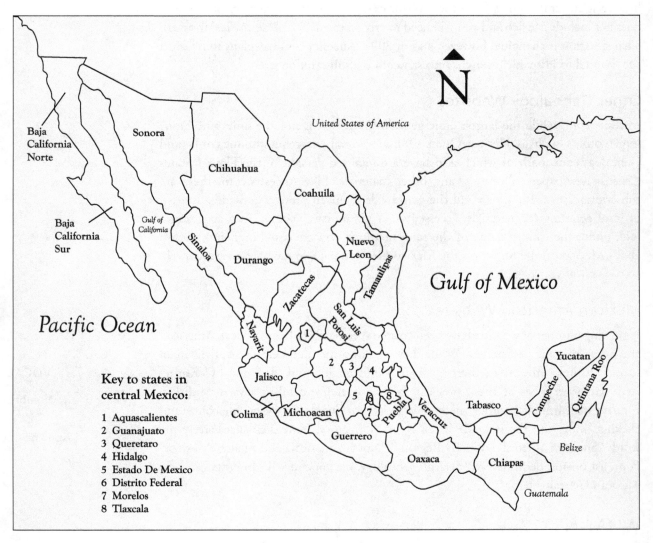

The current states of Mexico.

2

FINDING AND WORKING WITH MEXICAN RECORDS

To use this chapter, begin by helping you find the following information about your immigrant ancestor:

- Name and surname(s) of ancestor*
- His/her parents
- Approximate date of birth and/or marriage*
- Date of border crossing
- Spouse's name
- Specific place of birth or marriage in Mexico*
- Other information

If you know those items marked with an asterisk you are ready to look for Mexican records. (If not, go to chapter 9, "Searching for Your Ancestors in United States Records.") Because they are generally of such excellent quality and detail, the first records you want to search will be government civil registration records or Catholic parish registers.

THE FAMILY HISTORY LIBRARY CATALOG

Although it may seem surprising, the best place to find microfilmed copies of either Mexican Catholic parish or civil registration records is a local Family History Center, operated by the LDS Church (The Church of Jesus Christ of Latter-day Saints, Mormon). These Family History Centers operate under the supervision of the Family History Library (FHL) in Salt Lake City, which has in its storage vault more than two and a half million rolls of microfilmed records. If you are not yet familiar with the Family History Center in your area, look in your phone book under The Church of

Jesus Christ of Latter-day Saints to find the phone number and location of the one closest to you, or check at FamilySearch.org.

A volunteer consultant at the Family History Center will be happy to help you by answering any questions you might have. Don't worry about your lack of experience in doing genealogy, and don't let concerns about religion make you hesitant about asking for help. The consultants offer their time and expertise free of charge, with their only goal to help you succeed in tracing your family lines. Family History Centers are used equally by members of the LDS Church and those who are not members, all sharing the common excitement of discovering more about their families.

Either before going to the Family History Center, or once there with the help of the consultant, you will first want to do an Internet search of FamilySearch.org. Once at the home page, click the "Library" tab and then the link to the "Family History Library Catalog." At this point several different search possibilities will come up. Click on the first one of these, "Place Search."

You will now see two fields, "Place" and "Part of." In the first field, type the place name, or the location in which your ancestor was either born or married. Note that this is not the name of the state in Mexico, such as Jalisco, but the town name, such as Guadalajara or Lagos de San Juan (see figure 2-1). In the second field, "Part of," type in either the state name or Mexico.

The screen that follows is called "Place Search Results." Click on the link to your area of interest. This will bring you to the "Place Details" page (see figure 2-2). Under the heading "Topics," you will generally get at least two possibilities: "Church

Figure 2-1: When doing a Place Search, type the name of the place in Mexico in which you want to search.

Records" and "Civil Registration." For the moment, even if other options are given, you will want to concentrate only on these two record types.

If both civil registration and parish records exist for your area, you may be uncertain which record type to research first. Both are generally considered excellent for their quality and quantity of detail when compared with similar record types for the same time period in the rest of the world. Civil registration will include microfilmed government vital records of birth, marriages, and deaths, and church records will include microfilmed parish records of baptisms, marriages, and deaths.

Mexican civil registration began in 1860 with a law passed under President Benito Juarez, and continues forward in time. Because these records are mandated by national law, the information they provide tends to be fairly uniform, although the date the records actually start will vary from one locality to another. Many times the volumes will be indexed.

The information in church records, on the other hand, can vary from one parish to another, depending on the time period and the priest. Many Mexican parish records continue back to the 1600s. Beginning researchers frequently find it best to work first in civil registration records, appreciating their consistency and organization. Then, when these records are no longer available before 1860, they turn to parish records.

As you look at the screen in the Family History Library Catalog, click on the record source you wish—either civil registers or parish records—and a description of all the available records of that type will be listed, with corresponding microfilm

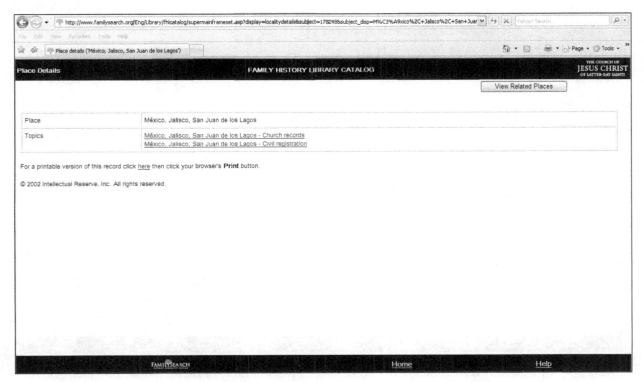

Figure 2-2: Once you find your place of interest, you will be given a choice of record types.

VOCABULARY

Rancho—Ranch, often large enough to form a separate community with its own name, and in some cases, its own chapel.

numbers (see figure 2-3). There may be duplication in years filmed. In some cases this is a second filming of the same records, but in many cases the filming is of a second set of records. Starting about 1875, Mexican law required that all civil registration records be hand copied each year. That copy was sent to state authorities. Often the description of the filming will say if it was done in the municipality or in the state archives. The second set of records may have entries that were lost from the first. You will be able to get a feeling for how large a geographical area is covered by looking at the years included in a microfilmed roll. For example, if a single year is covered by one microfilm, the municipality will undoubtedly be fairly large, perhaps covering a town and several small villages or *ranchos*. If the microfilm covers several years, for example marriages from 1807 to 1812, it's likely the locality is smaller, with fewer entries per year. The page listing these records will include a printing option, so you can print a copy to keep in your files.

Your next step will be to order the rolls of microfilm you desire. Again, the consultant can help with this process. For a small cost, these microfilms will be sent to your Family History Center where you can work with them.

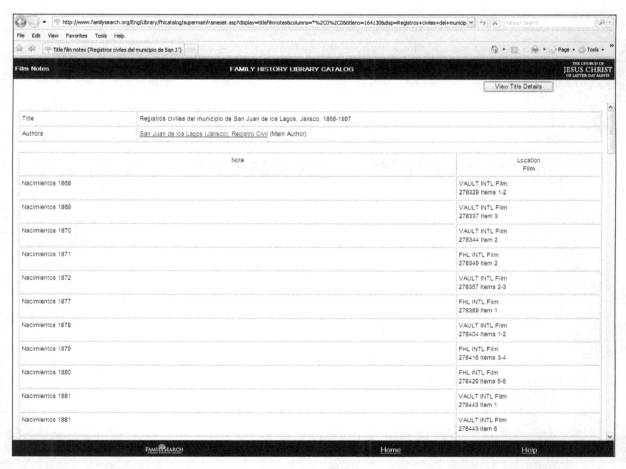

Figure 2-3: After selecting the record type you want, you can peruse a list of available records with their corresponding microfilm numbers.

In determining what record years to search, remember that the goal of research is always to go from the *known* to the *unknown*. For example, if you have found the date for your grandfather's birth on his naturalization record as 20 August 1880 and his birth place as Panuca, you would want to order the microfilm for that place and year in order to find the exact entry for this event. One word of caution is not to be dismayed if the actual date is in fact different from the one given in your source. For that reason, you may want to order films within a broad enough time period to allow you to search at least a couple of years before and after the one you have identified.

NO MATCHING PLACES FOUND

Some researchers might find that when they type in the place name of the locality in Mexico the results come back, "No matching places found." If this happens to you, don't be discouraged. Several things might have happened.

Make sure the spelling is accurate according to your source. Look up the locality on a map or atlas to be certain the name is correct. Sometimes place names have changed slightly with time (for example, "Michoacanejo" is later spelled "Mechoacanejo"). Remember that in some instances the clerk or other person filling out a document may not have been familiar with either Spanish or Mexican geography, and might have written the name incorrectly. Perhaps the handwriting on the document giving the place name is unclear. Most of these challenges can be solved by consulting a good map or atlas, especially if you have some idea of where the locality in Mexico should be found.

Perhaps the place name you have is neither a municipality (the likely location for civil registration) nor a parish, but a small area within them such as a *rancho*. These terms are explained more completely and a solution for this problem is discussed in chapter 5, "Finding the Place in Mexico."

A third possibility, although less likely in dealing with Mexico, is that neither civil registration nor parish registers exist for the locality of your ancestor because they were destroyed. If this is the case, chapters 6 and 7 in this book will give you further ideas of places to search.

With your microfilms ordered, there is still a lot you can do while you are waiting for them to arrive at the Family History Center. Read chapter 3, "Civil Registration Records," and chapter 4, "Parish Records," which will give you background about civil registers

A Catholic church in Lagos de San Juan.

and parish records and specific helps in working with them. Since many of the same suggestions will apply to either source, reading both chapters will prove helpful even if you plan to begin with only one record type.

WORKING WITH MEXICAN RECORDS

By this point you should feel understandably anxious to finally begin the process of researching in "real" Mexican records. The following ideas should help give you a feeling of confidence as you begin this new process.

The world of family history and genealogy is filled with people who remember that sense of nervous anticipation as they first approached research in original records,

---

LEARNING TO READ OLD HANDWRITING

Learning to read old handwriting in a foreign language can be frustrating to a beginning researcher. However, by learning a few guidelines and being persistent, you will soon find your abilities increasing. The following steps can be used as guidelines:

1. Study a new handwriting carefully.
Each person's writing is unique. By carefully studying a new document and those surrounding it, you can become familiar with the writing of the person creating those records.

2. Begin with those familiar portions of the record.
If you know the record was created in a certain locality, look first for that place name to see how the letters of those words are formed. Next look for the date, another familiar point. Start with the words that are easy to pick out.

3. Use the surrounding text as a guide.
Understanding the context of the document(s) you are working with will help in puzzling out unusual words or phrases. Many of the legal or ecclesiastical phrases will be repeated in other documents, giving you points of reference not only for help with handwriting, but also to alert you to places of genealogical importance.

4. Remember that there may be inconsistencies.
Most documents will be from a time period when punctuation and

spellings—even of surnames within a single document—were not always consistent.

5. Use an alphabet chart to compare any unknown letters.
Using an alphabet chart can help with any unknown letters.

6. Don't spend too much time on difficult letters or names.
If you cannot decipher a name or word after reasonable efforts, trace or copy it down. Write down your best guess or guesses as to what the word may be, and then go on. The word, especially if it is a name, will most likely appear again. When it does, it may be much clearer the second time or you may be better able to decipher it in the new context. If it does not appear a second time, then you can go back and look again at the word, having had more experience with less difficult words in that same individual's handwriting.

7. Be aware of unique challenges with handwriting.
Using the hints discussed above will help with any particularly difficult letters or words.

8. Be patient with yourself!

and who today find it irresistibly fascinating. Your enthusiasm and interest in learning more about your family is a far more important qualification than "expertise." That comes in doing it.

Research Strategies

A person doing document research—in any language—wants to *copy the information exactly as it is given*, and *preserve this information in a way that allows for easy retrieval and analysis.*

Your choice of method for getting an exact copy of the document information you are working with will probably vary, depending on the document type and archive in which you are working. Photocopies, digital copies, or simply copying the information down by hand exactly as it is given may each be options at differing times and in differing circumstances. The important thing to remember is to *always* make a true copy of the document, generally in the most efficient way possible. You will find yourself continually needing and wanting to refer to it in the research process.

You will quickly find yourself sensing the need to preserve your growing family information into some type of database that allows you to organize it, work with it in various formats—such as family groups, pedigree charts, name lists, and so on—and perhaps create smaller files for specific purposes such as sharing with others. Several excellent genealogy database programs have been created for this purpose.

An added challenge for those doing research in a foreign language is the problem of translation. Especially in cases where your only document record will be handwritten, you need to preserve a *true* document copy. Rather than translating as you read ("He left children Jose, Maria, Ysabel, and Juana."), copy the document exactly as it is written, including punctuation (or the lack of it), putting quotation marks to let you know your wording is exact ("Dejó hijos José María Ysabel y Juana"). Notice, for example in the previous example, that from the punctuation in the English translation, it would seem there were four children. The nonpunctuated sentence as written in the original Spanish, however, leaves several possibilities: a male child named José María followed by females Ysabel and Juana; a male named José followed by a female named Maria Ysabel and a female named Juana; or four separate children. Any of the options could be possible. Leaving the punctuation and wording exactly as the original allows you to make accurate deductions as your research progresses.

No document record is complete without source notes. These should be so complete that you or any other researcher could go back later and find exactly the same document using your written source description. If you were to cite a microfilmed record you would first indicate the *record type* and *original volume number* (found at the front of each item or volume on the film). This is followed by the *microfilm roll number*, the *item number* (if pertinent), followed by the *page number* and, if given, *certificate number* (for example, "Michoacanejo civil register birth, volume 13, FHL 0215473, It. 3, p. 29, #120"). Any genealogical database you use will have a place for source notes. Learning to correctly note your sources can save you, and possibly others, much time and frustration later.

COMMON CHALLENGES WITH LANGUAGE AND HANDWRITING IN SPANISH RECORDS

A. Interchangeable Letters:

i-y: Words such as *ayer, ya, Isabel, habiía,* and *iglesia* may be written *aier, ia, Ysabel, habya, yglesya*. This can make initial recognition of the word difficult. As with many other challenges described below, by simply pronouncing the word it will become evident what the original says.

b-v: In Spanish the "b" and the "v" stand for the same phonetic sound. Even today, it is not at all uncommon to find words such as *había* and *venía* spelled *havía* and *benía*. The difficulty with the "b" and the "v" is further complicated because the written "v," which in Spain today is still called the "u-b," did not become clearly distinguishable from the "u," so that words which would normally have a "b" in them such as *había, habiendo,* and *abad*, could all be found as: *hauía, hauiendo,* and *auad*.

j-g-x: Examples of this may include *mujer/ mugger/ muxer* or *viaje/viagel/ viaxe* or even *Jiménez/ Giménez/ Ximénez*.

c, z, s, ss, ç, x: Keep in mind that where in modern Spanish words one might find a "c," "a," "z," or an "s," in early manuscripts one may find "c," "z," "s," "ss," "ç," or "x."

B. The Letter "h"

The letter "h" became silent relatively early in the development of the Spanish language and can present difficulties for the reader of manuscripts because it is often omitted or added arbitrarily, or substituted by a "g". Examples of this may include: *Enero/ Henero, Oyos/ Hoyos, oy/ hoy*, or something as simple as *Tomas/ Thomas* or *Toledo/ Tholedo, Catalina/ Chatalina*.

C. "Confusing" letters

Many letters may seem to look alike. The best way to discover which letter you are looking at is to sound the word out with various combinations of the letters to see if any make sense. Some letters that are easily confused or look similar include "f," "i," "j," "s" and "t;" "a," "o," "v," and "c;" or "r" and "x."

D. Double Letters

Be aware of the presence of double letters to avoid inadvertently converting one of the letters into another letter, especially where each of the letters in a double letter pair is written in a different style. Knowing that a double "s" is common, one reads *cossa*, not *cosia* or *cosja*. The "f," "t," "s," "m," "r," and "x" all frequently appear double.

E. Linking of letters

Perhaps one of the most difficult aspects of reading older Spanish manuscripts is the linking of the letters. Letters within a single word may or may not be linked together. Letters from the end of one word may also be linked with those at the beginning of the next. This can be particularly difficult when an abbreviation is involved. Reading the words out loud, and slightly run together, will frequently help suggest the correct alternative.

F. Flourishes

Writers frequently decorated their letters and words with flourishes. Such embellishments come most frequently at the end of the word, but can also come at the beginning, or on any letter in the middle. Generally a letter with a flourish will not be linked with the next. However, one must be careful, because occasionally a flourish that may appear to have no meaning can indicate an abbreviation or serve some other function.

G. Alternate spellings

Several different spellings of the same word may occur in a single document, and even in the same sentence. Also, because of the number of interchangeable letters and the variety of writing styles for the various letters, there may not be a regularity as to the use of a particular spelling.

H. Capitalization and Punctuation

There are no definite patterns for the use of upper case or capital letters: they can appear at the beginning, in the middle, or at the end of a word. Names can be found capitalized at one point in the document and not in another. If you are simply looking for a capital letter to find a name, you could easily miss it entirely.

One possible difficulty the researcher may encounter is that capital letters found in the middle of a word will frequently not be linked with the letter before it, thus appearing as the beginning of a new word. Once again, the best way to handle this situation is to read with care and pronounce the words out loud and slightly run together.

As with capitalization, there were not set rules for punctuation. Note that generally there will be no type of punctuation where today one finds a hyphen when a word is split at the end of a line and continues on to the next line. To understand such words, read the documents as if there were no lines.

I. Accent Marks

Probably the most significant point about the accent mark is its absence in the majority of cases in older Spanish manuscripts. Don't expect accent marks, and when they are found, be aware they may have a different form or be placed where they will not be found today.

J. Numbers

Be careful with the numerals 1, 3, 5, and 7, which are at times very similar in appearance and can be confused.

K. Abbreviations

The frequent use of abbreviations can pose a real challenge. Many words, especially names and places, will be abbreviated in the documents you read. They are generally consistent, however, and you will quickly learn to recognize them. See figure 2-4 for examples of abbreviations.

Keeping a good research log will help you to remember both the records you have already searched and the information (or lack thereof) that you found in those records. A sample research log appears in appendix C, "Research Forms," although you could make your own if you prefer. Tracking information such as the date of your search, record source looked at, research purpose, and findings can jog your memory at a later date.

You will find as you read civil registers and parish records that, although much of the information given is valuable in tracing your family lines, other parts are repetitive and have no genealogical value. Your goal as a researcher is to cull, or extract, the important genealogical facts from the document. Appendix C contains copies of extract forms designed specifically to use with Spanish language civil registration or parish records: one for baptisms or births, another for marriages, and a third for deaths. These can be photocopied and used for your personal research if you wish. (You may still want to make document copies as well, particularly if they are for direct line families.) As will be shown in working with civil registration records and parish registers, these forms were designed to help researchers working with these record types move through them accurately, but efficiently.

As discussed previously, the purpose of the extract is to copy information *exactly* as it appears in the original—to know unquestionably what the record says, with wording and abbreviations unchanged. For example, in the example given in figure 2-4, the mother's name would be recorded in the extract form as Dª Mª del Refugio Ontiveros, rather than writing it out as Maria. Later, in putting the information into a computer database, that conclusion is made. Adopting this practice early in your research eliminates potential future confusion. One family found, in returning to their original extract, they had mistakenly interpreted the surname abbreviation Gᶻ to mean Gonzalez rather than Gomez. Copying the record exactly as they had found it allowed them to later go back and make this determination.

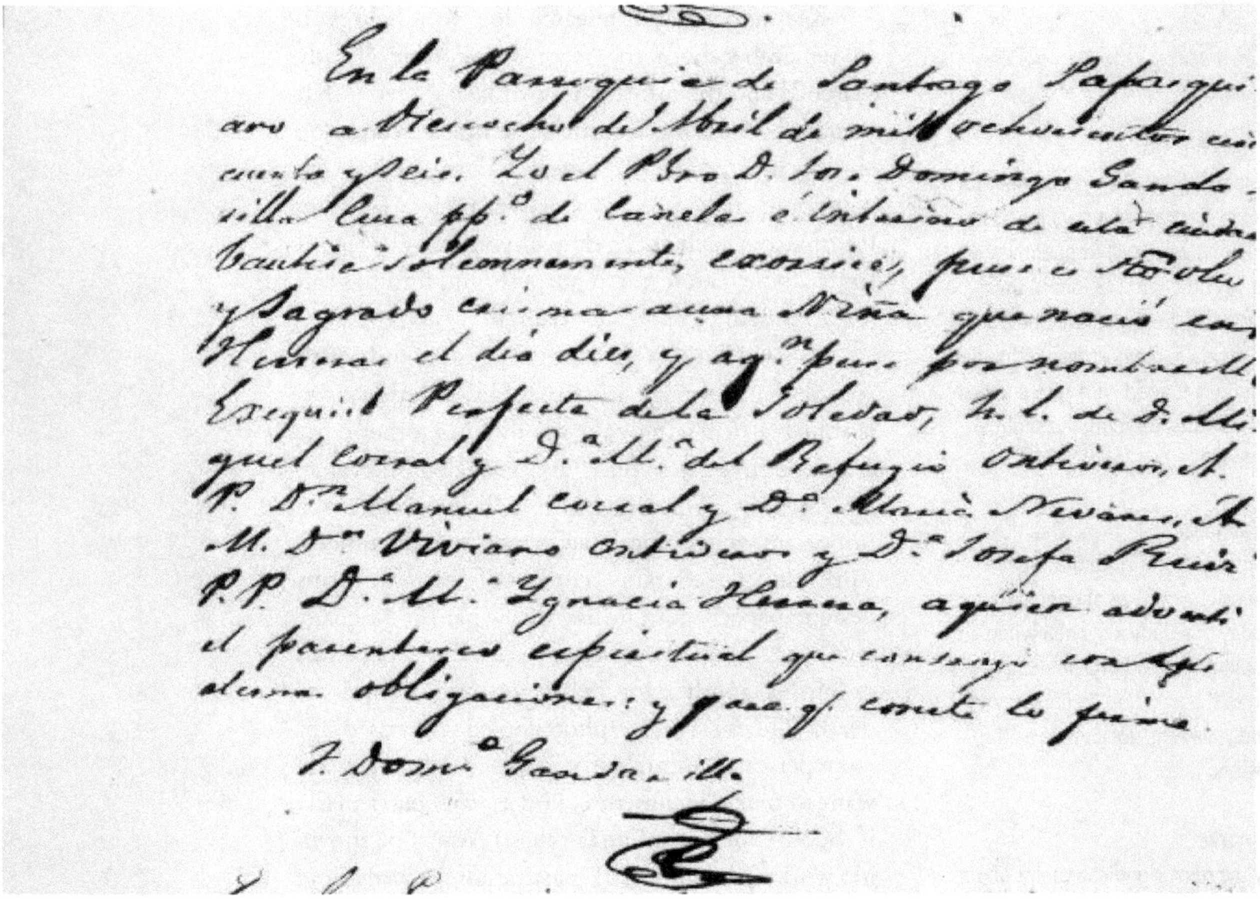

En la Parroquia de Santiago Papasqui-
aro a diez y ocho de Abril de mil ochocientos cincuenta y seis. Yo el Pbro D. Jose Domingo Gandarilla Cura pp.° de Canelas é Interino de esta Cabecera
bautizé solemnemente, exorcicé, puse el Sto Oleo
y Sagrado Crisma a una Niña que nació en
Herreras el dia diez, y a q.n puse por nombre M.a
Exequiel Perfecta de la Soledad, h. l. de D. Miguel Corral y D.a M.a del Refugio Ontiveros, A.
P. D.n Manuel Corral y D.a Maria Nevares, A.
M. D.n Viviano Ontiveros y D.a Josefa Ruiz
P.P. D.a M.a Ygnacia Herrera, a quien adverti
el parentesco espiritual que contrajo con la ahij.a
y demas obligaciones: y para q.e conste lo firme.
J. Domin.o Gandarilla

☒ P ☐ RC FECHA DE LA BUSCA ______ PERSONA QUE BUSCA ______

PARROQUIA Santiago Papasquiaro OBISPADO ______ PUEBLO Herreras Provincia/Estado ______

Fecha de Bautismo: 18 April 1856	Fecha de nacimiento: 10 —	Hora	Libro Folio Cart.: FHL 0658000, vol. 24, p.9
Primer Apellido y Segundo Apellido	~~Parentesco~~	~~¿Partida de defunción?~~	
Nombre de pila: M.a Exequiel Perfecta de la Soledad	M (F)	(Leg.) ileg.	Comentarios sobre el matrimonio de los padres
Padre: Miguel Corral	Natural de / Vecino de		Raza
Madre: D.a M.a del Refugio Ontiveros	Natural de / Vecino de		Raza
Abuelo paterno: D.n Manuel Corral	Natural de / Vecino de	¿difunto?	Raza
Abuela paterna: D.a Maria Nevares	Natural de / Vecino de	¿difunta?	Raza
Abuelo materno: D.n Viviano Ontiveros	Natural de / Vecino de	¿difunto?	Raza
Abuela materna: D.a Josefa Ruiz	Natural de / Vecino de	¿difunta?	Raza
Padrinos: D.a M.a Ygnacia Herrera			
Inscripciones marginales u otros comentarios:			

Figure 2-4: Be sure to extract information exactly as it reads on the document, as shown in the extract of this record.

READING SPANISH-LANGUAGE DOCUMENTS

The suggestions and guidelines in this chapter, as well as appendix A, "Glossary," which includes relationship terms, will help you gain a confidence in working with Spanish records. Remember, that while at first the concept of reading old handwriting in a foreign language may feel intimidating, Spanish is in fact an extremely consistent language in its pronunciation and has changed very little within the last centuries. It would be far more difficult to read an English language document written in the 1600s than to read a document from the same time period in Spanish. Most handwriting challenges can be solved by saying the words out loud. As your research continues you will find enthusiasm is a far more important requirement for successfully researching Mexican records than a vast knowledge of Spanish. With a minimum vocabulary and some patience, names can be found in original Spanish language records and you will be able to trace your family lines.

3

CIVIL REGISTRATION RECORDS

By now you will have gone through several phases of your research, first searching for and finding the place name of where your family lived in Mexico and then locating and visiting your local Family History Center to determine what records exist for that place. As discussed in the last chapter, the first record types you want to search will be civil registration and/or parish records, depending on what is available. If you have not already ordered the civil registration records for your ancestral hometown, return to chapter 2, "Finding and Working with Mexican Records," for help in doing so.

By this point you should feel understandably anxious to finally begin the process of researching in "real" Mexican records. Civil registration records are an excellent place to begin your research. Not only are they a valuable source of genealogical information, their consistent format allows even a beginning researcher with limited Spanish skills to be able to cull the facts they are seeking. Additionally, many of the volumes, especially for later years, will be indexed.

As mentioned in chapter 2, most Mexican civil registration began sometime in the 1860s, following a law passed during the administration of Mexican President Benito Juárez in 1859 (see the "Benito Juárez" sidebar later on the following page). A later requirement was added that copies of all civil registration records be sent to the state (see figure 3-1). You may find the microfilm you are reading is in fact one of these "copies," recognizable because all the handwriting on the page is the same. The entries often begin, "Marginal note reads . . ." or with a similar notation. Note that the marriage and death records shown in sidebars later in this chapter are handwritten copies of originals, and the birth record in the sidebar *is* the original. The actual date civil registration records begin, however, will vary from town to town and perhaps even from one record type to another within the same town.

BENITO JUÁREZ

Benito Juárez is considered
one of Mexico's greatest and
most beloved leaders. During
his political career he helped to
institute a series of liberal reforms that were embodied into
the new constitution of 1857.
That reform included the institution of civil registration in 1859.
During the French occupation
of Mexico, Juárez refused to
accept the rule of the Monarchy
or any other foreign nation,
and helped to establish Mexico
as a constitutional democracy.
He also promoted equal rights
for the Indian population, better access to health care and
education, lessened the political
and financial power of the Roman Catholic church, and cham-
pioned the raising of the living
standards for the rural poor.

Source: www.mexonline.com/
benitojuarez.htm

The civil register office, or *oficialía*, kept separate books for recording births, marriages, and deaths within the jurisdiction. As you begin working with these registers, you'll sense their value for giving a complete picture of individuals and families. Because the requirement of civil registration was national, the same facts are consistently reported in birth, marriage, and death entries, with less variation than can occur in parish registers where much of the record quality depended on the local priest serving at that time, or the rules of the local bishop.

You will find many of the same concepts and skills apply equally to reading civil registers as well as parish records. Read this chapter along with the one that follows on parish records. Carefully studying the document samples and translations should help answer any questions and bolster your confidence.

INDEXES

If the civil registration volume you are working with has an index, it will generally be found at the beginning of the book. Many times, especially in the case of birth registration, these indexes will be alphabetized by the child's *given* (first) name, rather than surname. For example, under the letter "M" you could find the names Manuela Gomez, Marcela Cruz, Miguel Jimenez, and so on, usually followed by a number (see figure 3-2). This number corresponds either to the item number or page on which the entry for this name will be found. You may even find the names indexed further by male and female.

While an index is always a welcome help, there are some things to be aware of, especially if you are looking for a specific person's given name. These issues can be resolved, however, by reading through the index completely.

Occasionally there will be cases where too many entries existed for a certain letter—for example, the letter "M"—and the "extra" names were indexed under another, less commonly used letter, such as "X." Another possibility, particularly if you are looking for a certain name, is that it has been spelled differently than you expected— "*I*sabel" rather than "*Y*sabel," or "*B*ibiano" rather than "*V*iviano," for example (see the "Common Challenges with Language and Handwriting in Spanish Records"

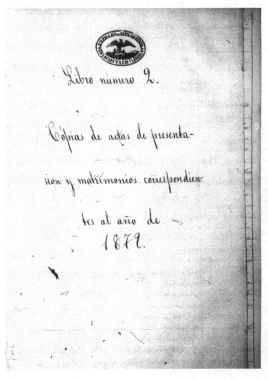

Figure 3-1: A cover like this indicates that the record is a copy.

sidebar in chapter 2). Reading through the entire index should help to solve this problem as well.

Especially in birth registers indexed by given name, researchers sometimes find that the person they are looking for is actually listed under another name. One person, looking for her grandfather named "Ignacio," felt disappointed when she couldn't find him listed on the page of names beginning with "I." She then searched on the page for names beginning with "Y," still with no success. As a final measure she searched the entire index, where she found him listed under the name "José." Reading the full entry, she learned her grandfather's given name at birth was José Ignacio, although she had only known him as Ignacio.

CIVIL REGISTRATION BIRTH RECORDS

The standard format for a birth registration begins with the date on which a person, usually the father, appeared (*compareció*) at the civil registry to announce the birth of a child. Generally this took place within days after the birth, although, especially in rural areas, this can vary. In some rare instances—generally in the more unpopulated, remote areas—the births of two or more children from the same family, covering a span of several years, are recorded on the same day.

VOCABULARY

Comparecer—to appear officially before someone, such as a judge, civil register secretary, or a notary.

Figure 3-2: Name indexes were often alphabetized by given names.

Nearly always the birth entry will then give the following information: the date and time of the child's birth, the child's name, the child's sex, his or her father's name, and his or her mother's name. In many cases the record will also give the father's profession, the father's age, the mother's age, and the location of their residence (usually the area of town). Other possible information, depending on the place and time period of the record, would be the grandparents' names, whether or not they are living, and their residence.

All civil registration records are witnessed by at least two people who, if they know how to write, sign their names at the end of the document. These witnesses generally have no relationship to the child.

Remember, although registering births was required by law, it was completed more effectively in some areas than in others. In some records you will find nearly all births reported no later than the following day. In smaller localities it may take several weeks or even months before births are recorded. Remembering this as a possibility, carefully check the sequential dates as you read. Even if you think you know the exact date of a birth, you may need to search the records of several months or even years to find it.

The sidebar "An Example of a Civil Birth Record" shows a civil registration birth record, found in the town of Tlaxcala, Tlaxcala, Mexico, accompanied by a transcription and translation. Note that an extract form for the record in this sidebar, as well as those for other similar sidebars found in this chapter and in chapter 4, "Parish Records," can be found in appendix C, "Research Forms."

THE CIVIL REGISTRATION MARRIAGE PROCESS

A couple's marriage record becomes a key piece of information in tracing that family. In Mexico, as in all Hispanic countries, the process of marriage was highly controlled by the Catholic Church—regardless of whether the ceremony took place in a local civil register office or a parish church. In both the civil register and the church, marriage was a process that ended with the ceremony and recording. First, the groom and bride gave their consent to the marriage and, if either party was under legal age (25 years), consent of his or her father was required as well. This was followed by a declaration that no impediments existed. (A further discussion of the marriage process is in chapter 4, "Parish Records." See the "Impediments to Marriage" sidebar in that chapter for a list of marriage impediments.)

Thinking of the marriage as a *process* rather than a single event will help in understanding the documentation involved. You may find times when a marriage civil register book will hold two types of documents mixed together: *informaciones matrimoniales*, which assure parental consent to the marriage and affirm that there are no impediments; and marriage records, a document of the marriage event itself. Knowing this is a possibility will eliminate confusion if the same couple appears in more than one entry. (Generally the *informacíon matrimonial* will precede the marriage entry by several weeks.) If the information in the marriage records you are looking at seems unusually sparse, check to see if a separate book of *informaciones matrimoniales*

VOCABULARY

Informacíon matrimonial—a bundle of papers or an entry in a parish book that originates from pre-marriage proceedings; for more information, see appendix A, "Glossary."

AN EXAMPLE OF A CIVIL BIRTH RECORD

Transcription

En el pueblo de Actopan, á las dos de la tarde del dia diez de Febrero de mil ochocientos se tenta y tres, fué presentada la niña Tomasa Candelaria del Carmen Dominguez, al 6° Juez auxiliary del registro civil, en cumplimiento de la ley: nacio en la congregacion de los Yiloles de este municipalidad, el dia veinticinco de Diciembre de mil ochocientos sesenta y tres: hija ligitima de José Dominguez y de Marcelina Grajales, difunta: abuelos paternos, Rafael Dominguez y Filomena Lagunes. Maternos, Antonio Grajales y Micaela Rosado: de cuyo presentacion fueron testigos Miguel Montiel y Pascual Barrados é el primero, de treinta y ocho años, casado, labrador, y vecino de este: el segundo, casado de treinta y cinco años, labrador, natural y vecino de este. Les da/Leida que les fué le presente acta y conformes con ella, la firmaron el declarante José Dominguez, y el testigo Miguel Montiel, no haciendolo Pascual Barraclos por no saber, haciendola para constan cia el referido Juez auxiliary de que doy fé.

José Dominguez
Jose Zalan
Miguel Montiel

Translation

In the town of Actopan, at two o'clock in the afternoon on the tenth of February of [the year] one thousand eight hundred seventy-three, there was presented a child [girl] Tomasa Candelaria del Carmen Dominguez, to the sixth auxiliary judge of the civil register, in fulfillment of the law: born in the congregation of los Yiloles of this municipality, on the twenty-fifth of December of one thousand eight hundred sixty-three [sic]: legitimate Child of José Dominguez y Marcelina Grajales, deceased: paternal grandparents, Rafael Dominguez and Filomena Lagunes. Maternal [grandparents], Antonio Grajales and Micaela Rosado: The witnesses of this presentation [are] Miguel Montiel and Pascual Barrados[,] the first, thirty-eight years, married, a laborer, and resident of this town: the second, married[,] thirty-five years, laborer, native and resident of this town. Having read this present act and in agreement with it, the declarant José Dominguez signed it, and the witness Miguel Montiel. Not knowing how [to sign his name], Pascual Barraclos did not. The referenced auxiliary judge signed it that it might be set forth, of which I give faith.

José Dominguez
Jose Zalan
Miguel Montiel

Note: The date of this civil registration of birth is 10 February 1873, while the date given for the birth itself is 25 December 1863, a ten year difference. Note too, that at the time it is reported, the mother is deceased.

Source: Actopan, Vera Cruz Civil Register, Nacimientos vol. 1873, #3. (FHL Microfilm 0782190, It. 2.)

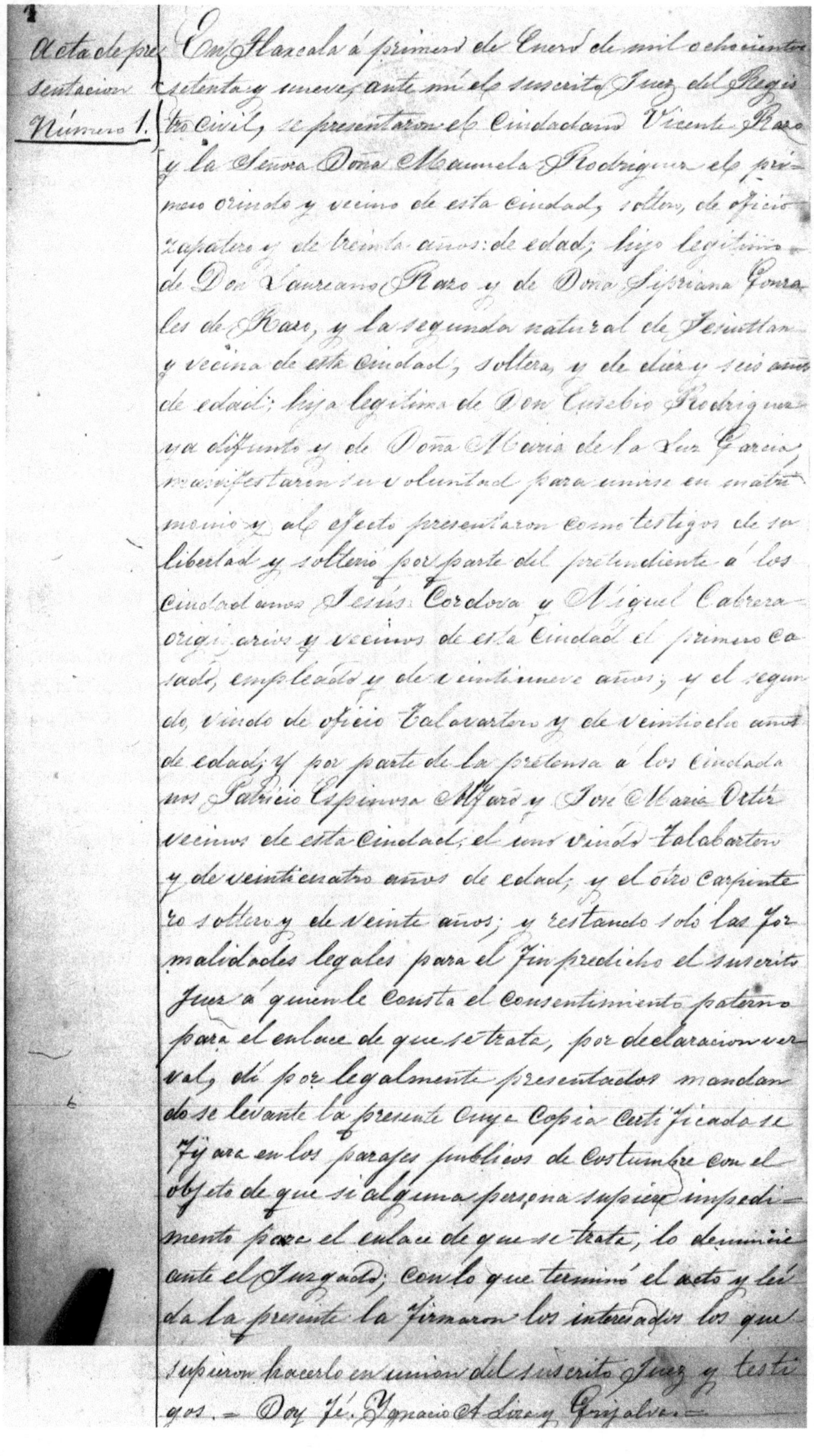

Acta de presentacion Número 1.

En Tlaxcala á primero de Enero de mil ochocientos setenta y nueve, ante mí el suscrito Juez del Registro Civil, se presentaron el Ciudadano Vicente Razo y la Señora Doña Manuela Rodriguez el primero oriundo y vecino de esta ciudad, soltero, de oficio zapatero y de treinta años de edad; hijo legitimo de Don Laureano Razo y de Doña Sipriana Gonzales de Razo, y la segunda natural de Ixcuitlan y vecina de esta Ciudad, soltera, y de diez y seis años de edad; hija legitima de Don Eusebio Rodriguez ya difunto y de Doña Maria de la Luz Garcia manifestaron su voluntad para unirse en matrimonio y al efecto presentaron como testigos de su libertad y soltería por parte del pretendiente á los Ciudadanos Jesús Cordova y Miguel Cabrera originarios y vecinos de esta Ciudad el primero casado, empleado y de veintinueve años; y el segundo, viudo de oficio Talabartero y de veintiocho años de edad; y por parte de la pretensa á los Ciudadanos Patricio Espinosa Alfaro y José María Ortiz vecinos de esta Ciudad; el uno viudo talabartero y de veinticuatro años de edad; y el otro carpintero soltero y de veinte años; y restando solo las formalidades legales para el fin predicho el suscrito Juez á quien le consta el consentimiento paterno para el enlace de que se trata, por declaracion verbal, dió por legalmente presentados mandando se levante la presente cuya copia certificada se fijara en los parajes publicos de costumbre con el objeto de que si alguna persona supiere impedimento para el enlace de que se trata, lo denuncie ante el Juzgado; con lo que terminó el acto y leída la presente la firmaron los interesados los que supieron hacerlo en union del suscrito Juez y testigos. — Doy fé. Ygnacio A. Diaz y Grijalva —

Figure 3-3: Note how much more information is in this informacíon matrimonial *than in the corresponding marriage entry in the sidebar on the opposite page. (Tlaxcala, Tlaxcala Civil Register, Matrimonios vol. 1873, p. 1, #2* Informacíon Matrimonial.*)*

AN EXAMPLE OF A CIVIL MARRIAGE RECORD

Transcription

En Tlaxcala, á diez y siete de Enero de mil ochocientos setenta y nueve, á las nueve de la mañana ante míel suscrito Juez del registro civil comparecieron los contrayentes C. Vicente Razo y doña Manuela Rodríguez con el objeto de celebrar el matrimonio que tienen concertado, en virtud de no haberse descubierto impedimento alguno, se procedió á el acta interrogándose á los contrayentas, si mutuamente se aceptaban el un por esposo y la otra por mujer á lo que contestaron que sé por lo que el suscrito Juez hizo que se dieran las manos, declarándolos en nombre de la sociedad quedar casados é imponíendoles el mismo Juez de los art.s del primero al cuarto y quince de la ley de veintitres de Julio de mil ochocientos cincuenta y nueve. Con lo que se dió por concluido el acto y firmaron los interesados, en union del suscrito Juez y testigos. Doyfé.=Ygnacio A. Lira y Grijalva = Vicente Razo.= José M. Ortiz.= Jesus Córdova. = Patricio Espinosa Alfaro. = Vicente Alarcon.

Translation

In Tlaxcala, on the seventeenth of January [of the year] one thousand eight hundred seventy and nine, at nine o'clock in the morning before me the undersigned judge of the civil register there appeared the contracting parties C[itizen] Vicente Razo and doña Manuela Rodriguez with the intent of celebrating their marriage, and by virtue [of the fact that] no impediment was found, I proceeded with the act[,] asking each of the contracting parties if they mutually accepted the other as husband and wife[.] And as they answered yes, the undersigned judge gave their hands [in matrimony], declaring them in the name of society to be married and the same judge placed upon them [the duties and privileges of] articles one to four[,] and fifteen from the law of the twenty-third of July of eighteen fifty-nine. With this he concluded the ceremony and those involved signed, along with the undersigned judge and witnesses. Of this I give faith. Ygnacio A. Lira y Grijalva = Vicente Razo.= José M. Ortiz.= Jesus Córdova. = Patricio Espinosa Alfaro. = Vicente Alarcon.

Source: Tlaxcala, Tlaxcala Civil Register, Matrimonios vol. 1873, p. 3, #2 matrimonio. (FHL Microfilm 0773818, lt. 2.)

exists in another location. Figure 3-3 is an *informacion matrimonial* taken from a register in Tlaxcala, Tlaxcala, Mexico. The sidebar "An Example of a Civil Marriage Record" is that couple's marriage record, with translation and transcription.

Unlike the civil registration of births, describing an event that has already happened, a civil registration record for a marriage is an account of an actual event taking place in the registrar's office. Between the *informacion matrimonial* and the marriage record itself, these records give at least the name of the groom and where he is from; his marriage status (single or widowed); the name of the bride and where she is from; her marriage status; and their parents' names. Additional information may include ages of the groom and bride; the groom's profession; names of former deceased spouses if applicable; and information about the parents, such as whether or not they were deceased, and their origin. As with so many records, the quality of marriage records is determined by the place and time in which they were kept, and who recorded them.

CIVIL REGISTRATION DEATH RECORDS

Some researchers question the need to search death records, feeling that birth and marriage records will bring quicker research results. For several reasons, however, death records should never be overlooked, as they do the following:

- *Close avenues of research.* Finding a person's death date in a civil register closes certain research options. Learning the death date of a small child, for instance, means that you will not find a marriage record; the death date of a spouse in a marriage of two adults in their childbearing years means that you will find no more possible children for them (although if the surviving spouse is the wife, there may be a child up to nine months beyond her husband's death date).
- *Verify what you already know, or have previously assumed.* As with obituaries today, many death records will give details of the person's life. Information such as the decedent's age, his or her parents' names, and the names of his or her spouse and surviving children can either confirm previous research or indicate gaps.
- *Give new information.* Death records are an excellent source for filling in previously unknown information. One family was surprised to find their ancestor not only had a deceased spouse they had not known about, but two sons from the marriage.
- *Trace back several generations.* The great variety in death record entries allows for many research possibilities. Finding the death record of an older adult can possibly move a pedigree back a generation or two, especially if parents' names are given.
- *Lead to other sources of information.* Knowing an adult's death date opens research options into other types of records, such as wills, death inventories, land sales, or guardianships of orphaned children.
- *Add human interest.* Occasionally a death record gives details that allow us a glimpse of our ancestors' lives at a particularly crucial time. One death record

AN EXAMPLE OF A CIVIL DEATH RECORD

Transcription

En Tlaxcala á treinta de Nobiembre de mil ochosientos sesenta y siete ante mí el Juez del Registro civil de esta Capital comparecio el Ciudadano Antonio Bautista natural y vesino del Pueblo de San Mateo Huesoyocan el que manifestó que hayer viernes á la media noche falleció en la Casa de su morada su padre Don Manuel de la Trinidad Bautista de idropecía de edad de sesenta y seys años que aquel fué viudo de María Ysabel madre del que habla. Presentes los testigos Ciudadano Manuel Soria y Marselino Sanches ambos del mismo Pueblo Casados de ejercicio leñeros y de teinta [sic] y dos años el primero y el segundo de veinte y nueve años de edad manifestaron previa la protesta de desir ser sierto lo espuesto por el esponente hijo de finado El suscrito Juez leyó la acta de la que quedaron conformes los interezados y no firmaron por no saber. Estendiendo la voleta para la hinhumacion en el Sementerio de su mismo Pueblo. José María Herrerias.

Translation

In Tlaxcala on the thirtieth of November of [the year] eighteen sixty-seven[,] before me the Judge of the civil register of this Capital there appeared the citizen Antonio Bautista[,] native and resident of the town of San Mateo Huesoyocan[,] who declared that yesterday Friday in the middle of the night his father Don Manuel de la Trinidad Bautista died in the home of his dwelling from dropsy[,] at the age of sixty-six years[.] He was the widow of Maria Ysabel[,] mother of the declarant. Present were the witnesses the citizen Manuel Soria and Marselinos Sanches both of the same town[,] married[,] their profession woodcutters[,] the first thirty-two years and the second twenty-nine years of age [who] manifested all was correct after hearing the declaration of the son of the decedent. The judge signing below read the act with which the parties were in agreement and did not sign as the know how, extending a ticket for burial in the cemetery of this town. Jose Maria Herrerias.

Source: Tlaxcala, Tlaxcala Civil Register, Fallecimientos 1867-1869, p. 10, #26. (FHL Microfilm 0773823, vol. 1867-1869, lt. 1.)

explains that the deceased was killed by Apaches. Another death record, listing a man's surviving children, added the comment that one son had gone to a foreign country and that nobody had heard from him since.

Because the information in a death entry varies far more than those from birth and marriage records, civil registration death records can differ dramatically in content and size. Generally a civil registration death record will give the following information: the name of the deceased, the date of his or her death, his or her age, the names of his or her parents (especially if the person is an unmarried child), the name of his or her spouse, his or her date of burial, the cause of death, his or her profession, and the names of any deceased spouses and surviving children. The sidebar "An Example of a Civil Death Record," is a copy of a death entry and its transcription and translation, also taken from the civil register in Tlaxcala, Tlaxcala, Mexico.

Working with civil registers is generally a satisfying, rewarding experience. You should find yourself developing both confidence in your research abilities, and a sense of your ancestors' lives as you find their names appearing in the records. You will likely have mixed feelings as you reach the period, probably sometime in the 1860s, when these records come to an end—disappointment at having reached the end of civil registration, but a sense of curiosity at what awaits as you turn now to parish records.

PARISH RECORDS

4

Researchers working in a predominantly Catholic country such as Mexico will find parish sacramental registers to be the backbone of their research. Unlike civil registers, which begin no earlier than 1860 in Mexico, some parish records go back as early as the 1500s. For example, records for the cathedral parish in Mexico City begin in 1536 and those for the cathedral parish in Puebla begin in 1545. These records of your ancestors' baptisms, marriages, and deaths bring with them a sense of intimacy, giving you a glimpse of their life at a pivotal point.

While researching "hands on" from an original parish book holds an unmistakable thrill, it also involves the cost and time of travel. Fortunately, the possibility of researching in Mexican parishes through the use of microfilmed records is readily available. Mexico is one of the best microfilmed countries in the world, with an astonishing 99 percent of pre-1900 parish records filmed.

As you read this chapter it is assumed you have already ordered microfilm copies of the parish records, as described in chapter 2, "Finding and Working with Mexican Records." Read this chapter as well as the preceding one as a unit, since much about the process of researching in either civil registers or parish records is the same.

READING PARISH RECORDS

The Council of Trent, a gathering of Catholic Bishops meeting in Italy in the 1560s, defined the concept of keeping parish records. Since then, each bishop has been responsible for maintaining good parish records in his diocese. As a researcher, this means you will find a similarity in format and information given in all parish records in a diocese, although there will be differences from one time period or location to another.

Within each parish, the priest recorded the sacraments of baptisms, confirmations, marriages, and burials in a leather-bound, thick-papered parish register, approximately the same size as a telephone book (for more information on sacraments, see the "Priests, Bishops, and the Sacraments" sidebar). Like phone books, these vary in thickness from less than one hundred pages to up to four hundred (see figure 4-1). Their state of preservation varies from excellent to rotting. Instead of the numbering system we are familiar with, pages are numbered on the front side of the page (*folio*) only, with the back carrying the same number followed by a "v" for the term *vuelto*, or verso (pages 1, 1v, 2, 2v, and so on).

At first glance, the prospect of reading parish records may seem daunting to a beginning researcher. The ink may be faded or blotched, and the writing filled with unfamiliar abbreviations. Don't despair—within a short period of time, reading parish records will become a familiar and satisfying experience. Along with the guidelines given in this book (see chapter 2, "Finding and Working with Mexican Records"), you may want to consult chapters 6 and 9 of the author's *Finding Your Hispanic Roots*. Another excellent source for learning to read parish records (which includes a series of workbook-style lessons) is *Spanish Records Extraction*, the manual originally written for those doing extraction work in Mexican records for the LDS Church. It is now out of print, but it is available online at the Center for Family History and Genealogy <http://familyhistory.byu.edu>. Knowing even a little about parish records and their format will help them seem less intimidating, and it won't be long before you find yourself thoroughly absorbed in the flow of their pages.

PARISH RECORD FORMAT

Using the format of the entry itself as a guide can prove reassuring and helpful in reading parish records. Nearly every entry begins with the date, written generally not in numbers but word by word, beginning with the day and followed by the month and year (see figure 4-2). The ordinance section of the sacramental information follows—words and phrases that remain fairly consistent from one entry to the next. (Use these repeated words to help you puzzle out any difficult handwriting in the remaining text.) You will quickly learn to find repeated phrases—*baptizé solemnemente á*, or *puse los santos oleos y crisma á* or similar wording for a baptism; *casé y velé en facie iglesia á*, or similar wording for a marriage entry. Following these, the entry wording will give the names of

VOCABULARY

Folio—a page of a book, notebook, or bundle (see "legajo" in appendix A, "Glossary."

Vuelto—verso, reverse side.

Figure 4-1: Parish books vary in size.

PRIESTS, BISHOPS, AND THE SACRAMENTS

In nearly all areas of Mexico, the initial activities of the Catholic Church were performed by missionaries sent and directed by the various religious orders: Franciscans, Augustinians, Dominicans, and Jesuits. As the population of Spaniards and latinized natives grew in a specific area the responsibility for the spiritual welfare of that population would pass to a bishop, appointed by the Pope from nominations submitted by the Spanish king. Juan de Zumárraga was appointed the first bishop of the newly created diocese of Mexico City in 1528. As the population expanded a second diocese was created in Michoacan ten years later and a new bishop was appointed. By the end of the colonial period (1821) ten dioceses existed in what is today the country of Mexico. By 1933, the number had expanded to thirty-three, all of which are still in existence.

As a means of supervision and in recognition of greater ecclesiastical and sometimes political importance, certain dioceses are designated archdioceses and are presided over by an archbishop. Initially all the dioceses of New Spain were under the supervision of the Archbishop of Seville in Spain. By 1548, Mexico City was made a separate archdiocese, the only one in Mexico during the colonial period. For information on the history of specific dioceses and archdioceses go to the online Catholic Encyclopedia at <http://newadvent.org/cathen/index.html>. Also see table 5-1 for a descriptive list of Mexican dioceses, their origins, and records.

Each diocese is divided into local congregations known as parishes. The bishop appoints ordained priests to serve as parish priests. More than one priest may serve in a parish, but only one, designated as the parish priest, has responsibility and authority over his parishioners and their ecclesiastical affairs. Although only the parish priest has authority to perform the sacraments of baptism and marriage within the geographical area of his parish, Mexican parish records clearly show instances that the parish priest could and did delegate that authority to others on an individual basis.

The Seven Sacraments of the Catholic Church

A sacrament is a "religious ceremony or rite. Most Christian churches reserve the term for those rites that Jesus himself instituted, but there are disagreements between them as to which rites those are. The Lutheran Church, for example, maintains that baptism and Communion are the only sacraments, whereas in the Roman Catholic Church and the Eastern Orthodox Church, there are five more:

confirmation; confession; anointing of the sick; the ordination of clergy; and the marriage of Christians."[1]

Since the middle ages it has been understood by Catholics that "[t]he first five sacraments are intended to secure the spiritual perfection of every man individually; the two last are ordained for the governance and increase of the Church. For through baptism we are born again of the spirit; through confirmation we grow in grace and are strengthened in the faith; and when we have been born again and strengthened we are fed by the divine food of the mass; but if, through sin, we bring sickness upon our souls, we are made spiritually whole by penance; and by extreme unction we are healed, both spiritually and corporeally, according as our souls have need; by ordination the Church is governed and multiplied spiritually; by matrimony it is materially increased."[2]

Some sacraments are performed by the parish priest at the level of the local church and others by the bishop (or his designated representative) who presides over the parishes that compose the bishopric or diocese he oversees.

SACRAMENT	BY WHOM	WHERE RECORDED
Baptism	Priest	Parish in Baptismal
	Register	
Confirmation	Bishop	Parish in Baptismal Register or in separate Confirmation register
Marriage	Priest	Parish in Marriage Register (and possibly in Diocese for pre-approval)
Communion (the mass)	Priest	Annually to Bishop
Confession and		
Absolution (Penance)	Priest	Annually to Bishop
Last Rites	Priest	Parish in Burial Register
Ordination to Priesthood	Bishop	Diocese

Notes

1. *The New Dictionary of Cultural Literacy, Third Edition* Edited by E.D. Hirsch, Jr., Joseph F. Kett, and James Trefil. (Houghton Mifflin, 2002).
2. Pope Eugenius IV. *Bull Exsultate Domine (Decree for the Armenians),* Council of Florence 1439 in *The Christian Faith in the Doctrinal Documents of the Catholic Church,* rev ed., ed. J. Neusner and J Dupuis, (New York: Alba House, 1982), no. 1737 (p. 506-507).

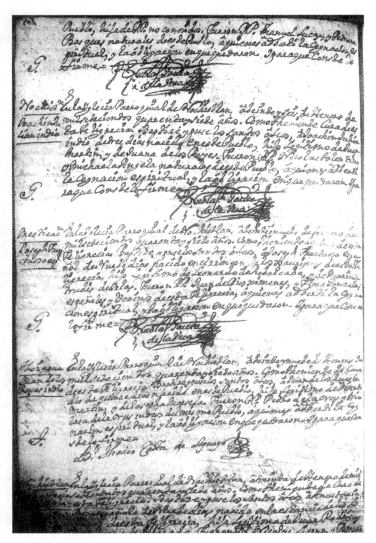

Figure 4-2: Parish records usually have marginal notations with names and sometimes places.

the baptized child or the persons marrying. This will be the part containing information of genealogical value.

Most likely because of the difficulty in obtaining paper and ink, and to speed up the time it took to write, abbreviations—particularly of repeated words—are a common occurrence in parish records. For example, the written months and years are nearly always shortened. The term "*hijo legitimo*" will often be shortened to simply "*h. l.*;" *natural* will appear as "*nl.*," and so forth. Names are also frequently abbreviated: Juan becomes *Ju°*; Francisco shortens to Fran*co*; Catalina to Cat*ª*, and so forth. Last names or surnames can also be shortened—Hernandez will become *Hz*, Garcia can be written either *Grª* or *Gª*. While these abbreviations may seem confusing at first, they will quickly become recognizable. Following the priest's handwriting from one entry to the next will help you to determine the abbreviations he commonly used.

Marginal notations giving the name of the baptized child, individuals to be married, or the deceased will frequently appear in the margin at the beginning of a new entry. Since many Mexican parishes cover more than one neighboring locality or *rancho*, the village name is also often noted in the margin along with the name of the baptized child in the entry. Another common marginal notation is a cross indicating that the person had died (often used for small children, although a date is seldom given). Many times marginal entries are made several years later. In one unique case, a marginal note next to one woman's baptismal record states she is the grandmother of the local priest serving at that time.

Even those who read Spanish fluently need to be aware that spelling was far less structured in the past than it is today. Even within a single document, the same word may be spelled differently. Fortunately, these variations in spelling make hardly any difference in the way the words are pronounced. Simply reading the document out loud should usually clear up any confusion.

Parish records show that a wide variety of nationalities and races are found among the ancestors of Mexican Americans, including Spanish, Portuguese, Arab, French, Anglo American, Italian, Irish, African, Japanese, Chinese and, of course, Native

VOCABULARY

hijo/ja legitimo/ma—
legitimate child; a child born
of a legal union.

American. A common practice in Mexican parish records during the colonial period was to give the racial designations of the parties involved. See the sidebar, "Racial Mixtures of Colonial Mexico," in chapter 10 for a list of those most commonly found. Also, in some areas during the colonial era, nearly 10 percent of the population was black or mulatto, both slave and free. Often, separate books of baptisms were kept for Africans, Native Americans, and those of mixed race. Unlike slaves in the United States, slaves in Mexico were often married in the Catholic Church.

PARISH BAPTISMAL RECORDS

A child's baptism in the Catholic Church could happen any time between the minutes after birth to several days after (or even, in some rural areas in Mexico, not for several months or years). Generally, however, most baptisms were performed within a few days. When there was fear that the child might not live, he or she was baptized immediately. This instance is usually recorded in the baptismal record with a phrase such as "*baptizó en caso de necesidad…*" (see the sidebar, "An Example of a Parish Baptismal Record").

Remember as you read these records that the priest's purpose was to record the sacrament of the child's baptism and not necessarily its birth information. Whether or not a date of birth was given will vary, depending on the priest and time period the record was made. The first date given in a baptismal entry, therefore, is the date of baptism—not the child's birth date. This will generally be followed by the standard sacramental wording until the "clue phrases" such as *baptizé solemnemente á*, or *puse los santos oleos y crisma á* indicate the name of the child being baptized will follow. The remainder of the entry should give the following information, although the order of it may vary: the parents' names and surnames; the parents' places of origin (*natural de*) and current residence (*vecino de*); and the name(s) and surnames(s) of godparents (*padrinos*).

While the above information is nearly certain to be given, the record may also give the date and time of birth; the names of the paternal grandparents (*abuelos paternos*) and the maternal grandparents (*abuelos maternos*); their places of origin and residence, and whether or not they are deceased. (Be aware of the difference between *natural de* "native of" and *hijo natural* ["natural" or illegitimate child]). As discussed in chapter 2, "Finding and Working with Mexican Records," you will want to make a true copy of this information recording *exactly* what the document says, without additional assumptions, such as surnames of the child.

While it may seem repetitive to recopy the given information for parents and grandparents in each baptismal entry, doing so gives details you might otherwise miss (a grandparent, for example, who has died since the last recorded birth). It is a good practice to also copy the *padrinos* names and any other information given about them. Many times they are related, or from a neighboring town that may turn out to have family members in it.

Every baptismal record will state in some manner whether the child is an "*hijo legitimo*," or "*hijo natural.*" This is not given to create a stigma on the child or for other social reasons. The church deemed this necessary information as certain

VOCABULARY

Natural de—native of; born in a given locality.

Vecino/na (de)—legal resident (of).

Padrino— godfather; pl. godparents.

Abuelos paternos/ maternos—paternal/ maternal grandparents.

Hijo natural—illegitimate child; a child born outside the marriage contract.

Baptizó en caso de necesidad—"he baptized in the case of necessity." This phrase indicates the child was baptized by someone other than a priest because it was thought the baby might die.

baptizé solemnemente á, or puse los santos oleos y crisma á—"I baptized and placed the holy oils and consecrated oil on…"

For more information, see appendix A, "Glossary."

AN EXAMPLE OF A PARISH BAPTISMAL RECORD

Transcription

Y [ten] En 5 de agosto del Año 1603. yo Ell^{do} di^o ortiz baptize A Jaçinta hija de Anton Catalan y de ysabel guerre ro estantes en este rreal fuero[n] sus padrinos Ju^o lopez vellido y Ana m^a su mujer vezinos deste rreal[1] Y[ten] Este mismo dia mes y año baptize a Ju^o meztizo hijo de la yglesia fue su padrino Ju^o de foronda vezino deste rreal—ell^{do} di^o Ortiz [rubrica]

Y[ten] En 19 de agosto del ano 1603. Yo Ell^{do} di^o Ortiz baptize a miguel hijo de la yglesia fueron sus padrinos alonso de Segura y mariana. meztiza esta[n]tes en este rreal de tlajuililpa—ell^{do} di^o Ortiz [rubrica]

This same day month and year I baptized Juan a mestizo son of the church.[2] His godfather was Juan de Foronda citizen of this mining town.—ell^{do} di^o Ortiz [rubric]

Y[ten] On 19 August of the year 1603. I the licensed Di[ego] Ortiz baptized Miguel son of the church.[3] His godparents were Alonso de Segura and Mariana. meztiza They [the godparents] were from this mining town of Tlajuililpa.—ell^{do} di^o Ortiz [rubric]

Source: Actopán, Hidalgo Parish Register Bautismos de españoles vol. 1546-1652, s/n. (FHL Microfilm 614336, lt. 1.)

Translation

Y[ten] On 5 August of the year 1603. I the licensed Di[ego] Ortiz baptized Jacinta[,] daughter of Anton Catalan and Ysabel Guerrero residing in this mining town[.] [The] godparents were Juan Lopez Vellido and Ana Ma[ria] his wife citizens of this mining town. Y[ten]

Notes

1. In this case rreal is a shortened term for real de minas, a silver mine held by the Crown.
2. An orphan abandoned at the church.
3. Ibid.

opportunities were not available to illegitimate children. For example, a man could not enter the priesthood if his birth was illegitimate. Occasionally, you will find a marginal note by a child's name indicating the parents were later married, legitimizing his birth.

PARISH CONFIRMATION RECORDS

From time to time, the presiding Catholic bishop would come to town and perform confirmations for all those who had not yet received that sacrament (for more information about the Catholic priesthood, see the "Priests, Bishops, and the Sacraments" sidebar). Records of this event, giving the name of each child the bishop confirmed along with at least the name of the father, are usually found mixed in with baptismal records (see figure 4-3). As confirmations were only performed by the bishop, how often these records appear depends on the frequency with which he visited. In many localities, this happened annually, although in one instance the bishop hadn't been to the parish for twenty-nine years. Going through confirmation records is a good way to be sure you have accounted for all of the children in a given family.

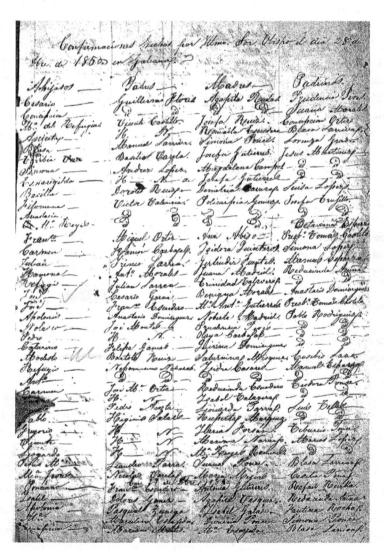

Figure 4-3: Confirmation records give lists of names of confirmed children. This example from 1850 also includes the names of fathers, mothers, and godfathers.

PARISH MARRIAGE RECORDS

A parish marriage record is an extremely valuable document. Beyond giving the date of the creation of a new family unit, it nearly always, in the event of a first marriage, gives the name of both parents in the older generation. If the bride and/ or groom is a widow/widower, the deceased former spouse is named. Since marriages traditionally took place in the bride's parish, this record can become a crucial means of obtaining the groom's information if he is from another town.

IMPEDIMENTS TO MARRIAGE

- Relatives within four generations, by blood or marriage*
- A godparent-godchild relationship*
- Impotence
- Crimes such as adultery or homicide
- A previous illicit relationship with a relative*
- A promise to marry another (by either party)*
- A previous vow of chastity (such as taken by a nun or monk)*
- An ordination to the priesthood
- A living spouse (of either party)*
- A bride or groom who had not reached puberty
- A bride or groom who was not Catholic*
- No banns were read*

* These could be dispensed or waived by decree of the bishop.

VOCABULARY

Investigación/diligencia matrimonial—premarital investigation conducted by parish priest.

An understanding of Catholic Church doctrine regarding marriage makes it easier to understand parish marriage records. As required by the same Council of Trent discussed earlier, before the sacrament of marriage could take place, the priest was required to perform an investigation, called an *investigación matrimonial* or *diligencia matrimonial,* to determine that no impediments existed on the part of either the groom or the bride. By canon law, a couple needed to give their consent to the marriage and, if either the groom or the bride were underage, the consent of his or her father (or mother, if the father was deceased) was also needed. In addition, the couple, their family, and members of the community needed to affirm that no possible impediments hindered the bride and groom from marrying (see the "Impediments to Marriage," sidebar). Mexico has the best preserved records of these investigations of any country in the world. The Family History Library Catalog often shows parish registers with two sets of marriage records covering the same dates, one the *informaciones matrimoniales* and the other the marriages themselves.

One researcher, finding the parish marriage record of his great grandparents, learned to his surprise that both the bride and the groom had been previously married and were widowed at the time of the marriage. Although he already had a lot of information about this couple, including names of all their children and both sets of parents, he had no idea either spouse had been previously married. Seeing in the Family History Library Catalog that *informaciones matrimoniales* existed for this same time period, he found, from approximately four weeks before the marriage ceremony, several pages of testimony by witnesses in the town giving information about the couple's previous spouses. Although much of the information given was the same as the marriage record, by careful reading he was able to get the name of the town in which the bride's deceased spouse was buried, giving him information about her past (and leads for further research) he had not previously known.

Informaciones matrimoniales often give more information than the marriage record itself, naming both the bride and groom, their place of residence and origin and their marital status, the names of both sets of parents and their places of residence and origin. As well, the investigation will discuss any impediments to the marriage that might have existed, as previously discussed. If you find yourself working with marriage records you feel are incomplete, check in the Family History Library Catalog for your locality to see if *informaciones* or *diligencias matrimoniales* exist.

Most marriage impediments could be removed by a special dispensation from the bishop. (Chapter 6, "Beyond the Parish: Church and Government Records," discusses bishopric ecclesiastical archives where these records may be found.) Whether or not these dispensations were granted was determined on a case-by-case basis. In one instance in the Mexican state of Coahuila, a dispensation was granted overlooking the impediment of consanguinity on the grounds that both the bride and groom, related in the third degree, were from the frontier town of Saltillo, which had no other suitable members of the opposite sex. Figure 4-4 shows pedigree from a marriage record where the groom and the deceased husband were third cousins.

Once the priest had determined both the groom and bride were qualified to be married, including the fact that no impediments existed, an announcement of their

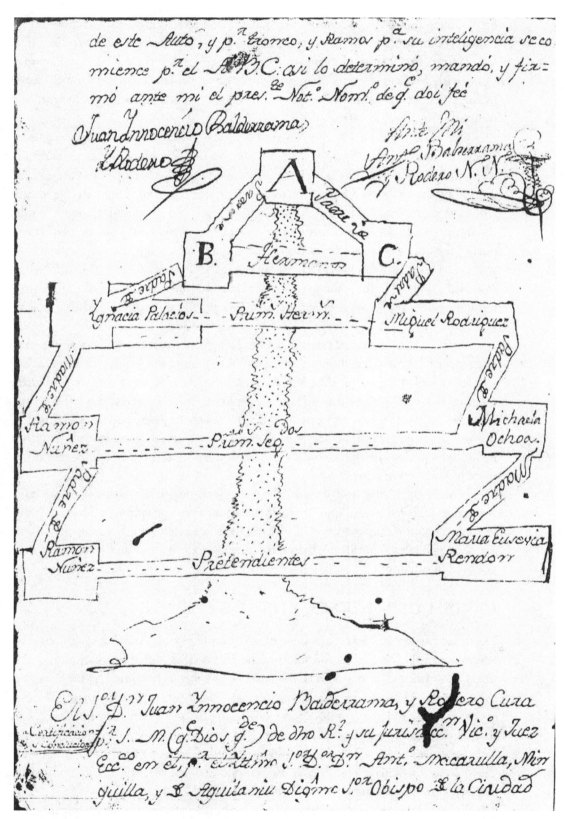

Figure 4-4: Pedigrees like this were often a part of a marriage dispensation record.

VOCABULARY

Amonestacíones matrimonial—proclamation published during three successive Sundays before marriages; banns.

Casamiento—marriage; wedding.

Velación—veiling ceremony of bride and groom in nuptial mass.

Viudo/da—widower/widow.

En facie yglesia—"in front of the church." Generally indicates that the marriage, and the mass that accompanied it, was done before the principal altar.

Párvulo/la—small child.

For more information, see appendix A, "Glossary."

forthcoming marriage was read in the parish for three consecutive holy days, generally Sundays, allowing for any objections to be raised on a local level. This process is called the reading of the banns, or *amonestacíones matrimonial*. See the sidebar "An Example of a Parish Marriage Record" for an example of an original marriage record found in the parish of Teocaltiche, diocese of Durango, and accompanying transcription, translation, and record extract.

The ceremony itself was comprised of two events, the marriage (*casamiento*) and a separate blessing. The Spanish word for the blessing portion is *velación*, stemming from the same Latin root as our English word "veil." During this part of the ceremony, the bride's veil was placed over the bride and groom. The marriage record will most likely read "*casé y velé*," meaning literally, "I married and blessed." While the marriage could be performed at any time, the *velación* could not be performed during the holy days of advent or lent. Occasionally in reading marriage entries you will find two records involving the same groom and bride. At first this may seem confusing, but a careful reading will probably show the first is the *casamiento,* and the later ceremony is the *velación*, performed after the holy days of advent or lent had ended.

A parish marriage record can give the following genealogical information: the date and place of the marriage; the given name and surnames of the groom; the given name and surnames of the bride; the place of residence (*vecino de*) and the place of birth (*original de* or *natural de*) for the bride and groom; their marital status, or whether either was a *viudo/viuda*, and usually the name of the former spouse; the names of the groom's parents; and the names of the bride's parents. Marriage records may also include the profession and age of the groom and bride, and the residence and birth place of both sets of parents.

As with all other parish records, the entry will most likely begin with the date and place, followed by the appropriate sacramental marriage language, indicating the procedures required by the Council of Trent have been followed. Look for the phrase "*en facie yglesia*" to appear just before the names of the groom and bride, and their personal information.

PARISH DEATH RECORDS

Death entries are the least consistent of any parish records, varying in format and length depending on the age and status of the deceased, as well as the discretion of the priest. A death record for a *párvulo/la* could be as short as two lines, giving no more than the date of burial and the parents' names. The death record for an adult could go on as long as two pages. Sadly, the deaths of small children happened far more frequently than those of the adults, so much so that in some cases a separate book was sometimes kept to record them. The sidebar "An Example of a Parish Death Record" shows four consecutive short death entries, one each for a single man who died in poverty, a priest, a young girl, and a widow.

Perhaps because of their lack of a definite format, parish death records are sometimes overlooked as a source of genealogical information. As the discussion on

AN EXAMPLE OF A PARISH MARRIAGE RECORD

Transcription

En 9 de Enero los veló el Padre D. Jose-Maria Gala-vis En la Parroquia de Teocaltiche á veinte y cinco de Diciembre de mil ochocientos Setenta y cuatro. Yo el Presbitero D. Jose Maria Galavis con lisencia del Señor Cura casé sin velacion infacie eclecie a Mateo Ramos con Yrinea Olmos originarios de Buena Vista: el primero Soltero de veinte años, hijo legitimo de Ambrocio Ramos y Norberto Santos: la Segunda doncella de dies y ocho años hija legitima delos finados Leocadio de Olmos y Estefana Ortis: justificaron su libertad para este matrimonio que se publicó inter missarum solemnia los dias veinte y cinco de Octubre, primero y ocho de Noviembre: fueron padrinos Seberiano Trujillo y Angela Trujillo: Testigos Bernardo San ches y Trinidad Alva y lo firmo para constancia.

—José Maria Rodríguez [rubrica], Jose M.ª Galvis [rubrica]

Translation

In the parish of Teocaltiche on twenty-five December eighteen hundred seventy-four,

I the Priest Don José Maria Galavis with license [authority] of the parish priest married without blessing in front of the church Mateo Ramos with Yrinea Olmos natives of Buena Vista, the first single[,] twenty years old[,] legitimate son of Ambrosio Ramos and Norberta Santos, the second single[,] eighteen years of age[,] legitimate daughter of the deceased Leocadio de Olmos and Estefana Ortis. They proved their liberty for this marriage [of] which [notice] was published between solemn masses on the twenty-fifth of October and first and eighth of November. The Godparents were Seberiano Trujillo and Angela Trujillo. Witnesses: Bernardo Sanches and Trinidad Alva. And I signed it that it be set forth.

—José Maria Rodríguez [rubric], Jose M.ª Galavis [rubric]

Source: Teocaltiche, Jalisco Parish Marriage Register, vol. 29, p. 2v. (FHL Microfilm 0639764, It. 1).

AN EXAMPLE OF A PARISH DEATH RECORD

Transcription

[Entry 4—Catharina de Sisneros]

Enla Ciudad delos Ang^{es}, en dies y ocho dehenero demil seicíentos y setenta y siete años se enterro en esta s^{ta} iglesia Cathedral   Catharina de Sisneros vezina de esta ciudad y viuda de Gabríel hernandes La qual no testo por que no tubo de que recivio los Santos Sacramentos—

Translation

In the city of los Ang[eles], on eighteen January of [the year] one thousand six hundred seventy and seven, was buried in this holy church cathedral Catharina de Sisneros resident of this city and widow of Gabriel Hernandez, who did not leave a will because she had nothing[.] [She] received the holy sacraments.

Source: Puebla de Zaragoza, Puebla, Sagrario Metropolitano. Defunciones 1673–1699, vol. 3, p. 50 (FHL Microfilm 0227800).

Mision de Guasavas en el Estado de Sonora.

Estado que manifiesta el número de bautizados, casados y muertos, comprensivo desde primero de Enero hasta último de Diciembre de 1847, y desde primero de Enero hasta último de Junio de 1848.

Año de 1847					Año de 1848				Enfermedades de que murieron.
Meses	Bautizados	Casados	Muertos adultos	Muertos parvul.	Meses	Bautizados	Casados	Muertos adultos	Muertos parvul.	
Enero	07.	00.	03.	03.	Enero	02	00.	00.	00.	De Sarampion - 73.
Febrero	13.	00.	00.	00.	Febrero	03.	02	03.	02.	De parto - 04.
Marzo	11.	00.	00.	00.	Marzo	06.	03	00.	03.	De Mancca - 05.
Abril	11.	00.	00.	03.	Abril	07.	00.	00.	00.	De otras enferm. 36
Mayo	08.	00.	04.	02.	Mayo	08.	03.	03.	04.	De repente - 02
Junio	08.	00.	13.	39.	Junio	06	02.	00.	00.	De Apaches - 10
Julio	06.	00.	03.	10.		37	10.	04.	07.	106.
Agosto	03.	03.	02.	03.						
Septiembre	12.	03.	02.	03.						
Octubre	07.	02.	..	03.						
Noviembre	03.	03.	00.	03.						
Diciembre	00	00.	03.	00.						
	78.	11.	26.	62.						

Nota

Este estado comprende la Hacienda de las Granadas como perteneciente á esta Mision.

Guasavas Noviembre 24 de 1848.

Fr. Agustin Zaldua

Figure 4-5: Death records can provide insight into life and death in a community, such as this mission entry, recording four deaths from childbirth and ten from an Apache raid.

death records in the previous chapter points out, however, death records not only give a concluding point in time to the potential of finding information on a person's life, but they can add previously unknown facts. One family found, in the parish death record of a great-grandfather, the name of a previously unknown spouse, as well as that of a child from that marriage. Another researcher found an entry in the parish death book where his great-grandmother came with two witnesses, her (previously unknown) father and grandfather, officially declaring the death of her husband three years earlier. The document was a part of the parish premarital investigation allowing her to remarry the following month.

Perhaps even more than other parish register types, death records give a sense of life in the community at that time. One researcher found several entries for people of all ages dying from "fever" within a matter of weeks. Figure 4-5 shows a summary of causes of death in a mission in northern Mexico where some deaths were caused by Apache Indian attacks.

A parish death record could give the following genealogical information: the name of the deceased; the date of death; the date of his or her burial; his or her place of origin; his or her place of residence at time of death; the names of the deceased's parents; the name of his or her spouse; his or her age at death; the cause of death; names of surviving children; and names of former spouses, as well as those of any surviving children from those marriages.

VOCABULARY

Collecturias—account books.

Por ser pobre, por no hay de que, por no tener de que—phrases that indicate that the decedent was poverty stricken.

Additionally, death records can give the crucial information of whether or not the deceased made a will and, if so, even the name of the notary making it—information that could lead to the possibility of finding notarial records for your family (see chapter 7, "Beyond the Parish: Notarial Records"). The alternative statement that the deceased did not make a will because he or she was too poor (*"por ser pobre,"* or *"por no hay de que"*), while not as helpful from a research perspective, is as compelling as it is blunt (see the sidebar "An Example of a Parish Death Record").

As with other types of parish registers, it's helpful to remember the cause for which death records were made. While we might view death registers as a means of announcing a parishioner's death, much in the same way we think of an obituary today, the primary purpose for most parish death records is to record the sacrament of burial and to give information about masses ordered and payments made. For this reason the burial date is often given first, with the date of death found later in the document (in many cases, it is not even included). Some parishes will have separate *collecturias* to record masses ordered and their payment.

PARISH RESEARCH USING THE INTERNATIONAL GENEALOGICAL INDEX AND MEXICAN VITAL RECORDS INDEX

The International Genealogical Index (IGI), containing 26 million baptisms and marriage entries extracted by volunteers from Mexican parish records, is an excellent starting point to help research your family lines.[1] It can also be helpful in identifying family members who came from, or moved to, a different locality. One researcher, using parent names from an ancestor's marriage record, searched in the appropriate time period for births of the bride and groom as well as their siblings. (Since no places of birth were given, the assumption was made that both families came from the marriage locality.) While several members of the bride's family were located, nothing was found for the groom's. A Parent Search in the Mexican IGI showed a couple with the same names as the groom's parents having children in a small town located in a neighboring state. A search in those records revealed the birth record for the groom as well as several siblings. Finding this family in a location so far removed from other known relations would have been impossible at that point in the research without the aid of the Mexican IGI, or time spent in doing a radial search.

While the advantages of using the Mexican International Genealogical Index as a research starting point are readily apparent, care must be taken. Since nearly all Mexican information comes from extracted original sources, the accuracy and reliability of the Mexican IGI is generally good; however, in some cases, information could have been either incorrectly extracted, or later incorrectly cataloged. Also, the parish records for your search locality or time period may not have been extracted. One researcher, doing a Parent Search, found children of a direct-line ancestor born in the years 1799, 1801, 1814, and 1816. A search of parish records in the intervening years revealed further children, but no information from those books is in the IGI. Never assume that if you can't find the information you are searching for in the Mexican IGI, it doesn't exist.

THE CATHOLIC MASS

The mass, sometimes called the Eucharist or Holy Supper of the Lord, is the central liturgical event in the life of a Roman Catholic. Celebrating the death and resurrection of Jesus Christ and his atonement for the sins of men, the priest offered the bread[1] and wine in front of, and in the name of, the community of believers in a ritual sacrifice *incruento*[2] to the Eternal Father, in union with Christ as head of the Church and motivated by the Holy Ghost. Under Tridentine ritual, the priest partook of the wine and then placed a piece of the bread in the mouth of each of the faithful who came forward, having previously confessed their sins. This was required of all faithful parishioners at least annually, and for many Catholics it was a weekly or even daily event. Mass also played a key part in marriage and funeral ceremonies.

The following terms referring to the mass are often found in Spanish documents:

- *Misa de oficio de cuerpo presente*—A funeral mass celebrated with the body of the deceased present in the church.
- *Misa del cabo del año*—A mass celebrated on behalf of a deceased person at the first anniversary of death.
- *Misa cantada* or *llana cantada*—A mass involving only a simple Gregorian chant, usually sung by the priest.
- *Misa cantada concelebrada*—A mass jointly celebrated and sung by several priests.
- *Misa rezada* or *privada*—A simple mass without music or pomp.
- *Misa Solemne*—A misa cantada celebrated by a priest, deacon, and subdeacon.

- *Misa de difuntos*—A mass celebrated on behalf of a deceased person; wills often specified that masses be performed for deceased spouses, parents, children, grandparents, and other loved ones.
- *Misa del alba, ~ de parida*, or *~ de purificación*—A mass performed the first time a woman returned to the church after giving birth, usually following the forty days of ritual confinement and purification.
- *Misa mayor* or *parroquial*—A mass celebrated in the parish, usually by the parish priest, on Sundays and holy or feast days at the hour in which the largest number of parishioners (in theory, all) would attend; on feast days it would often be followed or preceded by a procession.
- *Misa votiva*—A mass that was not a general parish mass, but offered for private devotion or for the dead; votive masses were often performed in hermitages and temples other than the parish church; many votive masses prescribed in wills were dedicated to specific saints and/or one's guardian angel.
- *En facie eclesie*—Latin phrase meaning "in front of the church," referring to the marriage mass performed in front of the community of the faithful.
- *Misas solemnarias*—A phrase in the marriage act describing the reading of the banns in conjunction with the Sunday or feast day mass.

Notes
1. In reality a thin wafer called the "host," in the past made by the priest on a hot pancake iron.
2. Meaning, symbolic and without blood.

Remember, too, that a hopscotch approach through parish records looking only for children of a direct-line ancestor already identified in the Mexican IGI will not yield the same sense of the family in the town at that time as a page-by-page search. For example, the life events for children of extended family members during the same time period will be missed, eliminating valuable research clues on the next generation back. No matter what results you get from the Mexican portion of the IGI, take the time to search the parish records page-by-page as well.

Using the Mexican International Genealogical Index

On the homepage of FamilySearch.org, click the "Search" tab. Using the headings on the left hand side of the page, click the one titled "International Genealogical Index." To do an Individual Search, type as much information as you know into the given fields. (Even if you think you know the exact date, give a wider range of possible years for it.) To do a Parent Search, enter *only* the parents' names and the region into the fields. Doing a Parent Search, in addition to an Individual Search, is an excellent idea because it will often provide the names of siblings.

Once you have located a name you are looking for, click the name's link. An IGI Individual Record will appear, with information about the event, location, and parties involved. Check the "Source Information" given at the bottom of the entry. This will

GENEALOGICAL INFORMATION ON PARISH RECORDS

BAPTISMAL RECORDS
Likely to be given
- Date of baptism
- Place of birth
- Child's name
- Father's name
- Mother's name
- Names of Padrino(s) [godparent(s)]

Possibly given
- Birth date
- Names of paternal grandparents
- Names of maternal grandparents
- Place of father's birth
- Place of mother's birth
- Place of grandparents' birth

MARRIAGE RECORDS
Likely to be given
- Date of marriage
- Place of marriage
- Groom's name
- Bride's name
- Names of groom's parents
- Names of bride's parents
- Birth places of groom and bride

Possibly given
- Possible restrictions
- Possible dispensation
- Race of bride and groom

DEATH RECORDS
Likely to be given
- Place of burial
- Date of burial and/or death
- Name of deceased

Possibly given
- Names of deceased's parents
- Marital status of deceased
- Name of current/former spouse
- Children's names
- Will information
- Indication of whether or not last rites were given
- Funeral masses given

include a Batch Number and Source Call No. (or the microfilm number). Click on the Batch Number to see the names extracted in that batch of records, listed alphabetically by surname (you can refine this search by adding the father's surname).

Some quick pointers in working with the Mexican naming system:

- Since each name listed in the Mexican IGI is based on a single parish entry, a person's name may vary in differing documents, depending on what was noted by the priest. The common Mexican practice of giving a child several names at the time of baptism allows the possibility that any one of those names could appear in later records. Take the time to try several search options, especially when entering the names of a couple.

- Instances where the Hispanic double surname system is used (in other words, the child carries the father's surname as his first surname, and mother's surname as his second) provide an excellent proof of relationship. Many times, however, especially in documents dating before about 1850, a surprising flexibility of surnames existed. Don't assume the existence of the double surname system as it exists today in any of your searches. Rather, be open to possibilities as you scroll down a list of search results, focusing in particular on any options from the parish in which you have been working, or areas close by. View the Mexican IGI as a resource in locating the parish records in which you will focus your research, not as a quick solution to your research.

- Return to the Mexican IGI intermittently during your research, especially as new information is found.

The time spent in becoming familiar with the search options of the Mexican International Genealogical Index will be well worth your efforts. If you are working at a Family History Center, the consultant on duty may not have had experience in working with the unique characteristics of the Mexican portion, or Hispanic surname system. If this is the case, use their knowledge of the IGI as a beginning platform on which to begin your search, but also try some of the techniques described in this section.

The Mexican Vital Records Index

An additional 2.2 million names have been added to the existing names in the Mexican International Genealogical Index in a separate database called the Mexican Vital Records Index.[2] When doing any search in the Mexican IGI, include a search of the Mexican Vital Records Index as well. A click on the heading "All Resources" at the top of the selections on the left hand side of the page will automatically include both the Mexican portion of the IGI and the Vital Records Index, as well as the other databases listed.

NOTES

1. John P. Schmall, "Mexican Genealogical Research," The Houston Institute for Culture, <www.houstonculture.org/hispanic/research.html>.
2. *Ibid.*

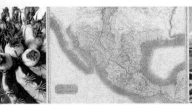

5

FINDING THE PLACE IN MEXICO

There are two reasons for reading this chapter. One is if you know the name of a place in Mexico but can't find it. The second is if you are interested in learning about the place in Mexico where your ancestors lived. To assist you in either of these, this chapter will explore basic concepts of Mexican geography and political and ecclesiastical divisions, and then discuss gazetteers, geographical dictionaries, atlases, and encyclopedias available for the Mexican researcher.

POLITICAL DIVISIONS OF MEXICO

If you have searched in the Family History Library Catalog for a place name as described in chapter 2, "Finding and Working with Mexican Records," you are already somewhat familiar with Mexican political divisions. The country of Mexico is divided into thirty-one *estados*, plus the *distrito federal* of Mexico City. Many times people refer to Mexico City simply as "Mexico," so if you are speaking with a Mexican national or reading something written by one, be aware that in referring to Mexico this person may be referring to the capital city rather than the country.

Mexico City itself is divided into *delegaciónes*—comparable to the boroughs of New York City—which today provide political organization at a more local level in this city of nine million people. Each *delegación* has an office of the civil register, where births, deaths, and marriages are recorded. In 1900, there were nineteen *delegaciones* in Mexico City, plus an additional eight municipalities with their own civil register offices.[1] The remainder of Mexico beyond the *distrito federal* is today divided into thirty-one *estados*. All of them are larger than the *distrito federal*, although they range in size from Tlaxcala, roughly the size of the state of Connecticut, to Chihuahua, roughly the size of the state of New Mexico. Since the creation of the original twenty

VOCABULARY

Municipio—municipality; the territorial jurisdiction that includes the inhabitants governed by a town council.

(Arz) Obispo—(arch) bishop; for more information, see appendix A, "Glossary."

states, each state has maintained a separate political government to handle executive, legislative, and judicial affairs for its area, with varying degrees of control from the central administration in Mexico City. Nearly all of these states have now created an archive in which official state governmental papers have been gathered (see appendix D, "Archives of the States of Mexico").

Each state in Mexico is divided into *municipios*. These *municipios* perform the same government functions handled by cities in the United States, and also serve as the unit for most record-keeping functions, such as voter registration, property ownership recordings, and civil registration handled by counties in the United States. An excellent place to go for information and maps of each state showing municipalities is <http://en.wikipedia.org/wiki/States_of_Mexico>.

Another important difference between cities in the United States and *municipios* in Mexico is that, unlike in the United States, *municipios* cover the entire area of each state. In other words, if you were to go from a town called "Redville" to another town called "Blueville" in the United States, while you were between those towns you may not be in one jurisdiction or the other. In Mexico, the area between towns is still part of the *municipio*. For example, there is no place in the large Mexican state of Chihuahua in which you are not in a *municipio*. In many cases, a rural *municipio* will be composed of several small villages that are miles apart, often with the largest of those providing its name.

Another important concept is that political boundaries may not necessarily be the same as church boundaries. Thus, one or more of the villages in a *municipio* may have a separate Catholic parish. This could mean that the town or village where you look for parish records may not be the same town or village where you look for civil registration.

Understanding the history of a particular municipal unit can be important in finding records such as civil registers and censuses. Many *municipios* were reorganized in the 1920s and the borders may have changed. Perhaps they were even once part of a separate municipality. Often, small villages formed separate *oficialías* of the municipal civil register in which births, marriages, and deaths were recorded.

CATHOLIC CHURCH DIVISIONS

As elsewhere in the world, in Mexico the Catholic Church is divided into administrative units known as dioceses or archdioceses. Each diocese is presided over by an *obispo*, and each archdiocese by an *arzobispo*. For the purposes of genealogical research, there is no difference between the records and powers of the bishop and archbishop. Dioceses are named for the city in which the bishop resides and has his cathedral, and often do not follow political lines. There may be more than one diocese in a single state, or a diocese may take in areas from more than one state. For example, the archdiocese of Durango, named after its capital city of Durango, includes cities within the states of Durango and Zacatecas. The map in figure 5-1 shows both diocese and state divisions in modern Mexico.

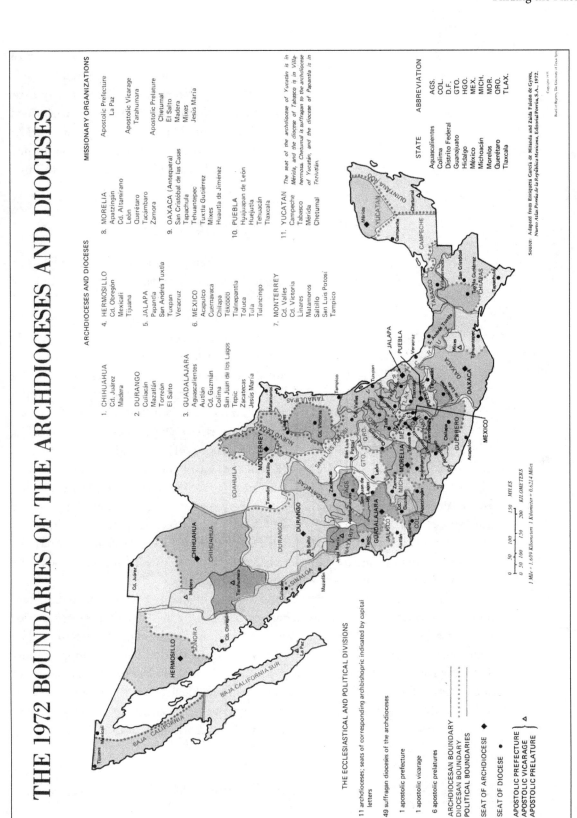

Figure 5-1: Knowing the Mexican state and diocese that your ancestor came from is vital to your success. (Map courtesy of the University of Texas Libraries, The University of Texas at Austin.)

Each of the dioceses and archdioceses of Mexico is divided into *parroquias*, local Catholic church units presided over by the *párroco* or *cura*. Within this local unit, masses are performed and communion provided at least weekly; baptisms, marriages, and burials are performed and recorded; catechism is taught; and first communions given.

HISTORICAL CHANGES

Numerous changes in both political and church organization have taken place throughout the history of Mexico. For example, the Mexican Constitution of 1824 divided Mexico into twenty states and four territories (see figure 5-2). Since that time there have been at least two major redivisions of state lines and literally hundreds of changes in municipalities. More detail about these can be studied in *Divisiones Politicas in Mexico* by Lyman Platt, as well as in publications of the Instituto Nacional de Estadísticas Geográficas e Información. Catholic dioceses have likewise changed. As Mexico has

Figure 5-2: This map shows the twenty-four states created by the Mexican constitution in 1824.

grown and the population increased, new dioceses have been created. A significant number were created in the 1880s as the Church opted to create more, smaller dioceses in order to increase administrative efficiency. Table 5-1, "Archives of the Catholic Church Created in Mexico before 1922," gives a list of dioceses in Mexico, with the date it was organized and from what diocese it originated.

Parishes have likewise been created, and in some cases even eliminated. Often, one of the challenges facing a researcher is determining where to look for records prior to the creation of the parish. Creation dates for specific parishes can be determined by referring to *Divisiones eclesiásticas de Mexico* by Lyman Platt. The "Locating Finding Tools for Mexico" sidebar at the end of this chapter identifies several categories of books that will prove helpful in locating a place in Mexico and learning more about it. Generally, before turning to these you should have a specific place name, given by a family member or taken from a document such as a marriage record or border crossing manifest.

LOOKING FOR JURISDICTIONAL INFORMATION IN THE FHLC

Perhaps you have already looked for the place in the Family History Library Catalog as described in chapter 2, "Finding and Working with Mexican Records," and did

VOCABULARY

Parroquia—parish; territory covered by the spiritual jurisdiction of a parish priest.

Párroco—parish priest.

Cura—parish priest; vicar.

Figure 5-3: Responses like this from queries in the Family History Catalog like this one for Teocaltiche can provide further place information.

not find it. If you did find your locality in the Family History Library Catalog, you now know a good deal of information about the locality, including the Mexican state to which it belongs. For example, if you had looked up Teocaltiche you would have learned that it is in the state of Jalisco. You would further have found there are church records and civil registration records for Teocaltiche. When you open the entry for civil registration you will find a box of information like that shown in figure 5-3. From this you can determine that Teocaltiche is a *municipio* with four *oficialías,* one in the town of Teocaltiche and three others located in the nearby villages of Belén del Refugio, Michoacanejo, and Ostotán.

If you click on Church Records you learn that there is a single Catholic parish in Teocaltiche. If you had typed the name of the village Mechoacanejo you would have learned it is in the state of Jalisco. No record of church registers appears, indicating there is no Catholic parish, and the entry for civil registration takes you to the material that appears in figure 5-3, telling you that Michoacanejo contains an *oficialía* of the civil register of Teocaltiche.

TABLE 5-1: ARCHIVES OF THE CATHOLIC CHURCH DIOCESES CREATED IN MEXICO BEFORE 1922

Dioceses	Date of Origin	FHLC Microfilms[1]	Origin of each diocese in México
1. Aguascalientes	1899	P	Diocese of Guadalajara
2. Antequera (Oaxaca)	1535	P	Original diocese
3. Campeche	1895	G P	Diocese of Yucatán
4. Chiapas	1539	P	Original diocese
5. Chilapa	1816	P	Archdiocese of Mexico and dioceses of Tlaxcala-Puebla and Morelia
6. Chihuahua	1891	G P	Diocese of Durango
7. Colima	1881	G P	Diocese of Guadalajara
8. Cuernavaca	1891	P	Archdiocese of México
9. Durango	1620	G P	Diocese of Guadalajara
10. Guadalajara	1548	G P	Original diocese
11. Huajuapam	1902	P	Dioceses of Antequera and Puebla
12. Huejutla	1922	P	Dioceses of Tulancingo, Tamaulipas and San Luis Potosí
13. León	1863	P	Diocese of Morelia
14. Linares (Monterrey)	1777	P	Diocese of Guadalajara
15. México	1530	G P	Original diocese
16. Morelia (Michoacán)	1536	G P	Original diocese
17. Papantla	1922	P	Dioceses of Veracruz, Tamaulipas, and Puebla
18. Puebla	1519	P	Original diocese
19. Querétero	1863	P	Archdiocese of México and diocese of Morelia
20. Saltillo	1891	G P	Diocese of Linares
21. San Luis Potosí	1854	G P	Archdiocese of México and dioceses of Morelia and Guadalajara
22. Sinaloa (Culiacán)	1883	P	Diocese of Sonora
23. Sonora (Hermosillo)	1779	P	Dioceses of Durango and Guadalajara
24. Tabasco	1880	P	Diocese of Yucatán
25. Tacámbaro	1913	P	Dioceses of Morelia and Zamora
26. Tamaulipas (Tampico)[2]	1870	G P	Diocese of Linares
27. Tehuantepec	1891	G P	Dioceses of Antequera and Veracruz
28. Tepic	1891	P	Diocese of Guadalajara
29. Tulancingo	1891	P	Archdiocese of México and diocese of Tlaxcala-Puebla
30. Veracruz (Jalapa)	1843	P	Diocese of Tlaxcala-Puebla and Antequerra
31. Yucatán	1561	G P	Original Diocese
32. Zacatecas	1862	P	Diocese of Guadalajara
33. Zamora	1863	G P	Diocese of Morelia

GEOGRAPHICAL DICTIONARIES, ATLASES, AND GAZETTEERS

If the place name you entered does not appear in the Family History Library Catalog, it is likely the name of a small village, hamlet, or ranch with neither a Catholic parish nor an office of the civil register. At this point you would turn to a gazetteer or geographical dictionary in order to determine the municipality and state to which the place name might pertain.

Several valuable locality reference works exist for Mexico. The first is a five volume geographical dictionary published at the end of the nineteenth century by Antonio Garcia Cubas, which can be ordered to a local Family History Center in two microfilm rolls, numbers 1102587 and 1102588. Each of the place name entries appear in a dictionary format with text describing the place. For example, if you had seen the place name of Aguatinta and wanted to learn more about it, you would find it identified as a *rancho* in the municipality of Paso de Sotos in the *cantón* of Teocaltiche (see figure 5-4). At the time this dictionary was published a *cantón* was a county-like division created in Mexico, and many of the small villages were given municipal status. In the early part of the twentieth century, this *cantón*-type of jurisdiction was eliminated and many of the smaller municipalities were combined into larger ones. In this case Paso de Sotos was merged into the municipality of Teocaltiche.

Reading the Garcia Cubas geographical dictionary entry gives the information that the ranch of Aguatinta

VOCABULARY

Cantón—jurisdiction of government beween municipality and state used in Mexico in the late nineteenth and early twentieth centuries.

Notes

As it is unlikely that research will be done in those dioceses created after 1922, no attempt has been made to evaluate the following dioceses: Acapulco, Apatzingán, Autlán, Ciudad Altamirano, Ciudad Cardenas, Ciudad Guzmán, Ciudad Juarez, Ciudad Obregón, Ciudad Valles, Ciudad Victoria, Matamoros, Mazatlán, Mexicali, San Andres Tuxtla, San Cristobal las Casas, San Juan de los Lagos, Tapachula, Tehuacán, Texcoco, Tijuana, Tlalnepantla, Tlaxcala, Toluca, Torreón, Tula, Tuxpan, and Tuxtla Gutierrez.

1. G means general records have been microfilmed. P means that parish records have been microfilmed.

2. Tamaulipas' name was changed to Tampico in 1958.

Sources

Bravo Ugarte, José. *Diócesis y Obispos de la Iglesia Méxicana (1519–1965)*. México, Editorial Jus.México, 1965. Text-fiche.

Galindo Mendoza, A., M. Sp. S. *Parroquias y Vicarias Fijas de la Iglesia Méxicana*. Tijuana, B.C., Vicario Apostolico de Tijuana, B.C., 1961. Text-fiche.

Galindo Mendoza, P. Alfredo, M. Sp. S. *Apuntes Geográficos y estadísticos de la Iglesia Católica en México*. México, D.F., Administración de la Revista "la Cruz," 1945. Text-fiche.

Iglesia Católica. *Directorio Eclesiástico de la República Mexicana*. ed. Jorge Durán Piñeyro. México, La Arquidiócesis, 1985.

Platt, Lyman De. *México Guía Gerneral: Divisiones Eclesiasticas*, 3 vols. Instituto Genealógica e Histórico Latinoamericano, 1989.

———. *Una Guía Genealógico-Histórica de Latinoamérica*. Acoma Books. Ramona, California, 1978.

Romero, José A., S.J., and Juan Alvarez Mejía, S.J. *Directorio de la Iglesia en Mexico*. México, D.F., La Buena, 1952. Text-fiche.

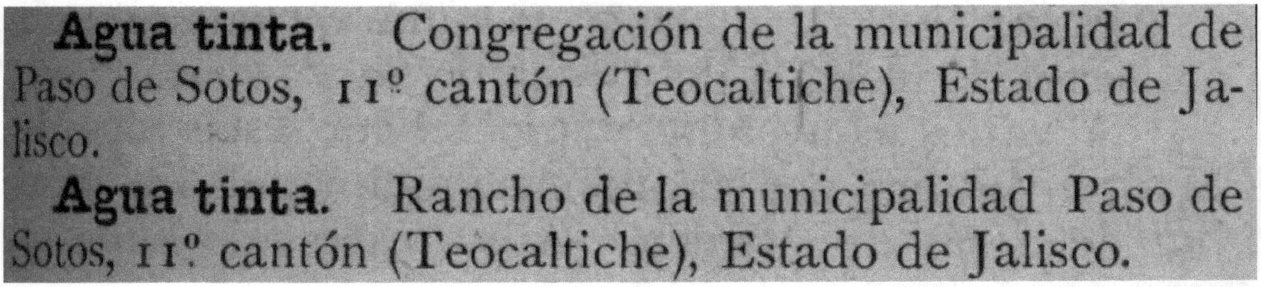

> **Agua tinta.** Congregación de la municipalidad de Paso de Sotos, 11º cantón (Teocaltiche), Estado de Jalisco.
>
> **Agua tinta.** Rancho de la municipalidad Paso de Sotos, 11º cantón (Teocaltiche), Estado de Jalisco.

Figure 5-4: Entries in geographical dictionaries like the one by Antonio Garcia Cubas help you find information about specific areas.

is within the municipality of Teocaltiche. However, other questions remain, such as to which of the modern *oficialías* of the Teocaltiche civil registers does the ranch of Aguatinta belong. Another approach for finding a locality would be to use a gazetteer, a book with long lists of place names and a minimal amount of information to identify and locate each particular place. Many gazetteers list geographical subdivisions smaller than the local parish and other natural features such as rivers and mountains, and provide latitude and longitude, making them a great help when the place you are looking for doesn't appear in an atlas or geographical dictionary.

Ironically, the best place to find a good gazetteer for Mexico or other Latin American countries is the *United States Board on Geographic Names Gazetteer*, prepared by the Office of Geography of the Department of the Interior. The number in this series referring to Mexico is fifteen. The most recent publication is a three volume series called *Gazetteer of México, Volumes I & II*. The same gazetteer is now available online at <http://gnswww.nga.mil/geonames/GNS/index.jsp>. You can download the entire directory for Mexico, or do a search online. Both of these alternatives take considerable time if you are using a dial-up modem. Continuing the search for the place name Aguatinta, you would find that it is a population center with the coordinates of 21° 32' 00" N latitude and 102° 40' 00" W longitude, found in the Mexican state MX14, or Jalisco, the fourteenth state in alphabetical order.

Another excellent place to search is the Archivo Historico de Localidades with an alphabetical search of all municipalities and localities. Typing in a place name will tell you the available online municipality (see <http://mapserver.inegi.gob.mx/dsist/ahl2003/index.html>.) This site also tells us that Paso de Sotos is now in the municipality of Teocaltiche.

This information could then be taken to one of three places to continue your search for Aguatinta. The first would be a collection of large topographic maps of Mexico, generally found in major public and university library collections. Another, possibly more effective source would be an atlas of Mexico, such as the *Nuevo atlas Porrúa de la república mexicana*. This single bound volume has a map for each Mexican state, several historical maps, an alphabetical list of all *municipios* by province, and an alphabetical index to all places on the maps.

In continuing your search for Aguatinta you would go to the map of Jalisco and, using the coordinate numbers located on the top or bottom and each side of the map, determine the location of Aguatinta. While the name of Aguatinta itself does not appear, the name of the larger village of Michoacanejo and municipality of Teocaltiche are located close by, indicating the sources for parish records and civil registration.

A third possibility would be an online search of a nineteenth century atlas published by the same Antonio Garcia Cubas discussed on page 61, found at <http://biblio2.colmex.mx/bibdig/dicc_cubas/base3.htm> Following the same procedure of using the latitudinal and longitudinal number coordinates on the side of the page, this locality could then be determined.

An excellent tool for attempting to more specifically locate the *rancho* of Aguatinta and its relationship with Paso de Sotos would be to check an atlas known as the *Enciclopedia de municipios de México.* This set of thirty-one volumes, one for each state in Mexico, contains three to four page articles about each *municipio,* with a map of the area showing the pertaining towns and villages and often even larger ranches. These volumes are not indexed, so you must know the current municipality. In the volume for Jalisco you could find Teocaltiche and then you would be able to determine the closest *oficialía* or civil registration office to Paso de Sotos.

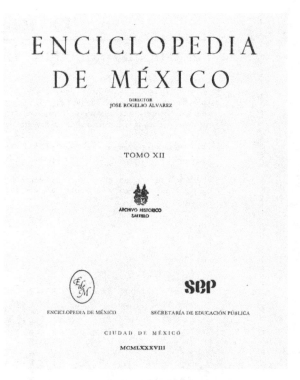

Figure 5-5: This encyclopedia gives detailed information on places in Mexico.

Figure 5-6 on pages 64 and 65 is a portion of the first page of the article for Teocaltiche, with a translation. (If language presents a problem, find somebody who can help you. Much of the vocabulary in this sample entry will be repeated in others, as each one essentially covers the same topics.) In the opening description we see a brief history of Teocaltiche, starting with the colonial period, covering the changes of the nineteenth and twentieth centuries up to the year 1994. A map on the second page shows that Paso de Sotos is located very close to Michoacanejo, which is therefore likely to be the appropriate civil registration office.

A further possibility is the *Enciclopedia de México,* which offers articles on the history of every state and diocese (see figure 5-5). Each state's article has a map showing all the municipalities in the state (see figure 5-7 for a page about Queretaro including a map of that state).

Remember, beyond looking for a specific place, a locality search is an excellent way to learn as much as possible about where your ancestors came from. As you search atlases and geographic dictionaries, be certain to copy the descriptions of the towns and information given about daily life. All of the sources mentioned above include descriptive sections about the places, generally including historical events, founding dates, crops raised, weather, and in some cases even details about nearby highways, railroads, and mail delivery. These kinds of details not only strengthen your research instincts, but make it easier to understand the lives of the people who lived there.

TEOCALTICHE

I PERFIL HISTORICO-CULTURAL

Cronología de la Ciudad

La fecha exacta de la fundación de Teocaltiche no se tiene, pero por las inumerables herramientas, utensilios y vasijas encontradas en el "Cerro de los Antiguos", data por lo menos de 20 siglos atrás.

Los historiadores manejan el año de 1187 fecha en que fueron dominados los indios (Tecuexes) por los Caxcanes.

Teocaltiche fue conquistado por los españoles en marzo de 1530 por el Capitán Cristóbal de Oñate y su segundo Miguel Ibarra.

Palacio municipal

En el año de 1532 se fundó la ciudad en el lugar que hoy ocupa, antes estuvo instalada en el lugar ya mencionado "Cerro de los Antiguos". Fue Fray Miguel de Bolonia quien arribó a este lugar y lo repobló.

Más tarde pasó a ser Alcaldía mayor de la Nueva Galicia en 1550, siendo su primer Alcalde Don Hernando de Martel.

Teocaltiche que significa "Lugar cerca o junto al Templo", fue elevada a categoría de ciudad por decreto Núm. 32 bajo el gobierno de Don Luis Vallarta.

Escudo de Armas

Con motivo del centenario del triunfo de la república el escudo de Teocaltiche fue oficialmente adoptado en ceremonia especial, el 15 de septiembre de 1967. Fue el ciudadano Martín V. del Mercado quien diseñó y donó el escudo al ayuntamiento en pleno.

Conforme a su significado el escudo consta de: El Cerro de los antiguos, al fondo; al sur, El Teocalli o Templo a la derecha de esta figura un (Macahuitl) o macana, arma ofensiva de las hueste pobladoras y al pie de tal alegoría el río de la ciudad.

En la cima del cerro de los antiguos, un chapulín, mote tradicional de los hijos de Teocáltiche: Chapulineros.

Ese cuadro se encuentra bordeado por un marco con los colores her[...] de verde, plata y oro; rematado en la parte superior con un águila nac[...] de frente.

Cronología de Hechos Históricos

1187 Fundación de Teocaltiche fecha en que fueron derrotados los [...] tecuexes.

1530 Mes de marzo, Teocaltiche es conquistado por los españoles.

1532 Fundación de la Nueva Ciudad de Teocaltiche.

1550 Teocaltiche pasa a ser alcaldía mayor de la Nueva Galicia.

1846 1 de septiembre, Teocaltiche es cabecera de departamento.

1861 22 de noviembre, se le concede título de ciudad.

1863 20 de enero, defensa de la Ciudad por Romualdo N. "El Caim[...]

1895 7 de marzo, motín del jueves santo. 30 de septiembre, homenaje [...] toriano Salado Alvarez.

Personajes Ilustres

Obispo Buenaventura Portillo y Tejeda
Lic. Rafael Pérez Maldonado
C. José María Carmona (1780-1885)
José María Alba (1805-1845)
Manuel de la Macusa (1833-1922)
Lic. Victoriano Salado Alvarez (1867-1931)
Escritor y Presb. José L. Larios.
C. Porfirio Martín del Campo (1885-1961)

Monumentos

Arquitectónicos: Ex-hospital, hoy casa de la cultura construida en el s[...] XVI; Templo de la Merced data del siglo XVII; Templo de San José co[...] truido en el siglo XVIII; Templo de Nuestra Señora de los Dolores, p[...] nervaduras estilo gótico en su interior, piso dulla frontis trabajado en ca[...] ra; Templo Parroquial de tres naves construido en el siglo XIX; Tem[...] de la virgen de Guadalupe del siglo XIX; palacio municipal, construc[...] muy antigua remodelada en 1981.

Históricos: Monumento a López Fonseca colocado en el atrio frontal [...] santuario; monumento en memoria a Don Benito Juárez; monumento [...] Independencia Nacional que se corona con un busto de Don Miguel Hi[...] go y Costilla y monumento en memoria de Don Venustiano Carranz[...]

Obras de Arte

Pinturas: La virgen del Refugio que se encuentra en el Templo de San J[...] realizada por Salvador Herrera, su presencia en Teocaltiche data del s[...] XVI; la pintura llamada del "Desprendimiento" que se encuentra en la [...] rroquia de Teocaltiche; "La Ultima Cena" pintura mural, ubicada en la [...] cristía del Templo de Jesús el Nazareno.

Literatura, Música y Poesía: En literatura destaca Victoriano Salado [...] varez con sus obras "La vida azarosa y romántica de don Carlos Ma. Bu[...] mante" y su ensayo de historia y filosofía denominado "De santa Ana [...] Reforma".

Fiestas Populares, Leyendas, Tradiciones y Costumbres

Fiestas Populares: 11 de noviembre feria local y festividades de la vir[...] de los Dolores.

Leyendas: "La de Jesús Nazareno", donde se cuenta que se hizo pe[...] y varios hombres no pudieron moverlo para sacarlo en procesión y se te[...] naran los temblores.

...ones y **Costumbres:** El día de muertos se acostumbra visitar en ...panteón de los Angeles; el sábado de gloria se acostumbra llevar el ...viviente por las calles; el día de Corpus Cristi se hace una proce-...las calles de la ciudad.

Templo parroquial

...ntos, **Dulces y Bebidas Típicos**

...ntos: Birria, pozole, mole, tamarindo y enchiladas.

...: Garapiñados, cocada, encurtidos, chilacayote, camote y biznaga.

... **Típicos**

... de charro y china poblana.

...anías

...dades de madera, hueso, sombrero de palma, sarapes, jorongos, re-...ceñidores, fajos, tilmas, camisas, escobetas, tejidos, bordados, alfa-...curtiduría de pieles y deshildados.

MEDIO FISICO Y GEOGRAFICO

...lización

...ipio se encuentra situado al noreste del estado y limita al norte con ...cipio de Villa Hidalgo y con el estado de Aguascalientes, al Sur con ...cipios de Jalostotitlán y San Juan de los Lagos, al oriente con el mu-...de Encarnación de Díaz y al poniente con el Estado de Zacatecas. ...ráficamente está ubicado entre las coordenadas 21°15'00'' y 21°43'30'' ...d norte y los 102°23'15'' y 102°47'30'' de longitud oeste con altura ...de 1,850 metros sobre el nivel del mar. Cuenta con 165 localidades ...cuales las más importantes son: Belén del Refugio, Michoacanejo, Hos-..., Huejotitlán, Villa de Ornelas, Rancho Nuevo, El Rosario y La Tri-

Figure 5-6: *The* Enciclopedia de municipios de México *contains information, maps, and other useful information for every* municipio *in Mexico.*

Templo de la Merced

Localización

Hidrografía

Sus recursos hidrológicos son proporcionados por los ríos y arroyos que conforman la subcuenca "Río Verde Grande de Belén", perteneciente a la región hidrológica "Lerma-Chapala-Santiago", teniendo como ramal el río Teocaltiche; así como también el San Pedro y Río Aguascalientes; en una multitud de arroyos tanto permanentes como temporales entre los que se pue-

QUERÉTARO

sitios se le invoca en vísperas de la temporada de lluvias.

QUERÉTARO, ESTADO DE. Fue erigido por la Constitución Federal del 4 de octubre de 1824 (Artículo 5°). Situado en la Mesa Central (parte sur de la altiplanicie), entre los 20° 01' 02" y los 21° 37' 17" de latitud norte, y los 99° 03' 23" y los 100° 34' 01" de longitud oeste del meridiano de Greenwich, limita al norte y noreste con San Luis Potosí; al este con Hidalgo; al sureste con el estado de México; al sur con Michoacán, y al suroeste, oeste y noroeste con Guanajuato. Conforme al Decreto núm. 19 de la Legislatura local, del 25 de julio de 1867, su nombre oficial es Querétaro de Arteaga. Tiene una extensión territorial de 11 269.7 km^2 y ocupa, en cuanto a superficie, el vigesimoséptimo lugar entre las entidades de la Federación, seguido por Aguascalientes (28), Colima (29), Morelos (30), Tlaxcala (31) y el Distrito Federal (32). El 8 de octubre de 1857, en el informe rendido ante el Congreso por el presidente Ignacio Comonfort, se anunció la determinación de agregarle el territorio de sierra Gorda, conforme a lo dispuesto en la recién promulgada Constitución Federal. El 1° de abril de 1900, el presidente Porfirio Díaz informó que los problemas de límites entre Hidalgo y Querétaro habían quedado resueltos mediante el decreto del 9 de diciembre de 1899. La entidad se ha regido por cuatro constituciones: del 12 de agosto de 1825, del 18 de enero de 1869, del 16 de septiembre de 1879 y del 9 de septiembre de 1917.

Según la *Relación de Michoacán o Códice escurialense*, el nombre original de la entidad es Quereta-Parazicuyo o Ychahtzicuyo, el cual, abreviado convencionalmente, se tornaría Querétaro, palabra que Eduard Seler interpreta como "juego de pelota". Maturino Gilberti, a su vez, advierte que el vocablo tarasco *querehte* significa pelota y que las palabras *taránduni*, *taránduquaro*, *queréhtaro* y *taránduqua* son sinónimos de juego de pelota. Fray Isidro Félix Espinosa afirma que en una escritura del primer virrey de México se le llamaba "Taxco y, en el traspaso de venta, Querétaro". En los *Anales del Museo de Michoacán*, con notas de Nicolás León, se lee que Taxco viene de Tlacho o Tlachco, que es juego de pelota. Parte de los territorios de Querétaro y de Tlachco (ahora Tasco, Gro.) fueron inva-

Municipios: 1. Amealco. 2. Pinal de Amoles. 3. Arroyo Seco. 4. Cadereyta. 5. Colón. 6. Corregidora. 7. Ezequiel Montes. 8. Huimilpan. 9. Jalpan de Serra. 10. Landa de Matamoros. 11. El Marqués. 12. Pedro Escobedo. 13. Peñamiller. 14. Querétaro. 15. San Joaquín. 16. San Juan del Río. 17. Tequisquiapan. 18. Tolimán

didos de modo casi simultáneo por los ejércitos de Moctezuma I (Ilhuicamina), según consta en la *Relación de las minas de Taxco*, formulada en 1581 por el alcalde mayor Pedro de Ledesma y publicada en el tomo IV de los *Papeles de la Nueva España* de Francisco del Paso y Troncoso; pero Querétaro jamás tributó a los aztecas, y sí, en cambio, Tasco, que fue conquistado entre 1440 y 1446 (*Códice mendocino*). Eduardo Ruiz dice: "Esta voz más bien debe ser Querétaro, que significa pueblo grande". Manuel Orozco y Berra, con apoyo en un documento del siglo XVI, indica que el nombre original fue Querenda ("piedra o peña grande") convertido luego en Querétaro. Coincide con él Nicolás León: "Querenda, piedra grande o peña, después Queréndaro o lugar o pueblo de piedras grandes o peñascos, luego convertido en Querétaro por modificación del vocablo original tarasco". En la mitología tarasca, Querenda Angápeti, nombre de una de las principales deidades, significa peña que se levanta en el llano; se le adora como casado con Peuame o Pavame

6741

Figure 5-7: A page like this, showing a map and providing useful information, can be a great aid in your research.

CHURCH GUIDES AND DIRECTORIES

So far the sources mentioned have concentrated on political jurisdictions. Information containing church divisions also needs to be located. The *Enciclopedia de municipios de México* mentioned earlier will also identify by name any parishes located in the municipality, often giving the date of their founding and some history. A second and perhaps more accessible source is Lyman Platt's *Divisiones eclesiásticas de México*, in which he lists all pre-1900 parishes for Mexico, providing information about the name and location of the parish, the bishopric to which it belonged, and the colonial civil divisions to which it belonged. Each of the entries is arranged under the state and then alphabetically by the name of the town. The date in which records begin for that parish is also provided. The introductory discussion of the history of the various dioceses is very helpful. Unfortunately, there is no general parish index at the back of the book, so you will need to know in what state the parish is found before the book can be used. This, of course, can be done in the several ways indicated above.

The Mexican Catholic Church also publishes church directories and other materials. Many of these can be found in a microfiche collection titled *Religiosity in Latin America*, published by K.G. Saur Company under the broader name of the CIDOC Collection. As this entire collection is available at many university libraries, including that of Brigham Young University, the easiest way to identify whether or not a specific directory is available is to go to <www.byu.edu>, look under the Harold B. Lee Library, and then go to the online catalog and search under the keywords "Mexico" and "CIDOC." This will then give you a list of 1,300-plus materials available in that collection. The list may be further refined by adding the word *directorio* or *historía*, and/or a specific state name. The individual books on microfiche may then be ordered through interlibrary loan if they are not available in a library close to you.

WHERE DO I GO FROM HERE?

Your reasons for reading this chapter will determine what you do next. If you had a place name but could not find it in the Family History Library Catalog, you will want to return to that catalog and look for records of the Catholic parish or civil register in the town or municipality which you have identified using the information in this chapter. Likewise, now that you know the municipality, state, and dioceses to which your ancestral hometown belonged, you may want to read about parish or civil registers in chapters 3 and 4. No matter where you go from here, you will undoubtedly find yourself gathering more information about your family's ancestral hometowns, making your family history richer and perhaps offering additional clues as to places to search.

NOTES

1. See Lyman Platt, *Genealogical Research in Mexico City* (IGHL, Salt Lake City, 1998).

VOCABULARY

Directorio—directory.

Historía—history; story.

RESOURCES ABOUT THE HOME LOCALITIES OF ACTIVITIES OF YOUR ANCESTORS

Would you like to know about what life was like for an ancestor who served in a *presidio* in northern Mexico, or who lived in Chicago in the early 1900s, or who lived on a *hacienda* near Saltillo, Coahuila, Mexico in the 1600s? These stories and many more are out there for you to find and incorporate into the family story you are compiling. Historians have written tens of thousands of books and articles about the history of Mexico and her people that

- can provide excellent detail for family histories,
- offer insights into the lives of one's Mexican ancestors, and
- give clues as to further research resources.

If you are new to Mexican history, consider first reading a general history book such as the following:

Meyer, Michael C., and William L. Sherman. *The Course of Mexican History*. 5th ed. New York: Oxford University Press, 1995.

Ruiz, Ramón Eduardo. *Triumphs and Trragedy: A History of the Mexican People*. New York: W. W. Norton, 1992.

If your ancestors lived in the northern frontier area of Mexico before 1848 you might start with the following:

Weber, David J. *The Spanish Frontier in North America*. New Haven: Yale University, 1992.

———. *The Mexican Frontier, 1821–1846*. Albuquerque: University of New Mexico Press, 1982.

You might also look at one of the many books that describe the history of a particular region or city, generally or in terms of a specific time or theme, such as the following:

Gutierrez, Ramon. *When Jesus Came, the Corn Mothers Went Away: Marriage, Sexuality, and Power in New Mexico, 1550–1846*. Stanford, CA: Stanford University Press, 1991.

Cuello, Jose. *Saltillo in the Seventeenth Century: Local Society on the North Mexican Frontier*. Ph.D. diss. [microform].University of California, Berkeley, 1981.

You can also find books that talk about a specific segment of people or a particular institution that may be relevant to your ancestors, such as the following:

Jackson, Robert H. *Indian Population Decline: The Missions of Northwestern New Spain, 1687–1840*. Albuquerque: University of New Mexico Press, 1994.

Moorhead, Max L. *The Presidio: Bastian of the Spanish Borderlands*. Norman: University of Oklahoma Press, 1975.

García, Juan R. *Mexicans in the Midwest, 1900–1932*. Tucson: University of Arizona Press, 1996.

LeVine, Sarah. *Dolor y Alegría: Women and Social Change in Urban Mexico*. Madison: University of Wisconsin Press, 1993.

Stagg, Albert. *The Almadas and Alamos, 1783–1867*. Tucson: University of Arizona Press, 1978.

How to Find Other Sources

Extensive bibliographies of histories can be compiled by searching online computer catalog services, especially those for large local public or university libraries and OCLC's First Search (also known as WorldCat <www.worldcat.org>). For general works, you should always perform a keyword search using key words such as, midwest, *mujeres*, *presidio*, and so on, followed by "Mexico." Researchers wanting books available for a specific locality of research in Mexico might also search one at a time under each of the following place names:

- State
- Municipality or town
- Capital city of the state
- Capital city of the local church diocese

Articles can be found by doing similar searches in a periodical index at a local library or online. Among the indexes that are particularly valuable for those doing Mexican research are *Hispanic American Periodicals Index* (HAPI) available at <http://hapi.gseis. ucla.edu/> and ABC Clio Historical Abstracts at <http://serials. abc-clio.com/active/start?_appname=serials&initialdb=HA>.

Most books and articles found can be ordered through Interlibrary Loan at a local library or are on film through the local Family History Center.

TOOLS FOR FINDING THE PLACE

Atlases

Nuevo atlas Porrúa de la república mexicana. García de Miranda, Enriqueta y Zaida Falcón de Gyves. México, D.F.: Edit. Porrúa, 1989.

Enciclopedia de los municipios de México. México, D.F. Imprenta Nacional, 1990.

Geographical Dictionaries

Garcia Cubas, Antonio. *Diccionario geográfico, histórico y biográfico de los estados unidos Méxicanos.* México, D.F.: Antigua Impr. de Murguia, 1888–91.(FHL film 1102587 vol. 1-3, 1102588 vol. 4-5)

Gazetteers

Gazetteer of México, Vol. I & II. 3rd ed. Washington, D.C.: Defense Mapping Agency, 1992.

Ecclesiastical Guides

Platt, Lyman D. *México: guía general: divisiones eclesiásticas.* Salt Lake City: Instituto Genealógico e Histórico Latinoamericano, 1989.

Historical Atlases, Maps, etc. (before 1848)

Gerhard, Peter. *A Guide to the Historical Geography of New Spain.* Cambridge, [U.K.]: Cambridge Univ. Press, 1972.

———. *The North Frontier of New Spain.* Norman, OK: University of Oklahoma Press, 1982.

———. *The Southeast Frontier of New Spain.* Norman, OK: Univ. of Oklahoma Press, 1993.

Encyclopedias

Alvarez, Josée Rogelio. *Enciclopedia de México.* México, D.F.: Secretaría de Educación Pública, 1987.

BEYOND THE PARISH
CHURCH AND
GOVERNMENT RECORDS

The emphasis of this book so far has been on finding and using Mexican parish sacramental and civil registration records. Many researchers may find they can effectively work in these records for long periods of time, in some cases running family lines back to the seventeenth century and beyond. In all cases where parish records exist before the beginning of civil registration in 1860, they will continue to be a mainstay of your research, even as you turn to other records as well.

You will have three reasons for reading this chapter. The first is to verify information already found in parish records. Perhaps you have reached the point that occurs even in some nineteenth century Mexican records where the information becomes less complete, sometimes insufficient to even reach a definitive level of proof of family relationships. The second is if parish records are missing, either totally or in a significant part, during a specific time period. A third reason is to add more interest and detail to the life stories of your ancestors than what appears in parish and civil registration records. Fortunately, the records of Mexico are extensive and rich and can assist you in accomplishing all three of these goals.

Mexico, unlike many other Latin American countries, has significant collections of other filmed records beyond parish and civil registration registers. Additionally, finding aids and, in some cases, public records or indexes exist to help locate and even directly consult these records. As discussed already, the first place to look for any type of record is the Family History Library Catalog, as the LDS Church has microfilmed extensive collections of records in Mexico. Many records have been filmed by other libraries and universities, particularly for the colonial period. Read chapter 10, "Research in Mexican Colonial Records" for ideas on finding these. The best way to locate the records filmed by the LDS Church is by first doing a Place Search under the name of the town where the parish and/or *municipio* is located. Also search under the name of the state, as records beyond parish and civil registers are often identified only as a collection for the entire state and not subdivided, even if they do contain significant information about specific people within towns in the state.

In some cases records for the entire state have been catalogued under the name of the capital city because the archive containing those records is found there, so check under the name of the state's capital city. Also check for the city that is the archdiocese for your ancestral hometown.

ARCHIVES: THE PLACE TO FIND ORIGINAL RECORDS

While much has been filmed in Mexico, the majority of records remains unfilmed (as in any other country in the world) and can only be consulted in Mexican archives themselves. In some cases where good catalogs and even indexes exist, and/or you find "genealogically friendly" archive personnel, records can be ordered from the archive upon payment of copying costs. For these reasons, understanding the organization of Mexican archives becomes helpful.

Simply defined, an archive is a place where records and historical documents are preserved. Initially an archive may be found in the place where the records were generated, under control of the generating entity—for example, the civil register office, parish house, or back room of a city hall. In many cases, records of several entities—such as all the various agencies of a state government and in some cases, cities within a state—will place their older records in a single separate historical archive designed to both preserve the records and provide access to them by interested historical researchers.

Municipal and State Archives

Government archives in Mexico are found at three levels: municipal, state, and national. Municipal archives hold records generated by the activities of city government, including such records as business licenses, tax lists, voter lists, censuses, and city legislation acts. Records created by businesses or families within the municipal limits may also have been donated to these archives. Generally municipal archives are found in the city hall, although in larger cities they may have been transferred to a separate building. In some cases, they are summarized or discussed online (see figure 6-1).

In some cases smaller municipal archives within a state have been transferred to central state archives where the possibility for preservation and access for researchers is better. The municipal archives of Mexico—especially those in capital cities such as Saltillo, Chihuahua, and Mexico City—are excellent, and many have rich historical collections, although unfortunately, they are often only cataloged and indexed at a rudimentary level. For information on material contained in specific city archives, see Patricia Rodríguez Ochoa's *Archivos estatales de México*. Indexes and archival guides for many specific archives may be located in university and large public libraries in the United States.

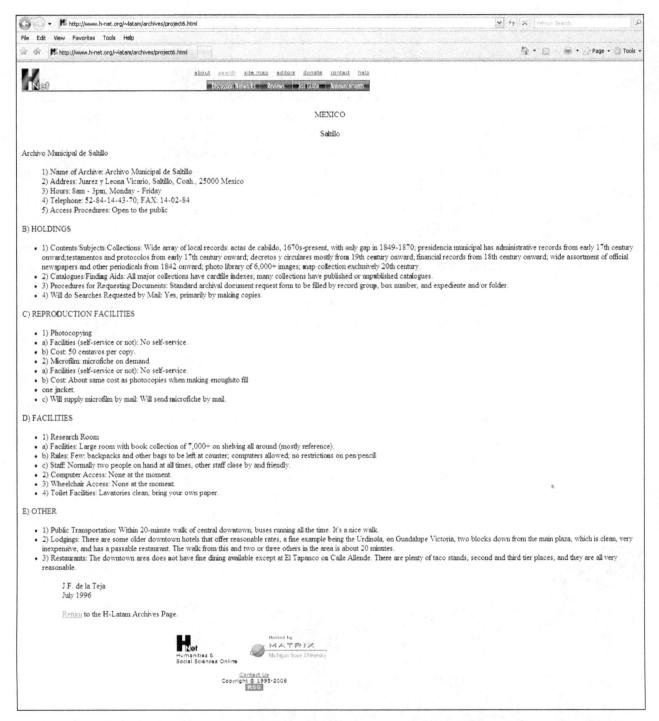

Figure 6-1: As shown by this summary of the Archivo de Saltillo, municipal archives are excellent places for finding information and are often described online, such as at this site at H-Net, <www.h-net.org/~latam/archives>.

During the middle years of the twentieth century, archives were organized in the majority of Mexican states to house accumulated records relating to state government agencies. Two categories of records generally comprised the core of these collections: judicial records and state administrative records (correspondence of the various governors, legislative acts, official state bulletins, court records, and so on). In many—although not all—states, notarial records for the national period were added. Some states sent in pre-1920 copies of civil registration records, generally beginning about 1875. Alternately, state copies of civil registration in states such as Chihuahua and Hermosillo are held by the central office of civil registration located in the capital city. Notarial records in some states have remained in a state office governing notaries, as in Chihuahua, or have been held in a separate archives held by the *colegio notarial*, as in Mexico City.

A few states, notably Chihuahua and Nayarit, have not yet created state archives. A list of the existing state archives with addresses and—where they exist—Internet sites, is found in appendix F, "Internet Sites for Mexican Genealogy." Ochoa's *Archivos estatales de México* also provides more specific information about each state archive. Even more detailed information can be found on the corresponding state archive website.

National Archives

In 1823, the National Congress of Mexico adopted legislation creating the Archivo General de la Nación, giving it the mandate to preserve the historical records of that great nation and make them accessible to the people of the United States of Mexico (see figure 6-2). At the time of its creation, the bulk of its records came from the archives of the Spanish Viceroy, housed in the General Archives of New Spain created in 1790.

During the 180 years since the creation of the Archivo General de la Nación, extensive records of the Mexican national government, from every administration beginning with that of Emperor Iturbide, have been transferred here, along with extensive private collections of materials relating to Mexican life and government. In 1977, a new facility for the archive was created by the conversion of an old prison with six spokes of cells and one of administration radiating from a central area which, as part of the conversion into the archive, was turned into a dramatic domed exposition area (see figure 6-3). One of the spokes houses all of the colonial records discussed in chapter 10, "Research in Mexican Colonial

Figure 6-2: The Archivo General de la Nación in Mexico City (shown here in an old drawing) provides access to a vast variety of records.

Figure 6-3: The Archivo General de la Nación was moved in 1977 to a new building, which used to be a prison.

Records" of this book. Other wings house the records of the nineteenth century through the end of the Porfirio Díaz era (1821–1910), the Mexican Revolution (1910–1920), and subsequent administrations of the twentieth century.

One entire wing of the Archivo General de la Nación houses a unique collection of microfilms, including not only government records but microfilmed copies of all pre-1900 Mexican parish records, obtained as part of the cooperative effort between the Genealogical Society of Mexico and the Genealogical Society of Utah (LDS Church). A beginning point for consulting records in the Archivo General de la Nación is the catalog ARGENA found at <www.agn.gob.mx./inicio.php> (see figure 6-4). The key to successfully locating records dealing with a specific locality in this collection is to make requests or searches under the name of the locality as well as specific surnames with or without given names. The archival personnel are excellent at responding to requests and, where the requests are specific enough, providing photocopies of requested records for a fee. See appendix E, "Researching in the Archivo General de la Nación from the United States," for microfilm copies available in the United States.

Since 2002, the national military archive, under the direction of the Mexican Department of Defense, has been open to researchers. This extensive collection of materials relating to military units in Mexico during the eighteenth, nineteenth, and twentieth centuries have yet to be explored in depth.[1]

Figure 6-4: The catalog ARGENA can be found on the Archivo General de la Nación's website <www.agn.gob.mx./inicio.php>.

Catholic Church Archives

An extensive and rich collection of Catholic Church records in Mexico exists beyond those of the parish (discussed in chapter 4, "Parish Records"). While parish records are recorded by individual parish priests, the role of bishops and archbishops is to oversee work done at a parish level, including the maintaining of parish records. In addition, their activities created records which are maintained at a diocesan level.

Table 5-1, "Archives of the Catholic Church Dioceses in Mexico before 1922," in chapter 5 is a chart of Mexican dioceses existing before 1922 with their creation dates, the diocese from which they originated on that date, and an indication as to whether or not there are microfilmed parish records or general diocesan records or both for that diocese. General records refer to documents that bishops or archbishops created by the bishop's courts and administrative agencies within that diocese and preserved in diocesan or archdiocesan archives. Each archive begins with the date of the creation of the diocese and contains records of genealogical significance such as marriage dispensations, censuses, and communion lists. For a more detailed discussion of the kinds of records located in these archives see pages 189 through 191 of Ryskamp's *Finding Your Hispanic Roots*. Although many of these records have been filmed, only limited work—primarily limited to marriage dispensations—has been done to index or even inventory them. One notable exception is the Archivo Histórico del Arquidiócesis de Durango, which has been microfilmed and indexed by the Rio Grande Historical Society located at New Mexico State University in Las Cruces, New Mexico. This index can be purchased at their website <http://archives.nmsu.edu/rghc/contents/contents.html>.

Archival Printed Materials

Most archives—local, state, or national—will have some type of published material explaining what they contain. It's helpful to think of these materials in the following way:

- *Guides*—If you were to walk into an archive that was new to you with somebody who was familiar with it by your side, they would probably begin by giving you an overview of what the archive held, saying things like, "The shelves in this section are where we keep inventories, this group of shelves deals with the Mexican Revolution," and so on. An archival guide serves the same function, giving an overview of what the archive contains.
- *Inventory*—Suppose this same person now takes you to a particular shelf or collection, going from book to book and pointing out the dates they cover. If this same information were written down it would be called an inventory. For example, when a state archive catalogs the names of all the notaries within a certain *municipio* and the dates their records cover, this is an inventory.
- *Index*—Now suppose this person takes a specific document from the shelf and goes through it with you, pointing out the names in it. This is the level of an index, which takes the documents in a section and at least gives the principal parties, such as the names of a child being baptized and his parents, or the people whose wills and contracts appear in a notarial book.

RECORD TYPES WITHIN MEXICAN ARCHIVES

Understanding the structure of Mexican archives leads to the question, "What records do each archive contain?" While it's unrealistic to try to cover all the record types within one discussion, some are more useful to genealogists and family historians, and/or more readily available. Among these are censuses, notarial records, city and administrative records, marriage dispensations, and diocesan administrative records.

Censuses

Following parish and civil registers, the record type likely to give you the most information about your family is the census. A census is a count or list of people in a city or rural district. While its actual purpose was usually to get a count of the people for taxes and military service, the specific nature of the census questions asked gave valuable family information. Unlike the United States system of taking a federal census every ten years (as discussed in chapter 9, "Searching for Your Ancestors in United States Records"), Mexican censuses in the late nineteenth and early twentieth centuries were taken less regularly on a nationwide basis. Only that of 1930 is readily available on microfilm through Family History Centers (see figure 6-5). Being aware that the 1930 Mexican Federal Census asked the following questions will let you know if this is in fact a source that could prove helpful to you:

- *Nombre/Apellido*—A census never indicates for certain all the members in a given family—it's your job to make that deduction based upon last names

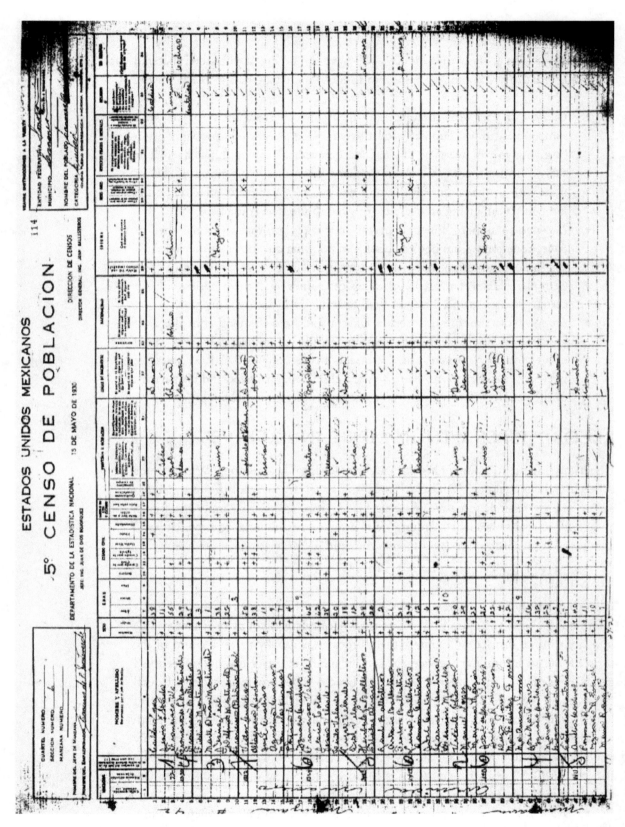

Figure 6-5: The columns of this 1930 census schedule correspond with the questions described on pages 77 and 79.

and ages. As you do so, remember the Hispanic surname system as it relates to women: the woman always keeps her birth surname throughout life, even after marriage, so the mother will have a different surname than her husband and children.

- *Sexo*—This column is divided into two categories, male and female.
- *Edad*—Beneath this heading are the three categories of years, months, and days.
- *Estado Civil*—This box refers to the person's "civil state," or in other words, marital status. Beneath this heading are six categories: Single; Married Civilly; Married by the Church; Free Union (living together without being married); Widow(er); Divorced. The distinction of being married civilly and/or by the church becomes more relevant when you think of the two record types, parish and civil registration. If a couple is listed as both, you should be able to find their marriage record in both parish registers and civil registers; if only civilly, you will find them only in civil registration.
- *Profesión u Ocupación*—A glance at the occupations listed in a census will give you a feeling for what the area is like where your ancestor lived.
- *Lugar de Nacimiento*—This category is especially helpful for researchers who do not yet know their ancestor's birthplace.
- *Nacionalidad*—This identifies those who are not Mexican citizens.
- *Idioma*—The first column under this category asks if the person speaks Castilian (Spanish.) The next column asks if another language or dialect is spoken.
- *Bienes Raíces*—This column indicates any real property owned.
- *Defectos Físicos o Mentales*—Physical and mental defects were noted in this column.
- *Religión*—As you would expect in an Hispanic nation, the majority of people will be Catholics, although not all.
- *Sin Trabajar*—This last column gives employment information by asking how long a person has been without work.

It's easy to see how a census record listing an ancestral family can be a valuable find. With even minimal study and imagination, you should find yourself piecing together new information and understanding about your family members and the locality in which they lived.

During the nineteenth century, censuses gave less information. Many in the eighteenth and nineteenth centuries, however, contain good information, including the names of family members and their ages. Such is often the case even in censuses from the 1700s and early 1800s (see figure 6-6).

Where Can I Find Census Records?

As with other sources, you can begin your search for Mexican censuses online at FamilySearch.org. Look first in the Family History Library Catalog under your ancestor's locality. Look under both the name of the town by itself and the name of

VOCABULARY

Nombre/apellido—name/ surname.

Sexo—Sex.

Edad—age.

Estado civil—marital status.

Profesión u ocupación— profession or occupation.

Lugar de nacimiento— place of birth.

Idioma—language spoken.

Bienes raíces—real property owned.

Nacionalidad—nationality.

Defectos físicos o mentales—physical or mental defects.

Religión—religion.

Sin trabajar—without work.

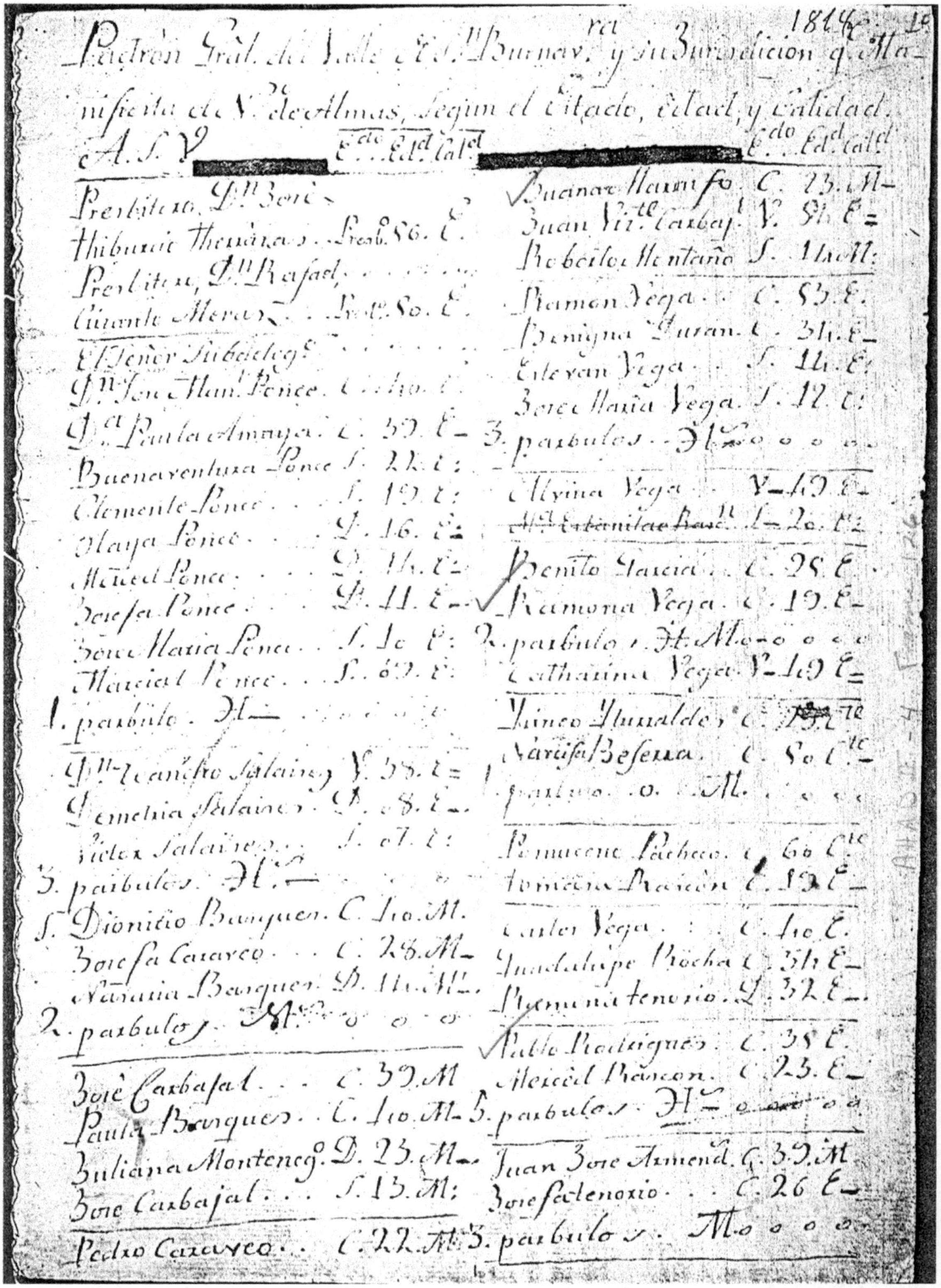

Figure 6-6: Early censuses, like this one from 1814, also provide valuable information, including name and age.

the *municipio* for that town. Most often the 1930 census will appear under the name of the *municipio*. Others will appear under either heading, as censuses were taken by both government and church units. Many are available on microfilm through any Family History Center.

If you don't find census records in the Family History Library Catalog, look up your town in the book *Latin American Census Records* by Lyman Platt, a listing of hundreds of Mexican censuses the author found while working as director of microfilm acquisition in Latin America for the Genealogical Society of Utah. Even this large list is not exhaustive, as many censuses held in Mexico in municipal, state, and church archives do not appear. If you do not find the census you need, consider writing to one of these archives to ask if they have any censuses for the years that interest you.

Records Found in the Diocese

As part of his responsibilities, the local Catholic bishop creates and maintains many types of records, some with the potential of helping with your family history. Records you will want to be aware of are described by the following.

- *Marriage Dispensation Records*—A couple that married in the Catholic Church who were related within the fourth degree of consanguinity (having a common great-great-grandparent) needed to have a marriage dispensation from the local bishop. (See chapter 4, "Parish Records," for a more detailed discussion of the marriage process.) Since these documents were created at the bishopric level rather than the local parish, they are stored in the diocesan archives. The length of a marriage dispensation varies from one or two pages to several. As a part of the format, the person making the document asks questions to people in the town—generally the older citizens—getting their testimony as to how the bequeathed couple were related. In many cases the dispensation includes a family tree showing connecting generations to the common descendant (see figure 6-7).

- *Ordinations to the Priesthood*—A careful record was kept of anybody ordained to the priesthood. Again, since these records were made by the bishop who had the authority to ordain priests, they are kept

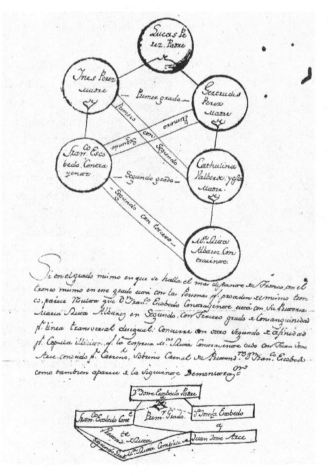

Figure 6-7: Family trees like this one are often found in marriage dispensation records.

in diocesan archives. If one of your ancestors had a sibling who became a priest, information in these records could contain a glimpse into your family history.

- *Parish Census or Communion Lists*—These records will look much like civil census records, except they indicate if a person has taken communion and confessed during that year (see figure 6-8). Unlike a civil census, they often do not list small children who have not yet received their first communion.
- *Other Bishop's Court Records*—Apostolic or ecclesiastical notaries worked in the curia (diocesan offices), preparing documents for presentation at canon law courts, as well as various petitions sent both to Rome and the local Bishop. In addition, they prepared any contracts and testaments involving the church and its property. Many of these documents, such as testaments and contracts, closely parallel those prepared by public notaries. Most are kept in either diocesan or cathedral archives.

Government Administrative Records

Both municipal and state archives have extensive records of government activities, with many of those at the municipal level containing records of potential value to family historians.

- *Tax Lists*—While today we think of tax lists as pertaining mostly to land, these documents record taxes assessed on such things as wine, wool, and cattle, in addition to property. One community even assessed a tax to pay for the new piano teacher. You can find tax lists in archives at all government levels (see figure 6-9).
- *Government Employee Records*—These records can be found in either municipal, state, or national archives. If one of your ancestors or a sibling worked for the government, perhaps you could find added information about your family here.
- *Cemetery Records*—City or municipal cemeteries were first created at the end of the colonial period. (Before that time, burial took place in the church.) Since they are found within each city, cemetery records will usually be found in municipal archives.
- *Land Records*—Your ancestors may have owned land. If so, you could perhaps find documents in property registers or notarial records concerning the sales of land and water rights, land ownership registrations, and land tax records pertaining to your family. You can find these in archives at the municipal or state level, or even at the Archivo General de la Nación in Mexico City.

Court Records

Containing a variety of judicial proceedings, court records are generally found in state archives, although they may also be found at the municipal level. Among them are records of criminal prosecutions, lawsuits about contracts or land disputes, and, for some time periods, divorce proceedings. Prepared by judicial and governmental

Figure 6-8: Parish census records provide similar information to their civil counterparts.

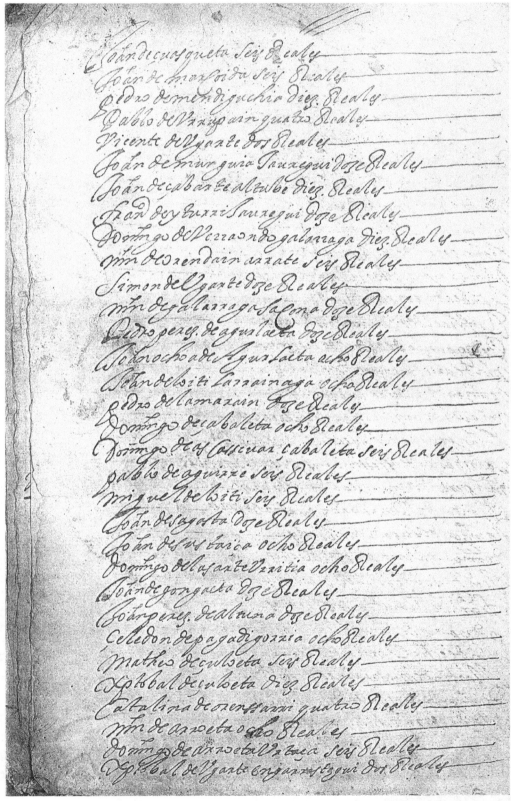

Figure 6-9: Tax lists give clues as to what your ancestors owned and where they lived.

scribes or notaries, these records are prepared almost entirely for the presentation of a particular court case, or for the filing of a petition with an administrative body. Since they are not well indexed as to particular individuals involved in the cases, you will most likely find it practical to consult these documents only if you know a particular ancestor was involved with a suit in a specific court, or with a petition to a specific governmental council.

NOTES

1. At this point, the only detailed information about the military records are two articles found in *Balance y Prospectiva de los Archivos Históricos de México*: Eulalio Fonseco Orozco's "Creación, organización y desarrollo del Archivo Histórico de la Secretaría de la Defensa Nacional" and Gloria Marin's "Situación y perspectivas del Archivo Histórico de la Secretaría de la Defensa Nacional," (D.F.: Archivo General de la Nación, 1994).

7

BEYOND THE PARISH
NOTARIAL RECORDS

As in other civil law countries, *notarios* in Mexico went beyond the scope of what United States attorneys traditionally do. *Notarios* in Mexico performed functions much like a contract attorney today in the United States, drafting wills, land sale contracts, prenuptial agreements, and many other types of documents. By signing these documents, *notarios* gave legal validity to them. They then provided permanent recording or safekeeping by arranging them chronologically and binding each year's documents in a book called a *protocolo*.

The prospect of reading legal documents in a foreign language can feel intimidating. Notarial records are not the place for beginners. However, as your confidence level increases in working with the other record types discussed in this book, and particularly if your geographic area of interest is lacking in some of these record types, the potential value for finding genealogical information in notarial documents makes the effort of reading them well worth it. With time and patience, the format of notarial documents will become familiar, and the possible glimpses of detail about the town and perhaps even the daily life of your ancestor can be enormously rewarding.

Unlike most other record sources, which deal with a specific event such as a birth, marriage, or death, notarial records cover a full range of documents. From wills to dowries, from sales of land to the sale of slaves, from apprenticeship papers to contracts with teachers, the list is nearly endless "because it would be difficult to find any human act in private or public life in which the pen of the *notario* did not intervene to give faith and testimony [to that act]."[1] Many Mexicans did not have reasons to use the *notario* to provide legal validation of transactions, but for those whose ancestors had sufficient social or financial status, these records will provide an incredible amount of human interest and information about the daily lives of their ancestors. From the center of Mexico City to the farthest small towns on the northern

VOCABULARY

Notario—notary; authorized official for preparing and certifying public actions, contracts, deeds, bonds, wills, etc.; for more information, see appendix A, "Glossary."

Protocolo—a book generated and preserved by a notary public.

Figure 7-1: Hernán Cortés, shown here with his interpreter Doña Marina, was trained as a notario before he came to the Americas.

frontier with the United States, notarial records have provided key genealogical information and a wealth of human interest materials to family history researchers in Mexico.

The connection between Mexico and its notarial system runs to its founding in 1521. In fact, Hernán Cortés trained as a *notario* in Salamanca, Spain and served as one in Santiago de Cuba before leading his expedition of conquest against the Aztecs (see figures 7-1 and 7-2). Since that time, throughout Mexico, *notarios* have been documenting legal transactions in accordance with specified formats and binding those documents in *protocolos*. Even in many frontier areas where *notarios* did not exist, the local *alcalde* or military *comandante* prepared legal documents and maintained them in formats just as a *notario* would. Those interested in the history of the notarial system in Mexico should read Bernardo Pérez Fernández del Castillo's *Derecho Notarial*.

ORGANIZATION, INDEXING, AND FORMATTING OF *PROTOCOLOS*

Protocolos are nearly always arranged under the name of the *notario* who produced them (see figure 7-3). Frequently, until the late eighteenth century, documents for a specific year were tied together in *legajos* . After that time period *protocolos* are generally found in bound volumes containing all the documents drafted by a single *notario* during a specific year or series of years.

Most historical archives have an alphabetical surname listing of the *notarios* whose *protocolos* appear in their archives, indicating the years they cover as well. Filmed collections like that of the records of Guadalajara are similarly arranged (see figure 7-4). Although the Guadalajara list does not, these lists may also include the name of the locality in which the *notario* or *escribano* served.

Occasionally there may also be a second index of all the towns from which *protocolos* have been assembled in a particular archive. Following the name of each town, the name of the *notario* or *notarios* from that town whose records are listed in the archive will be listed, generally with an indication as to the years their particular *protocolos* cover. You will find a system of call numbers in each archive with a number identifying each specific bundle or bound volume, covering one or several years of documents produced by a particular *notario*. A name index of those who are parties to the individual contracts may exist. Sometimes these are published, but more often they are in manuscript or card form at the archives.

In spite of the many differing types of legal transactions they can cover, a system of standard forms and practices developed for notarial documents, helping to assure

VOCABULARY

Alcalde—mayor.

Comandante—military commander.

Legajo—a bundle of loose papers that are tied together because they deal with a common subject.

Escribano—notary.

For more information, see appendix A, "Glossary."

407.—2 de marzo de 1527.—II, fols. 77 v y 78 r. CLXXXI v y CLXXXII r.

Antonio Cantero, estante en Tenustitlán, reconoce deber a Francisco López, carpintero, 20 pesos de oro, "por rrazón de vna esclava yndia de la tierra, que ha nombre Juana, que de vos resçebí conprada".

408.—3 de marzo de 1527.—II, fol. 78 r y v. CLXXXII r y v.

Miguel de Zaragoza, vecino de la Villa Rica de la Veracruz, estante en Tenustitlán, hallándose gravemente enfermo, confiere poder para testar a Pedro Valenciano, vecino de la misma ciudad, señalando por su heredero a su hijo Juan de Zaragoza y de Beatriz García, su legítima mujer, y por albaceas al citado Valenciano y a Juan de Salcedo, asimismo vecino de la misma ciudad.

409.—4 de marzo de 1527.[21]

Medellín. Pedro de Madrid, estante en la villa de Medellín, en la Nueva España, otorga poder a Leonor de Sanabria, viuda de Juan de Requena, para cobrar de Juan de Cuevas, estante en la ciudad de México, 150 pesos de oro, importe de la venta de cierta ropa, y de Alonso Lucas, boticario, "la parte que yo tengo en vna botica que el dicho Alonso Lucas tiene, con lo que se a ganado e proçedido después que entre mí y el dicho Alonso Lucas se hizo conpañía en la dicha botica, más vos doy e trespaso el asyón e derecho que yo tengo a vnas casas que yo arrendé de Salamanca, sastre, para que las podáys arrendar"...

410.—4 de marzo de 1527.—II, fol. 79 r y v. CLXXXIII r y v.

Gonzalo Hazán, vecino de Tenustitlán, reconoce deber a Antonio de Segovia, estante en dicha ciudad, 46 pesos de oro "por razón de vn sayón de terçiopelo negro nuevo e de çiertas joyas de oro, que de vos resçebí comprado".

[21] Esta escritura se incorporó entre las hojas del registro.

411.—4 de marzo de 1527.—II, fols. 79 v y 80 v. CLXXXIII v y CLXXXIV v.

Francisco de Figueroa, estante en Tenustitlán, entra a servir como minero con Hernando de Torres, vecino de Tenustitlán, y con Martín Jiménez, vecino de la villa de Colimán, por tiempo de 16 meses, "para que en este dicho tienpo yo el dicho Francisco de Figueroa ande coxendo oro en las minas de Çacatula o en otras qualesquier partes que me dixerdes e mandardes, con vna quadrilla de esclavos de çiento hasta ochenta personas..., e que vos los dichos..., seáys obligados en todo este dicho tienpo 2 me dar de comer e bever, e casa e cama en que esté e duerma sano o enfermo conveniblemente, segúnd vso e costunbre de la tierra, e más que me avéys de dar... çiento e veynte pesos de oro de minas".

412.—6 de marzo de 1527.—II, fols. 80 v y 81 r. CLXXXIV v y CLXXXV r.

Diego de Medina, sastre, estante en Tenustitlán, otorga poder a Hernán García, estante en Tenustitlán, para que éste cobrase de Juan de Báybar, calcetero, nueve pesos de oro que le debía.

413.—7 de marzo de 1527.—II, fol. 81 v. CLXXXV v.

Pedro de Villanueva, vecino de Tenustitlán, confiere poder a Juan Páez, vecino de Santiago de Guatemala, estante en Tenustitlán, para cobrar de cualquier persona cualquier cantidad

414.—7 de marzo de 1527.—II, fol. 82 r. CLXXXVI r.

Pedro Sánchez Farfán, vecino de Tenustitlán, otorga poder a don Luis Vaca, obispo de Canarias, del Consejo de Su Majestad, para comparecer ante el mismo y presentar una carta por la que Luis de Berrio renunciaba en su persona el oficio de regidor, y solicitar se le hiciera merced de dicho cargo.

415.—7 de marzo de 1527.—II, fols. 82 v y 83 v. CLXXXVI v y CLXXXVII v.

Testamento de Miguel de Zaragoza otorgado por Pedro Valenciano, en virtud del poder contenido en el documento núm. 408.

Figure 7-2: Two pages of extracted notarial records from Mexico City during the years under Cortés. (Agustin Millar, Carlos and Mantecos, Jose L. Indice de Protocolos. *Mexico D.F. Colegio de Notarios, 1927.)*

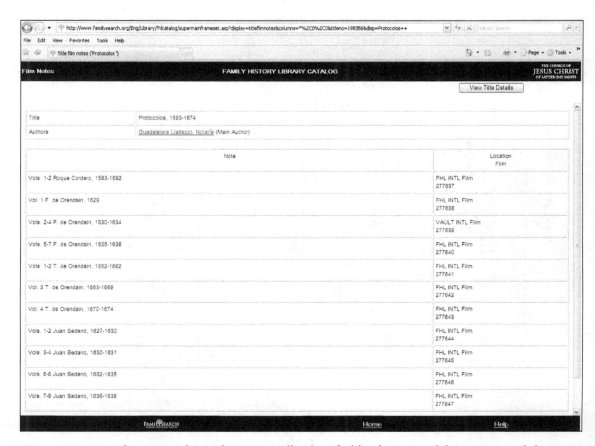

Figure 7-3: Note that notarial records are generally identified by the name of the notario *and the years covered in the* protocolos *he has written.*

that recorded transactions were legally recognized and binding. First, all documents from 1673 on had to be drafted on specially stamped paper, the cost of which varied, depending on the document type. The cost of these represented a revenue tax by the crown on legal transactions. A stamped paper bearing the particular year of issue had to be used. Only in circumstances of isolation will you find paper used from a preceding year—which in itself may indicate an interesting but difficult period in local history.

By the time of the 1519 conquest of Mexico, a basic format for writing notarial documents had developed, with every notarial document containing the following six elements:[2]

1. Date and locality of the transaction
2. Reception of the parties by the *notario*
3. Identification of the parties (usually by given names, surnames, and residences, and often marital status and/or occupation or title)
4. Standard legal language specific to the type of transaction (these were so standardized that by the sixteenth century books were published setting forth specific formats for the *notario* to copy)

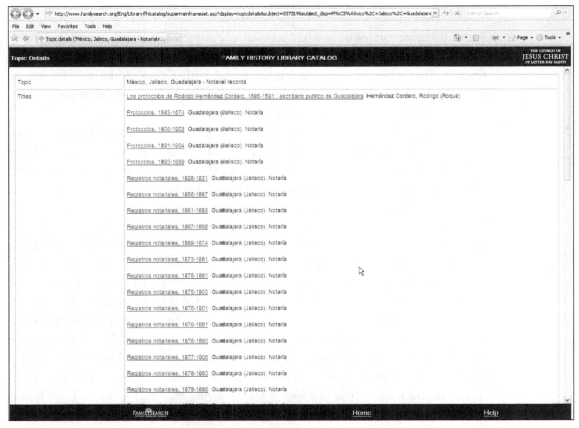

Figure 7-4: Many filmed notarial records, such as these from Guadalajara, Jalisco, can be found in the Family History Library Catalog.

5. Witnesses to the transaction (with identification similar to that of the parties involved)
6. Authentication of the transaction by the *notario*

Knowing that all notarial documents contain these common elements will make them feel less intimidating to work with. Generally a brief description or summary of the document appears in the margin or at the top of the first page. If it is a contract or other transaction between two parties, the names of both parties will generally appear here. If not, this information will be in the first paragraph.

Like the top of the page, the body of differing notarial documents also follows certain formats. As you become familiar with some of the more significant types of documents and their basic formats you'll find yourself increasingly able to evaluate the information they contain, knowing which ones should be read carefully and in their entirety.

Because of the uniformity of notarial documents, a researcher can quickly survey a large number of them in looking for those that relate to his particular family. This is fortunate, since practically no general indexes exist as to the names of the parties involved, and for many volumes even yearly inventories do not appear.

VOCABULARY

Testamento—a will; for more information, see appendix A "Glossary."

En el nombre de Dios, Amén—"In the name of God, Amen." This is the phrase with which wills usually began.

Wills

One of the most common notarial documents of interest to a family history researcher is a will (see figure 7-5). The Spanish word for will is *testamento*, similar to the word "testator" (the name of the person making the will). Knowing the specific format of a notarial *testamento* allows you to concentrate your efforts on those parts of the document most likely to give genealogical information.

You can quickly identify a will as it usually begins with the words "*En el nombre de Dios, Amén.*" The next sentences give the place, the name of the testator and, if he or she is married, the name of the spouse, as well as whether or not the spouse is deceased. If the testator never married, the record often gives his or her parents' names.

After the testator is identified, he or she will state how they want to be buried. In Mexico—as with all Hispanic countries—most people were Catholic, which is reflected in the requests for masses they wished performed on their behalf as well as for previously deceased family members. These requests may give you new information about the family. For example, names of former spouses might be given, or the names of children who have already died. This part of the will also gives directions for burial.

Once the religious requests have been dealt with, the testator then specifies what he would like done with his property. This is a fascinating part of the will for you as a family historian, as it gives some indication about your ancestor's lifestyle. Remember that in Mexico both men and women owned their own property. One study of the wills of twelve women living in New Mexico during the years 1715 to 1768 found that eleven of the twelve owned property.[3] This statistic gives a perspective on the lives of women who lived during this rugged time, and an understanding of the potential value of the wills of both women and men.

Because most people owned so little, everything had value. Wills dealt with property such as land and buildings, but could also include small items such as a hoe, a spoon, or stockings. One will left "a pitcher used for chocolate." Many times articles of clothing were given. Generally these items were left to family members, whose names and relationships are specified. The names of stepchildren might be mentioned, or names of family servants who were also given property. Watching for these details gives not only family information but a glimpse into the testator's life.

At the conclusion of this part of the will, the executors and heirs are nearly always named. If the testator's child is deceased but has living children, names of those grandchildren might be given.

Even the closing of a will, which reveals whether or not he or she was able to sign his or her name, can tell you about your ancestor. Frequently the testator was unable to do so, an indication of the education level at that time. None of the women in the New Mexico study mentioned above signed their name. One of them even stated that she did not sign because she did not know how.

Other Notarial Record Types

It is impossible to even briefly review the many document types found in a *notario's protocolos* (see figure 7-6). The sidebar, "Types of Notarial Documents," lists only the

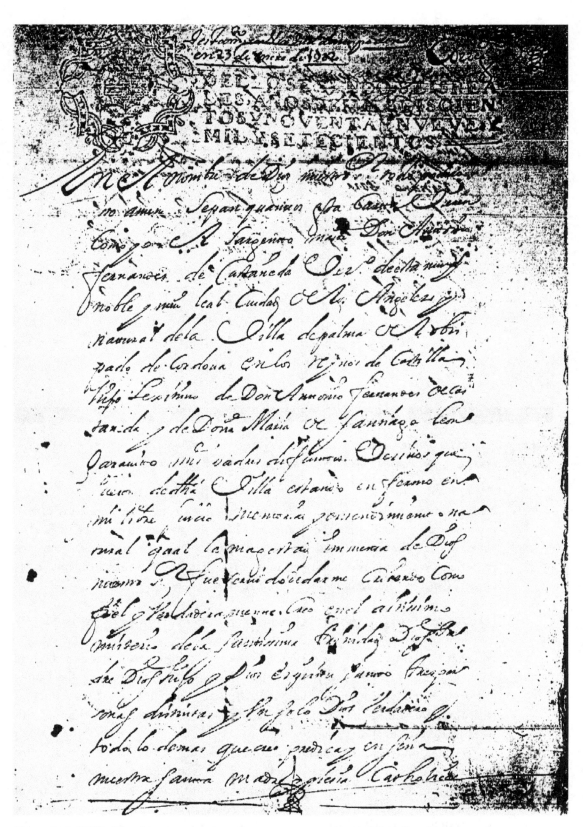

Figure 7-5: Wills, like this one on stamped paper, can give detailed family information.

Figure 7-6: Collections of notarial records can be very large. The example shown here in the Family History Library Catalog shows a collection comprising 1,060 rolls of microfilm.

principal ones, but as you begin your own research you will likely find many others. If you are puzzled as to what they are, check either the glossary in the back of *Finding Your Hispanic Roots*, or a good unabridged Spanish language dictionary from past centuries, such as the one published in Madrid, Spain by the Real Academia de la Lengua Española, found in facsimile form at <www.rae.es>.

WHERE CAN I FIND NOTARIAL DOCUMENTS?

Fortunately, many notarial documents, including wills, have been microfilmed. Once again you can order these to your Family History Center by checking the Family History Library Catalog in a Locality Search under the name of the state (such as Jalisco), and/or the capital city of the state (such as Guadalajara) for the topics of Notarial Records or Wills.

Parish death records are potential sources for leading you to the will of an ancestor as they may tell you if the deceased made a will and if so, with which *notario*. Be sure when reading death records to copy this information if it is given. With the name of the *notario*, you can then find his records by doing an Author or Keyword search in the Family History Library Catalog. Once you are actually researching in notarial

TYPES OF NOTARIAL DOCUMENTS

Spanish	English
Testamento	Will
Poder	Power of Attorney
Inventario de Dote	Dowry Inventory
Venta Real	Land Sale
Capitulación Matrimonial	Marriage Contract or Prenuptial contract
Compra-Ventas	Sales of Property (all types)
Donaciones	Gifts
Prueba de Nobleza	Proof of Nobility
Certificacion	Certificate of Status
Truecos y Cambios	Trades and Exchanges
Escritura de Censo	Annuity contract
Traspasos	Transfers
Cobdicilios	Codicil
Limpieza de Sangre	Purity of Blood Proof
Inventario de Bienes de Difunto	Inventory of the Assets of the Deceased
Tutela	Guardianship
Partición	Partition (division of assets, often among heirs)
Renuncias	Revocations or Renunciations
Protocolos	Books of notarial documents

records, use your ancestor's death date as a starting point for the search and move backward in time.

Locating notarial records that have not been microfilmed can feel challenging, but is possible. In any locality, three different archives will potentially have them:

- *State Historical Archives*—These archives generally contain records created after Mexican independence in 1821.
- *Notarial Archives or Office*—Either because a state archives has not been set up, or local pride and/or interest of local historians has discouraged the practice of submitting records to the government historical archives, state or federal district notarial offices may hold the notarial records for certain localities. Such is the case in Nayarit, Chihuahua, and Mexico City.
- *Municipal Archives*—Notarial records, especially for the colonial period before 1821, are often found in municipal archives. If you are looking for a notarial record from a particular city, it may be necessary to consult their local municipal archive. At this local level, the record preservation varies

dramatically, from ordered and well-protected collections in a proper library setting to a random or careless storing of the records in any available space, most frequently in the local city hall.

If the notarial records you are looking for have not been filmed, write to the Archivo Municipal or the Archivo Estatal in the town and/or state where your ancestor lived and ask if they have notarial records for the time and place in which you are searching. Generally, this should be done in Spanish. Most archival personnel are extremely helpful. They should not only answer, but be willing to allow you access to the records themselves if a trip to Mexico can be arranged. In some cases, such as in the city of Saltillo in the state of Coahuila, wills and other notarial records have been indexed and those indexes are published. If you are unable to personally consult the records and they have not been microfilmed and made available in the United States, you could obtain the services of an experienced Mexican historian, genealogist, or record searcher. The potential value of notarial records for adding detail and depth to your family's history makes them well worth the search.

NOTES

1. Miguel Muñoz de San Pedro, *Reflejos de siete siglos de vida estremeña en cien documentos notariales* (Caceres, 1962), 485.
2. "Bibliografía del Notariado en España," *Estudios históricos y documentos de los archivos de Protocolos* (Barcelona: Colegio Notarial de Barcelona, 1974), 195–198.
3. Angelina F. Veyna, "It Is My Last Wish That . . . A Look at Colonial Nuevo Mexicanas Through Their Testaments," in *Building With Our Hands: New Directions in Chicana Studies*, ed. Adela de la Torre and Beatriz M. Pesquera (Berkeley: University of California Press, 1993), 91–108.

8

SEARCHING FOR YOUR MEXICAN SURNAMES

Much research on Spanish surnames has already been done by others, including considerable genealogical research about Mexican families. While original sources for Mexico are not as readily available online as those for the United States are, an individual working both online and in a larger public or university library can find considerable information about Mexican and Spanish families.

This process of identifying what others may have written about your Mexican family is divided into three steps:

1. Searching for individuals of your same surname in large selected databases
2. Searching for family histories and biographies
3. Searching for histories or descriptions of your surname and its origin

SEARCHING FOR INDIVIDUALS

The first place to check for information about specific family members would be at FamilySearch.org, where you will find a collection of database indexes, two of which—the International Genealogical Index (IGI) and the Vital Records Index-Mexico—contain the names of millions of persons born and/or married in Mexico, generally before 1900. Although some of these names were submitted to the database by specific individuals, the great majority are there as a result of a volunteer program, which extracted data from Mexican Catholic parish baptism and marriage records.

Once you are on the home page for FamilySearch.org, click the "Search" tab. From here, you can fill in information on the family members you are searching for. On the left hand side of the screen you will see a listing of several database indexes. The default setting, "All Resources," allows you to search all of these databases at one time, which will give you more complete results. Be certain, after you have entered the family member's information, to limit your search to Mexico. (Of course, if you are not certain whether the person was born or married in the United States or Mexico, then conduct the search for both places.) If you are dealing with a common surname such as González, Díaz, or Martín, limiting the time period of the search will help. Note that once the search comes up you can also limit the entries you look at to those from the part of the Mexican state from which your ancestors came.

The websites Ancestry.com and Genealogy.com have databases of a comparable size to the IGI, but unfortunately, as these databases have been compiled from the information given by individual subscribers and from the extraction work done from records within the United States, at this time they contain relatively little Mexican material. As more Mexican Americans do genealogy research and submit their information, that database will increase. Remember though, that while there may not be large amounts of Mexican American material, you will find specific instances where considerable information can be found. The message boards on these sites often contain Hispanic surnames, sometimes with hundreds of messages from others doing their own genealogical research and looking for "cousins." Also, as mentioned previously, Ancestry.com is launching a site for Hispanic research in 2007.

Database materials, which can be located by doing a Google search or going to Cyndi's List <www.cyndislist.com> or Ancestry.com, are abundant for those with ancestry in New Mexico, especially for certain branches of families from the colonial period with extensive descendants in the United States, and for those whose ancestors come from Catholic parishes in small towns like Mier and Camargo situated on the Mexican side of the Rio Grande River. The New Mexico and colonial records appear because of researchers who have done significant amounts of research for these places and time periods and have submitted the results to share with others. The last category of parish information from the Mexican side of the Rio Grande River appears on Ancestry.com as a result of a volunteer project by members of the Spanish American Genealogical Association in Corpus Christi, Texas.

A small but growing number of very good databases can be found relating to research in Mexico, containing databases of genealogical research done by Mexican Americans. One of these is Elanillo.com (see figure 8-1). Spending half an hour exploring each of these sites will be well worth the effort. These sites provide message boards and access to a growing number of individual family sites created by researchers wanting to share the excitement of discoveries they have made in their family history. Sites relating to Mexican genealogy can also be located by checking at Cyndi's List in the general Hispanic category or the category for Spain. Searching for a surname, or even the names of specific individual members of an ancestral family, can also be done at Google.com.

SEARCHING FOR FAMILY HISTORIES AND BIOGRAPHIES ONLINE

In the same way some researchers and volunteers have significantly contributed to online databases, others have written and published their family history in journals

Figure 8-1: Websites like Elanillo.com focus on Hispanic genealogical research.

and books. You can look for information regarding your family by going again to FamilySearch.org and searching in the Family History Library Catalog. Unlike the Place Search described in chapter 3, "Civil Registration Records," conduct this search in the Surname Search section. Type in the surname of interest and it will give a list of books and films in the Family History Library Catalog collection containing information about persons of that surname. As with any catalog entry, this does not identify every individual mentioned in those books, but only those surnames for which there were significant enough numbers of individuals that the cataloger noted them as he created the catalog entry. While the books in the Family History Library in Salt Lake City do not circulate, many of them are found in other collections, such as that at Brigham Young University. If the book is more than seventy-five years old, the Family History Library may be able to make a microfilm copy of it and send to a local Family History Center.

Other online library catalogs should also be searched, even for books you found in the Family History Library Catalog. Libraries such as those at the University of Texas at Austin, the University of Arizona, Arizona State University, New Mexico State University at Las Cruces, the University of New Mexico at Albuquerque, Tulane University in New Orleans, the University of California at Berkeley, as well as the Los Angeles Public Library, Dallas City Public Library, and the Clayton Library in Houston, Texas, all have significant collections of material relating to Mexican American history research and therefore significant numbers of family histories. You can search each of these libraries separately, or you can go to a major library that has access to a Library Consortium (such as WorldCat or RLIN) and look at all of them in a single search along with thousands of other libraries worldwide. Once you have identified a book you want, it can be ordered through Interlibrary Loan to a library near your area that participates in the online library catalog system.

In searching for family histories, remember to look not only for books, but for articles in journals. Note, in the sidebar "Published Surname Sources," the number of published genealogical journals relating to Spanish language research. Unfortunately, at this time there is no central index of these materials, although the Allen County Public Library in Ft. Wayne, Indiana has expressed interest in adding these to PERSI, its online index to genealogical periodicals found at Heritage Quest <heritagequest. com> (a paid service). Watch that index for the possibility of such periodicals appearing in the future. Another place to look for family histories published both in books and articles is the book *Hispanic Surnames* by Lyman Platt, an excellent collection of references to more than five hundred different published family histories dealing with Latin America. As in the search for individuals, remember the possibility of doing a search for your surname at Google.com <www.google.com> or at Cyndi's List <www.cyndislist.com> and finding a link to a recently published online family history.

PUBLISHED SURNAME SOURCES

Atienza, Julio de. *El Diccionario heráldico de appellidos españoles y títulos nobiliarios.* M. Aguilar: Madrid, 1948.

Basanta de la Riva, Alfredo. *Sala de los Hijosdalgo, Catálogo de todos los plietos y expedientes y probanzas.* 2a. ed. Hidalguia: Madrid, 1956.

Bermudez Plata, Cristobal. *Catálogo de Pasajeros a Indias.* Vol. 1: 1509–34; Vol. 2: 1535–38; Vol. 3: 1539–59. Imprenta Editorial de la Gavidia: Sevilla, 1940.

Boyd-Bowman, Peter. *Indice geo-biografico de 56 mil pobladores de América* Fondo de Cultura Económica: Mexico, D.F., 1985.

Garcia Carrafa, A. *Enciclopedia Heráldica y Genealógica Hispano-Americana.* 88 vols. AA-URR. Madrid, 1920–63.

____. *El Solar Catalán, Valenciana y Balear.* Libreria Internacional Churruea: San Sebastian, 1967.

Heredero Roura, Federico, and Cadenas y Vicent, Vicente. *Archivo General Militar de Segovia: Indice de Expedientes Personales.* 9 vols. Ediciones Hidalguía: Madrid 1959–63.

Herrero Mediavila, Victor and Aquayo Hayle, Lolita Rosa. *Indice Biográfico de España, Portugal e Ibero-América.* 4 vols. K.G. Saur: New York, 1990.

Magdaleno, Ricardo. *Catálogo XX del Archivo General de Simancas, Títulos de Indias.* Patronato Nacional de Archivos Historicos: Valladolid, 1954.

Matilla Tascon, Antonio. *Indice de Expedientes de Funcionarios Publicos, Viudedad y Orfandad, 1763–1872.* Hidalguia: Madrid, 1962.

Nuñez Alonso, Pilar. *Inventario de la Sección de Hidalguía del Archivo de la Real Chancillería de Granada.* Real Maeztranza de Caballería: Granada, 1985.

Platt, Lyman D. *Hispanic Surnames.* Baltimore: Genealogical Publishing Co., 1996.

Querexeita, Jaime de. *Diccionario onamástico y heráldico basco.* 6 vols. La Gran Enciclopedia Vasca: Bilbao, 1970–75.

Another possibility for finding information about a specific ancestry would be a collection of biographies or a biographical dictionary, such as the *Indice biográfico de España, Portugal e Ibero-América* by Victor Herrero Mediavila and Lolita Rosa Aquayo Hayle. This four-volume index identifies about two hundred thousand historical individuals from Roman times to the early twentieth century, compiled from 306 biographical encyclopedias, dictionaries, and collective works covering seven hundred original volumes published from the seventeenth to the early twentieth centuries from Latin America, Spain, and Portugal. Those works were photocopied and the articles from all seven hundred volumes were then separated and arranged in alphabetical order. That alphabetized collection was then filmed on 1070 microfiche and is available at Family History Centers (Microfiche sets #6002170-6002172), as well as at many large public and university libraries, such as the Brigham Young University library or the Bancroft Library at the University of California, Berkeley. A second series, on 984 microfiche, adds significant other works to the collection, including all entries for the Garcia Carraffa Encyclopedia discussed below. (Microfiche sets #6131531-6131558.) These microfiche collections are also included in the *World Biographical Index* published on CD by the K.G. Saur company, which covers thousands of biographical dictionaries and collections from all over the world, including two Hispanic series. The Internet version, known as the World Biographical Information Systems, is available as a paid service at large libraries.

SEARCHING FOR HISTORIES OR DESCRIPTIONS OF YOUR SURNAME AND ITS ORIGIN

A wide variety of biographical and genealogical encyclopedias and dictionaries exist for Spanish surnames. Perhaps the most famous and extensive, Garcia-Carraffa's *Enciclopedia heráldica y genealógica Hispano-Americana* currently includes eighty-eight volumes published from 1920 to 1967, covering the letters AA through URR. The first two volumes of this series are a study of the science of heraldry, and the remainder of the volumes are an alphabetical list of noble and semi-noble families from throughout Spain and her former American colonies. These are listed according to surnames, and involve a brief account of the history of each family, tracing it down to its most recent noble member. Most entries also include illustrations of coats of arms, and frequently have a limited bibliography, which can lead to more extended monographic family histories. An additional fifteen-volume series prepared by Endica de Mogrobejo has completed the missing names from URR to the end of the alphabet.

The Library of Congress has indexed fifteen thousand surnames found in these two sets combined at <www.loc.gov/rr/hispanic/geneal/index_gc.html>. This collection is reproduced among the entries in the second series of the Archivo *Biográfico de España, Portugal e Ibero-América*. It is also available at the following locations:
- Family History Library (Salt Lake City)
- Library of Congress
- Boston Public Library
- California State Library

- Getty Center Library
- Harvard University
- The Hispanic Society of America
- New York Public Library
- Princeton University
- University of Illinois
- University of Pennsylvania
- University of Tennessee
- University of California, Berkeley
- University of California, Berkeley, Bancroft Library
- University of California at Santa Barbara
- University of Michigan
- University of Nevada (Reno)
- State University of New York at Buffalo

Lyman D. Platt offers Hispanic surname histories online at <www.infowest.com/personal/l/lplatt/platt.html>. Many of these histories, which have a heavy Spanish American emphasis, originally appeared in *Vista* magazine. Each provides a brief history of the surname, its etymology, and a series of references to individuals with that surname who have been famous or found in Spanish American regional sources. A similar series has appeared in the Orange County, California newspaper *Excelsior*, and has been compiled and published by the Society for Hispanic Historical and Ancestral Research <www.somosprimos.com>.

Almost every Hispanic country has national and regional dictionaries and encyclopedias, which can often be of even greater value to the researcher because they include many families and surnames that are not noble in origin. Mexican examples are the *Diccionario biográfico de Tamaulipas* and *Diccionario biográfico de Saltillo*.

Another type of regional series is typified by the *Diccionario onomástico y heráldico vasco* by Jaime de Querexteta, a six-volume series listing in alphabetical order nearly all of the Basque names that can be found. While it does not give a family history for most of them, it will indicate if the name is unique to a particular region, and may be a clue in locating the particular area in which one should search. For example, the surname *Anacaba* is listed as meaning *pastizal de gamones* (feeding grass of small mountain goats) and originating in the area of the province of Vizcaya. Perhaps more helpful would be a reference such as that for the surname *Mendiguchía*, giving the town of its origin as Elgueta.

Other books dealing with surnames and biographical data on immigration would include Peter Boyd Bowman's *Indice geobiográfico de más de 56 mil pobladores de la América hispana*, listing the earliest immigrants to the Spanish colonies. The bibliography at the end of chapter seventeen in the third edition of *The Source* illustrates the kinds of books that can be used as a starting point to identify your own areas and periods of research.

9

SEARCHING FOR YOUR ANCESTORS IN UNITED STATES RECORDS

Some Mexican American researchers may have ancestors in the United States going back twelve or thirteen generations. Far more, however, descend from families that came to the United States more recently—many within a generation or two. Obviously, the amount of U.S. research required will vary depending on the length of time your family has lived here. As with the home search, you will want to approach the process of doing U.S. research with two thoughts in mind. The first is to learn as much as you can about members of your family. The second is to determine the exact place where your ancestors lived in Mexico, as knowing where your ancestors were born and lived will open vast possibilities of church and government records in Mexico. With that thought, this discussion will focus primarily on U.S. resources most likely to give a place of birth or assist in finding other records that do.

BORDER CROSSING RECORDS

Immigrants crossing into the United States by land from Mexico and Canada throughout most of the nineteenth century were not registered (see figure 9-1). Immigration regulations that were initiated in 1882 and included the use of passenger lists of immigrants entering through seaports, however, brought attention to the significant, uncontrolled entry of aliens into the United States via land ports. From this came the creation of systems to control and register those crossing into the United States by land.

Beginning in 1895, immigration officials recorded all entries through Canadian land ports.[1] Working with Canadian governments and railroads, they achieved control over the substantial flow of immigrants who came to the United States through Canadian ports. A decade later, similar controls were put in place on the border

Figure 9-1: Even the many Mexican immigrants who crossed the border by train will appear in border crossing records after 1900.

between Mexico and the United States, beginning at El Paso, Texas in 1903 and following at other major crossing points by 1905 or 1906. Rather than preventing the entry of illegal immigrants as is the case today on that border, immigration control efforts of this period centered on recording names of immigrants and assuring they met required health standards.

As border crossing controls began, the Immigration and Naturalization Service kept records of both immigrants and non-immigrants crossing the Mexican border, using individual one-page manifests or two-sided cards. Those crossing the border were also classified as statistical or non-statistical, based in large part on whether they were required to pay the alien head tax, but also on factors such as how long they intended to stay, if they had been in the United States before, and their reason for coming (see figure 9-2). (Before 1930, residents of Mexico were not counted as immigrants if they planned to enter the United States for less than six months.) In a short summary:

> Statistical arrivals were immigrants or non-immigrants who were subject to the head tax and generally not from the Western Hemisphere. By contrast non-statistical arrivals were immigrants and non-immigrants who usually were natives of the Western Hemisphere and not subject to the head tax. Although arrival of the latter was not included in immigration statistics, a record of that arrival may still have been made. It cannot be said with certainty that the definitions of statistical and non-statistical arrivals were applied uniformly at any particular port on the Canadian or Mexican Borders.[2]

This means that researchers looking for ancestors who crossed the border from Mexico into the United States between 1903 and 1954 would need to check both statistical and nonstatistical records, and both temporary and permanent admission.

Not surprisingly, most immigrants who came across the border were Mexican citizens, but there were also significant numbers of Europeans. Many other nationalities appear on border crossing records, including Syrians, Japanese, Guatemalans, Koreans, Palestinians, Canadians, and Filipinos. After the closure of United States ports to most Europeans in 1926, sufficient numbers of Europeans entered Mexico en route to the United States that at one point, the American Consul was directed to make a record of all European immigrants entering Mexico destined for that purpose. In some cases even United States citizens were recorded on border crossing manifests.

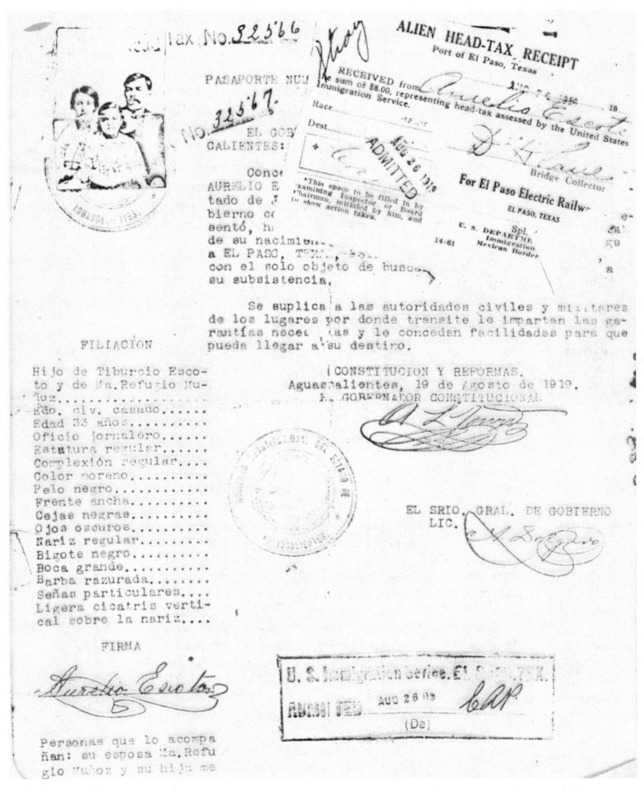

Figure 9-2: Most immigrants from Mexico were required to pay an alien head tax, and thus received receipts, like this one.

In order to work with border crossing records you will need to know the point(s) where your ancestral family crossed the border. One of the functions of the "Mexican Border Crossing Records" sidebars throughout this chapter is to provide a listing of all the crossing points controlled by U.S. immigration officials.

All of the original border crossing manifest records were microfilmed in the late 1950s and later destroyed. Although varying slightly in content depending on the time period, they will give the place of entry into the United States, the date, and some or all of the following information: the person's name, age, place of birth, who he or she was traveling with, whether or not the immigrant had ever been to the United States and, if so, for how long. Additionally, some type of physical description is given. This information was recorded on a single card or one-page manifests (see figure 9-3). Regardless of which form was used, the information remained basically the same.

MEXICAN BORDER CROSSING RECORDS—ARIZONA PORTS

Crossing Point	Dates	Record Type	NARA Call #	FHL Film #
Aros Ranch, AZ	1908–1909	List of Arrivals	A3365, rolls 3–4	2342416
Douglas, AZ	1908–1952	Manifests and Index to Arrivals	M1759, rolls 1–4	2241245-2241248
Lochiel, AZ	1908	List of Arrivals	A3365, rolls 3–4	2342416
Naco, AZ	1906–1910	List of Arrivals	A3365, rolls 1–5	2342416
	1908–1952	Index to Manifests	A3372, rolls 1 –? (18 rolls total)	n/a
	1908–1924	Statistical Manifests	A3372, rolls ?–?	n/a
	1924–1952	Manifests for Permanent Residence	A3372, rolls ?–?	n/a
	1924–1952	Manifests for Temporary Admission	A3372, rolls ?–?	n/a
Nogales, AZ	1906–1909	List of Arrivals	A3365, rolls 1–5	2342416
	1905–1926	Index to Manifests	M1769, rolls 1–? (74 rolls total)	n/a
	1905–1924	Statistical Manifests	M1769, rolls ?–?	n/a
	1924–1952	Manifests for Permanent Residence and Crossing ID Cards	M1769, rolls ?–?	n/a
	1927–1952	Manifests for Temporary Admission	M1769, rolls ?–?	n/a
San Luis, AZ	1929–1952	Manifests for Permanent Residence	M1504, roll 1 (2 rolls total)	n/a
	1929–1952	Manifests for Temporary Admission	M1504, roll 2?	n/a
Sasabe/San Fernando, AZ	1919–1924	Index to Manifests	M1850, roll 1	2241236, item 1
	1919–1924	Statistical and Permanent Residence Manifests	M1850, roll 1	2241236, item 2
	1924–1952	Manifests for Returning U.S. Residents	M1850, roll 1	2241236, item 3
	1927–1952	Nonstatistical and Temporary Manifests	M1850, rolls 2–3	2241237-2241238, item 1
	1919	Statistical and Permanent Manifests	M1850, roll 3	2241238, item 2

Occasionally the card manifest will have a photograph of the immigrant or immigrant family attached on the back that may, in the microfilmed version, prevent reading the personal information given under the photo. Those microfilmed copies were "lost" for over two decades until discovered in the National Archives about ten years ago by an INS historian. Since that time, work has progressed steadily to clean up, catalog, reprint, and distribute them. As is evidenced on the "Mexican Border Crossing Records" sidebars throughout this chapter, much of that process still remains to be completed, as records for the period from 1910 to 1924—the time of heaviest Mexican emigration, resulting from the Mexican Revolution—are not yet available for most ports.

Manifests are arranged alphabetically or chronologically by the crossing date. Those arranged chronologically have manifest numbers assigned that are used on the indexes and even appear on subsequent manifests as a way of cross-referencing multiple crossings. Indexes likely exist for all collections of chronologically arranged manifests, although they may not yet be available. Researchers will want to search these indexes first, since if they do exist they will give the specific date of the crossing and applicable manifest number

Figure 9-3: Border crossing manifests like this one provide information about a person's migration to the United States.

for that person. With that information, the researcher should then find the date of crossing in the chronologically arranged manifests and look for the specific manifest number. In using the index, remember the following:

- Cards are arranged alphabetically by surname and then by given name.
- Double surnames were filed as if the second surname did not exist, but if you do not find someone and know the maternal surname, check under that to be certain.
- All given names beyond the first were ignored.
- Women usually appeared in crossing manifests under their maiden surname rather than their husband's, as that was the surname system they knew.
- Surnames beginning with *de, del,* and *de la* were filed under the main surname rather than the preposition.

Remember to search all the categories of records for a single port of entry, as there is no way to be certain under which category a person may have been placed when he or she arrived. Once you have found the right manifest, be sure to look at the records of all those who crossed that day, as families and friends often traveled together. (You may want to note the names of those who came in a group from the same town as your ancestors, as they could later turn out to have some connection to your family.) If you do not find the manifest you are looking for, check before and after the indicated date, as manifests have occasionally been misfiled. The same is true for some index cards.

As indicated on the "Mexican Border Crossing Records" sidebars throughout this chapter, border crossing records are available through the National Archives in Washington, D.C., and can be consulted there or at several of the Regional NARA branches. For more information go to <www.archives.gov>. Watch that same site for information about new collections as they are released. The films are also available for purchase, if an individual or library wishes to do so, at a cost of $38.00 per film. Some, but not many, large university libraries have added them to their collection. Check on a library consortium such as WorldCat for specific libraries where this is the case.

Perhaps the easiest way to consult border crossing records would be to order the desired films to a local LDS Family History Center. Due to an incredible inconsistency in cataloging, however, these records can be hard to find through traditional "Locality" or "Subject" searches. The "Mexican Border Crossing Records" sidebars throughout this chapter gives the film numbers for those microfilms held by the Family History Library Catalog at the date of publication of this article. Search in the Family History Library Catalog at FamilySearch.org under the beginning film number of the collection of interest for further details about all the films in that particular collection. As the FHL has a policy of regularly ordering these films, check periodically in the Family

MEXICAN BORDER CROSSING RECORDS—CALIFORNIA PORTS

Crossing Point	Dates	Record Type	NARA Call #	FHL Film #
Andrade, CA	1911–1924	Index to Manifests	M2030, rolls 1–2	2138429-2138430
	1911–1952	Manifests	M2030, roll 3	2138431
Campo, CA	1911–1924	Index to Manifests	M2030, roll 4	2138432, item 1
	1912–1954	Manifests for Temporary Admission	M2030, roll 5	2138433, item 2
	1910–1952	Manifests	M2030, roll 4	2138432, item 1
	1946–1952	Applications for Crossing ID cards	M2030, rolls 4–5	2138433, item 2– 2138433, item 1
San Ysidro, CA	1908–1952	Manifests	M1767, rolls 1–18	2242997-2243014
	1923–1924	Nonstatistical Manifests with a Paid Tax	M1767, rolls 19–20	2243015-2243016

History Library Catalog for these acquisitions under "Mexico-Emigration Records" or "United States-Immigration Records."

One researcher, looking for the border crossing record of his grandfather, found he came to the United States with a group of eleven other family members, among them his great grandmother. Although he had previous information about her, he learned from her border crossing manifest that she had been born in a different town from other members in the family, located in a neighboring state. Border crossing records had not only given him a view of his family members on a pivotal day of their lives, but opened previously unknown research possibilities for him. The vast amount of information given on border crossing records makes it well worth the effort of searching them out.

UNITED STATES FEDERAL CENSUSES

In an effort to track its citizens and learn more about them, the United States government began taking a federal census of citizens in 1790 and has done so again every ten years since (see figure 9-4). This type of record, which has always available to researchers, has now become even easier to search since commercial companies such as Ancestry.com or Heritage Quest <heritagequestonline.com> have digitized and indexed them and made them available online at. These are paid services and you will first need to become a subscriber or go to a place offering their services.

If your ancestors came to the United States any time before or during the years 1900 to 1930, they will likely appear in one or more of the U.S. Federal Censuses taken in 1900, 1910, 1920, or 1930. Your ancestor may appear is later censuses as well, but privacy laws protect the information provided by the census for seventy-two

MEXICAN BORDER CROSSING RECORDS—NEW MEXICO PORTS

Crossing Point	Dates	Record Type	NARA Call #	FHL Film #
Columbus, NM	1924–1952	Statistical Manifests	A3370, roll 1 (9 rolls total)	n/a
	1917–1944	Statistical Index and Manifests	A3370, roll 2	n/a
	1917–1926	Nonstatistical Manifests	A3370, rolls 2&6	n/a
	1917	Statistical Manifests	A3370, roll 3	n/a
	1919–1924	Sheet Manifests	A3370, roll 3	n/a
	1924–1954	Temporary Admissions	A3370, rolls 4–6	n/a
	1953–1954	Permanent and Temporary Admissions	A3370, roll 6	n/a
	1924–1954	Citizen Admissions	A3370, roll 6	n/a
	1945–1952	Application for Crossing ID Cards	A3370, rolls 8–9	

years after it was taken, and so you will not be able to access that information until the government releases it.

While the questions varied slightly from year to year, the procedure for taking the census remained the same. A census-taker would go from door to door in a neighborhood, talking to a member of each household and recording the required information. The system, of course, had its flaws. Whether or not the recorded information for a family was accurate depended on the person giving it. (For example, ages, particularly of adults, may be off by several years.) There is the additional possibility of the census-taker either misinterpreting or misspelling what was said, particularly if the informant had an unfamiliar accent. Knowing this, many researchers, having tried unsuccessfully to find the name of a particular ancestor, then tried the name again using several different spellings and were successful. For all their weaknesses, however, federal censuses remain a mainstay for anybody tracing his or her family history in the United States.

The questions asked in a census vary from one schedule or census taking to the next, reflecting the interests and concerns of the government at that time. For example, although censuses began in 1790, it wasn't until 1850 that a census listed each person's name in a household, rather than naming only the family head. Census schedules through the year 1860 asked for information about slaves. The 1930 census lists whether or not the person has a "radio set."

With the end of the Civil War in the 1860s, as immigrants continued coming to the United States from throughout the world, the government became aware of the need to record immigrant information. The census of 1880 is the first that asks for the birthplace of the informant and his or her parents. Those for the years 1900, 1910, 1920, and 1930 list the birthplace of the informant and parents and those who are foreign born, the year of their immigration into the United States, and whether or not they are naturalized citizens. (The census for the year 1890 was destroyed as a result of a fire.) Be aware, however, that "birthplace" refers to the country only ("Mexico," for example) and will not give the name of a state or town within the country.

Besides immigration information, these censuses give the person's name; his or her relationship to the family head; and his or her sex, race, age, and marital status. Depending on the census year, other questions concerned such topics as occupations, property ownership, the ability to speak English, school attendance, and literacy.

The easy access and convenience of online census research has forever changed the nature of it. However, while it is now possible to do an online search of a given census by simply typing in a person's name, the results of most searches would be overwhelming and far too complicated to narrow down to the one person who is your ancestor. For example, the 1920 census lists 151 matches for the name Miguel Garcia. Knowing the place your ancestor lived during the census year makes the search far more manageable. By narrowing the search for Miguel Garcia to Texas, nineteen matches appear. Looking for a Miguel Garcia in Laredo, Texas, narrows the possible matches to three. Once you have found the person you are searching for, take the time to look up and down the page at the names of surrounding entries. Particularly in the past, families tended to live close to each other, and you might find the names of married siblings or parents who live close by. Looking at the surrounding names and nationalities can also give you a feeling for the area and neighborhood in which your family lived.

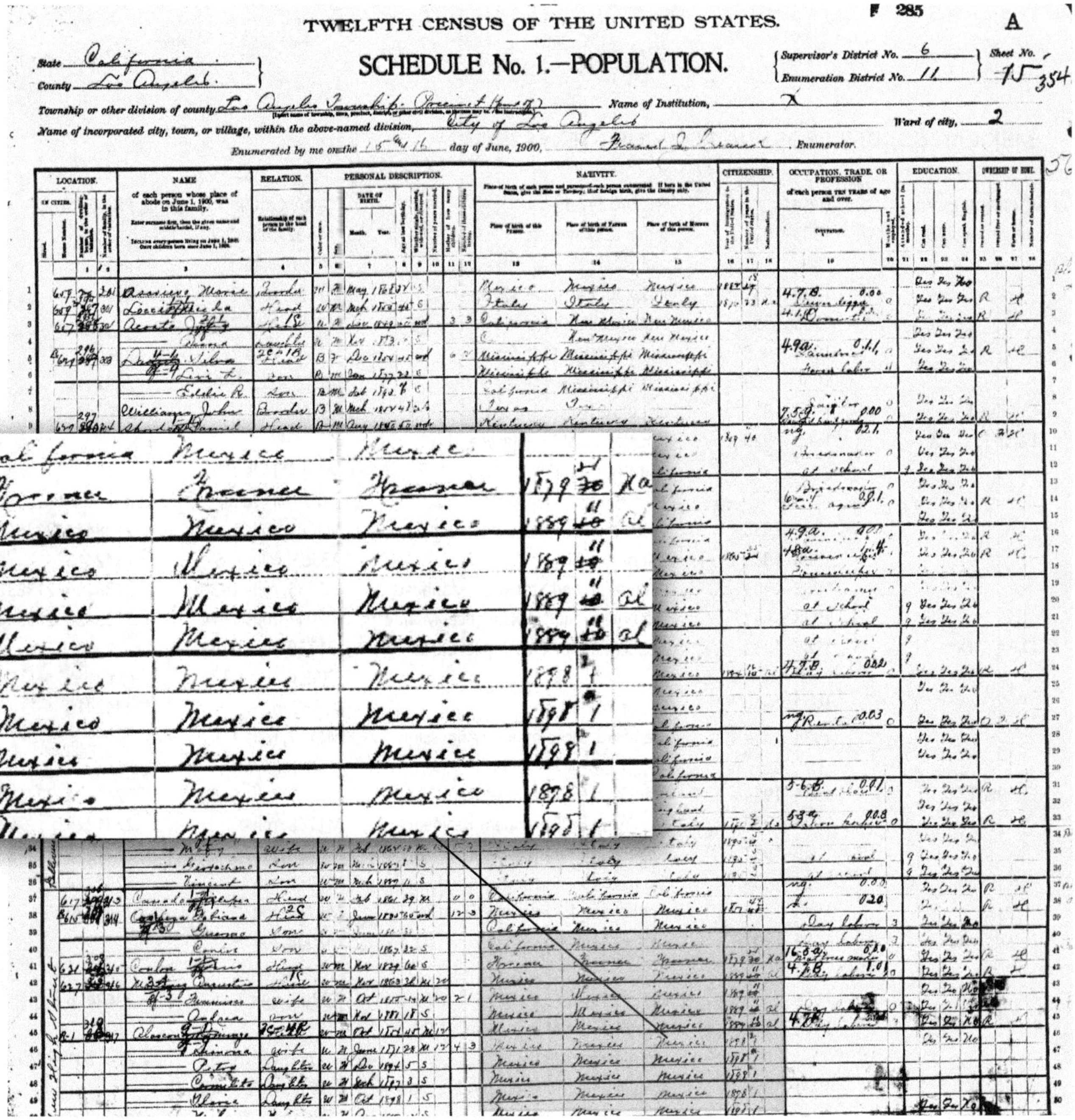

Figure 9-4: The United States federal censuses are always a good place to look for immigrant ancestors in the U.S. Note the columns in this 1900 census page from Los Angeles giving nativity and citizenship information, including year of arrival in the United States.

MEXICAN BORDER CROSSING RECORDS—TEXAS PORTS

Crossing Point	Dates	Record Type	NARA Call #	FHL Film #
Brownsville, TX	1905–1929	Index to Manifests	M1502, rolls 1–?	
			(40 rolls total)	n/a
	1929–1952	Index to Statistical Manifest	M1502, rolls ?–?	n/a
	1905–1952	Statistical Manifests	M1502, rolls ?–?	n/a
	1929–1953	Nonstatistical Manifests	M1502, rolls ?–?	n/a
	1906–1909	List of Arrivals	A3365, rolls 1–4	2342416
Del Rio, TX	1906–1909	List of Arrivals	A3365, rolls 1–4	2342416
Eagle Pass, TX	1905–1929	Nonstatistical Manifests and Statistical Index	M1754, rolls 1–27	
			(27 rolls total)	n/a
	1929–1953	Index to Manifests	M2040, rolls 1–2	2138434–2138435
	1906–1909	List of Arrivals	A3365, rolls 1–5	2342416
	1905–1953	Permanent and Statistical Manifests	M1755, rolls 1–30	2138296–2138325
	1928–1953	Temporary and Nonstatistical Manifests	M2041, rolls 1–14	2138436–2138449
El Paso, TX	1945–1952	Application for Crossing ID Cards	M1756, rolls 1–62	
			(62 rolls total)	n/a
	1903–1909	List of Arrivals	A3365, rolls 1–5	2342416
	1924–1954	Manifests for Temporary Admission	M1757, rolls 1–97	
			(97 rolls total)	n/a
Fabens, TX	1924–1954	Manifests for Temporary Admission	M1768, rolls 1–3	2241222–224124
	1924–1952	Manifests for Permanent Residence	M1768, roll 4	2241225
	1945–1952	Application for Crossing ID Cards	M1768, rolls 5–7	2241226–2241228
Fort Hancock, TX	1924–1954	Manifests for Temporary Admission	M1766, roll 1	2241229
	1945–1952	Application for crossing ID cards	M1766, roll 2	2241230
Laredo, TX	1903–1907	List of Arrivals	M2008, roll 1	
			(1 roll total)	n/a
	1906–1909	List of Arrivals	A3365, rolls 1–4	2342416
	1929–1955	Non-Mexican Manifests for Temporary Admission	M1771, rolls 1–5	2241231–2241235
	1929–1955	Manifests for Temporary Admission	M1772, rolls 1–66	
			(66 rolls total)	n/a
Los Ebanos, TX	1950–1955	List of Arrivals	A3377, rolls 1–2	
			(2 rolls total)	n/a
Presidio, TX	1908–1909	List of Arrivals	A3365, rolls 3–5	2342416

Crossing Point	Dates	Record Type	NARA Call #	FHL Film #
Progresso, TX	1928–1952	Index to Statistical Manifests	M1851, rolls 1–? (6 rolls total)	n/a
	1928–1952	Statistical Manifests	M1851, rolls ?–?	n/a
	1928–1955	Non Statistical and Temporary Manifests	M1851, rolls ?–?	n/a
Rio Grande City, TX	1908–1909	List of Arrivals	A3365, rolls 3–4	2342416
	1908–1952	Index to Statistical Manifests	M1770, roll 1	2241239
	1908–1952	Statistical Manifests	M1770, rolls 2–4	2241240–2241242
	1916–1955	Non Statistical Manifests	M1770, rolls 4–6	2241242–2241244
Roma, TX	1907–1908	List of Arrivals	A3365, roll 2	2342416
	1929–1954	Index to Statistical Manifests	M1503, rolls 1–? (5 rolls total)	n/a
	1928–1929	Manifests	M1503, rolls ?–?	n/a
	1929–1954	Statistical Manifests	M1503, rolls ?–?	n/a
	1928–1955	Non Statistical and Temporary Manifests	M1503, rolls ?–?	n/a
San Antonio, TX	1944–1952	Lists of Arrivals	M1973, roll 1 (1 roll total)	n/a
Yseleta, TX	1924–1952	Statistical and Permanent Manifests	M1849, roll 1	2138421
	1924–1954	Manifests for Temporary Admission	M1849, rolls 2–3	2138422–2138423
	1945–1952	Application for crossing ID cards	M1849, rolls 4–7	2138424–2138427
Zapata, TX	1929–1950	Index to Statistical Manifests	M2024, roll 1	2138450, item 1
	1923–1950	Statistical Manifests	M2024, roll 1	2138450, items 2–3
	1923–1929	Manifests	M2024, roll 1	2138450, item 4
	1929–1952	Manifests	M2024, rolls 1–2	2138450, item 5– 2138451, item 1
	1945–1953	Application for Crossing ID Cards	M2024, roll 2	2138451, item 2

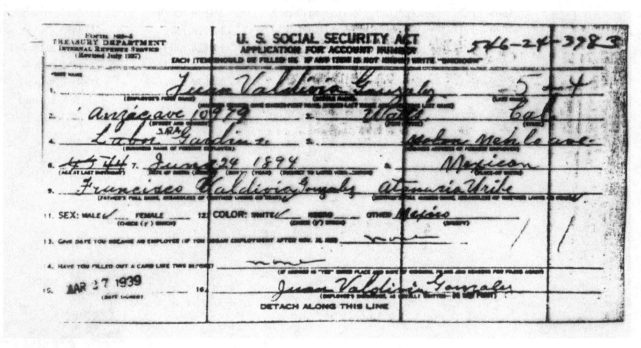

Figure 9-5: Social Security records are another good source of information about Mexican immigrants in the United States.

NATURALIZATION RECORDS

The process of becoming a citizen in another country always involves paperwork. If your ancestor became a citizen before 1906, this process was handled in local courts in the city or county in which he or she lived, and the paperwork should be available there. Check under the name of this locality in the Family History Library Catalog to find these records.

If your ancestor became a citizen after 1906, the process was handled by the Immigration and Naturalization Service, now called the United States Citizenship and Immigration Service (USCIS). These records can be ordered at the local regional office of the USCIS in the area where you live, although a request may also be sent to the national office at the following address: U.S. Department of Justice, Immigration and Naturalization Service, 425 I. Street N.W., Washington, D.C. 20536. The packet will include documents such as a Declaration of Intention, with detailed information about the immigrant and his naturalization process.

WORLD WAR I MILITARY DRAFT REGISTRATION

All males between the ages of seventeen and forty-five living in the United States in the years 1917 or 1918 during World War I should appear in this registration, whether they were citizens at that time or not (see figure 9-6). You can find these records in the Family History Library Catalog by doing a "Subject Search" for "World War I" on the Family History Library Catalog page on FamilySearch.org. Ancestry.com also has these records available online. Click the "Search" tab, and then click "WWI Draft Registration Cards" under the heading "Military" in the "Browse Records" column on the right side of the screen. The draft record will tell the place and date of birth and may even tell if the person served in the army in Mexico.

ALIEN REGISTRATIONS OF 1940

With the prospect of another World War in the early 1940s, the United States began registering all aliens. (An alien is a person living in a country in which he is not a citizen.) Although this was done for the purpose of tracking people who had come to the United States from countries with existing political conflict, thousands of Mexican Americans were also registered. You can obtain copies of these records by writing to the United States Citizenship and Immigration Service.

MILITARY SERVICE RECORDS

Many Mexican Americans have served in the United States military, some as early as the Civil War. Since World War I, more than forty Americans of Mexican descent have won a Medal of Honor. Military service and pension records are excellent. Those for soldiers serving from 1860 to 1900 are mostly found at the National Archives in Washington, D.C. (see NARA's website <www.archives.gov>) and after 1900, at the

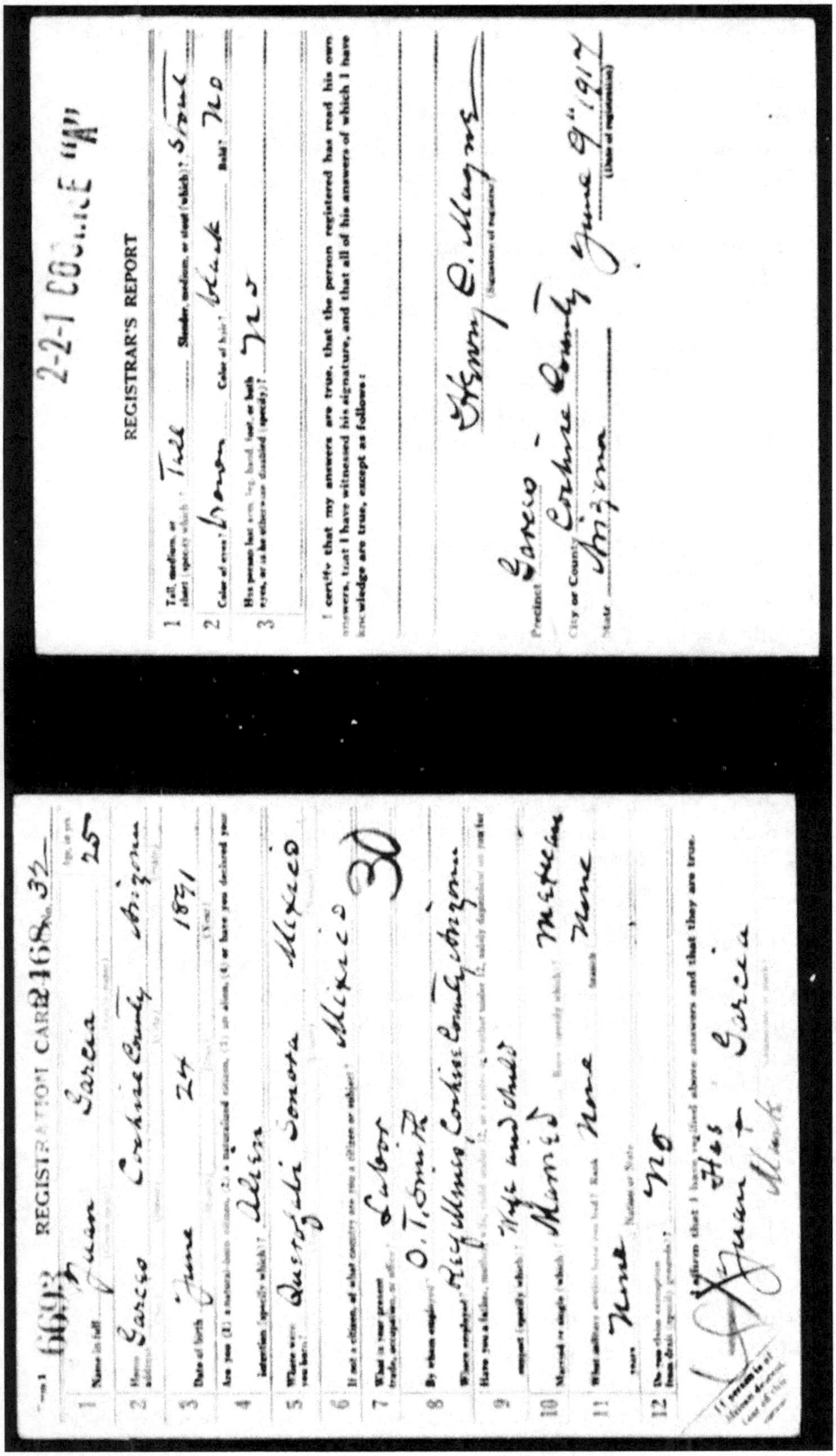
REGISTRATION CARD 2168 No. 32

1 Name in full: Juan Garcia — Age, in yrs. 25
2 Home address: Garcio Cochise County Arizona
3 Date of birth: June 24 1891
4 Are you (1) a natural-born citizen, (2) a naturalized citizen, (3) an alien, (4) or have you declared your intention (specify which)? Alien
5 Where were you born? Queregali Sonora Mexico
6 If not a citizen, of what country are you a citizen or subject? Mexico
7 What is your present trade, occupation, or office? Labor
8 By whom employed? O. T. Smith — Where employed? Cochise County Arizona
9 Have you a father, mother, wife, child under 12, or a sister or brother under 12, solely dependent on you for support (specify which)? Wife and child
10 Married or single (which)? Married — Race (specify which)? Mexican
11 What military service have you had? Rank None — Branch None
12 Do you claim exemption from draft (specify grounds)? No

I affirm that I have verified above answers and that they are true.
Juan His Mark Garcia

REGISTRAR'S REPORT
2-2-1 COCHISE "A"

1 Tall, medium, or short (specify which)? Tall — Slender, medium, or stout (which)? Stout
2 Color of eyes? Brown — Color of hair? Black — Bald? No
3 Has person lost arm, leg, hand, foot, or both eyes, or is he otherwise disabled (specify)? No

I certify that my answers are true, that the person registered has read his own answers, that I have witnessed his signature, and that all of his answers of which I have knowledge are true, except as follows:

Henry C. Magee
Precinct: Garcio
City or County: Cochise County
State: Arizona
June 5 1917

Figure 9-6: Male ancestors who were over seventeen years old during World War I may have a draft card like this one, giving a birth place in Mexico.

St. Louis Personnel Center. Many Mexican Americans also served in state militias or National Guard units. For detailed information about military records and their use in family history, see James Neagle's *U.S. Military Records.*

RAILROAD PENSION RECORDS

Many Mexicans coming to the United States in the early 1900s, especially to places in the midwest, worked as railroad employees. Researchers with ancestry among this group can check the heading "Railroad Pensions" as part of the Social Security Death Index on Ancestry.com. Another possibility for finding railroad employees is *The Directory of North American Railroads, Associations, Societies, Archives, Libraries, Museums and Their Collections*, written by Holly T. Hansen.

CATHOLIC CHURCH PARISH RECORDS IN THE UNITED STATES

An immigrant's attitude about religion would most likely have remained the same after crossing the border, perhaps even taking on a higher significance amid the change and uncertainty of life in a new place. Nearly all Mexicans arriving in this country were Catholic and would have found and settled into a local parish, recording family baptisms, confirmations, marriages, and deaths.

You will find United States Catholic parish registers an excellent potential source for finding exact place names in Mexico, or any other foreign country (see figure 9-7). In contrast to government records, made in offices where recently-arrived immigrants would have dealt with busy clerks having little or no idea of Mexican geography, parish records were made by the local priest who knew his parishioners on a more personal level. Additionally, a priest realized the need for giving the exact location of a potential record source in Mexico, since it might be needed for ecclesiastical reasons later. So while many government records might give only the country name, or perhaps

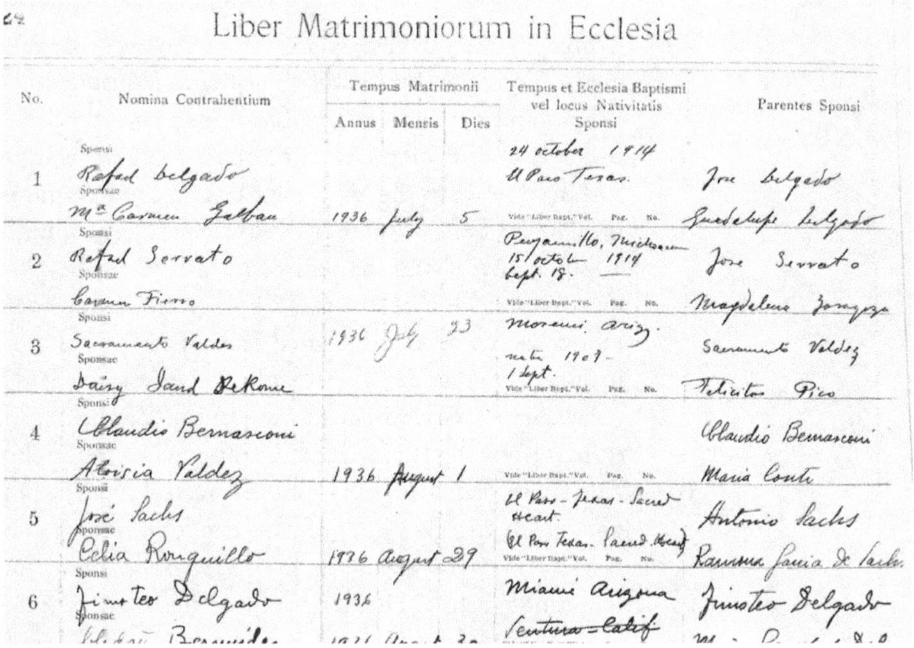

Liber Matrimoniorum in Ecclesia

No.	Nomina Contrahentium	Tempus Matrimonii Annus	Mensis	Dies	Tempus et Ecclesia Baptismi vel locus Nativitatis Sponsi	Parentes Sponsi
1	Sponsi Rafael Delgado Sponsae Mª Carmen Galban	1936	July	5	24 october 1914 El Paso Texas.	Jose Delgado Guadalupe Delgado
2	Sponsi Rafael Serrato Sponsae Carmen Fierro				Purandillo, Michoacan 15 octobre 1914 bapt. 18.	Jose Serrato Magdalena Zaragoza
3	Sponsi Sacramento Valdes Sponsae Daisy Sand DeKome	1936	July	23	Morenci. Ariz. nata 1907- 1 Sept.	Sacramento Valdez Feliciti Pico
4	Sponsi Claudio Bernasconi Sponsae Aloisia Valdez	1936	August	1		Claudio Bernasconi Maria Conti
5	Sponsi José Sachs Sponsae Celia Ronquillo	1936	August	29	El Paso - Texas - Sacred Heart. El Paso Texas. Sacred Heart	Antonio Sachs Ramona Garcia de Sachs
6	Sponsi Timoteo Delgado Sponsae	1936			Miami Arizona Ventura Calif	Timoteo Delgado

Figure 9-7: Since most Mexicans coming to the United States were Catholic, searching in U.S. Catholic parish records can yield spectacular results.

the Mexican state, parish records often give the *municipio* from which the immigrant came. A page from the 1926 marriage register of one Los Angeles parish lists the grooms' birthplaces from such varied locations as Rio Florida, Mexico; Port-of-Spain, Trinidad; Marseille, France; and Arizona.

Because of policies set by the Council of Trent in the 1500s, the format for recording parish registers will remain much the same in the United States as it is in Mexico, Spain, or any other place Catholic records are kept. A more detailed discussion of what you will find in parish records and how to use them is found in chapter 4, "Parish Records."

UNITED STATES VITAL REGISTRATION RECORDS

Similar to civil registration records in Mexico, United States vital records are the government recording of births, marriages, and deaths. Because these documents play such an important role in daily life, they have already been discussed as among those items likely to turn up in a home search (see chapter 1, "Getting Started: Home, Family, and Internet Searches"). Remember that the recording of all births, marriages, and deaths is a law in the United States, regardless of citizenship status. This law went into effect on a state-by-state basis, so the earliest records will vary from one state to another. These records are made and kept at a county level. See the website United States Vital Records Information <www.vitalrec.com> for places to write and state-by-state information about vital records.

OTHER UNITED STATES RECORD SOURCES

While not likely to give a place of birth, many other valuable records exist that can help give a picture of your family. For example, using city directories, one researcher was able to find the address for a Los Angeles meat market owned by his uncles. Another researcher, also using city directories, was able to locate the house her grandparents had lived in when they first came to this country and estimate their year of entry into the United States. Another researcher in Texas found his grandfather's name in the 1920 census, giving the year of his arrival in the United States as 1916. With that information he looked up the border crossing records for his grandfather, who he found had come to the United States with a group of several other family members, including his grandmother. Her border crossing record gave the name of her birthplace in Mexico as Nochistlan in the state of Zacatecas, information he had not known earlier. Knowing this opened up entirely new research possibilities for him.

Try to search as many different record types as possible, recognizing that finding one record can give clues of where to look next. Undoubtedly, you will not find any single document giving all the facts you want to know, but each source will add something helpful. Reading any of the many excellent books available about the Mexican immigrant experience is another way to understand and appreciate your ancestors' lives. The more information you can find the richer your family history will be, and the more likely will be your success in tracing your roots.

NOTES

1. For a detailed discussion of Canadian Border Crossing records see Marian L. Smith, "By Way of Canada: U.S. Records of Immigration Across the U.S.-Canadian Border, 1895–1954," *Prologue* 32, no. 3 (2000), <www.archives.gov/publications/prologue/2000/fall/us-canada-immigration-records-1.html>.

2. For this and other information, go to "Mexican Border Crosssing Records," on the NARA website <www.archives.gov/genealogy/immigration/border-mexico.html>. This web page is adapted from Claire Prechtel-Kluskens, "Mexican Border Crossing Records (3 parts)," *National Genealogical Society Newsletter*, Vol. 25, Nos. 3–5 (May–Oct. 1999).

10

RESEARCH IN MEXICAN COLONIAL RECORDS

As your research progresses, you will move back into the time when Spain ruled the colony of New Spain, or the area now called Mexico. This is known as the "colonial period," beginning with the conquest of the Aztecs, and covering the years from 1521 to 1821. By 1800, the Spanish population had reached 26,800 in California, Texas, Arizona, and New Mexico (twenty thousand in New Mexico alone) and over 6.8 million in what is now Mexico.[1]

For more than a century before the beginning of American and French colonization, this Spanish colony had established an active and dynamic frontier. In the eighteenth century these three frontiers collided, as the British, French, and ultimately the Americans crossed into, settled among, and interacted with the Spanish administration and people. As a result many early American, British, and French settlers appear in Spanish records alongside an extensive number of Spanish subjects.

Always dedicated document keepers, the Spanish kept extensive and detailed records of governmental administration and daily life. Aided by the Catholic religion, Spanish records are generally more extensive than their English counterparts during the colonial period, providing an excellent amount of material of interest not only to those with ancestral lines among the Spanish settlers, but those with ancestors who lived in areas under Spanish rule.

This chapter reviews the types and locations of records generated during the colonial period, as well as by the Mexican government in Texas north of the Nueces River until 1836, and for Arizona, California, and New Mexico until the end of the Mexican war in 1848. You will find you can research much more effectively in this time period if you understand the history of Spanish colonial development in Mexico. Many excellent books have been written about this time period, a sampling of which is given in the "Books about the Mexican Colonial Period" sidebar on page 140.

MEXICAN COLONIAL RECORDS AND JURISDICTIONS

As Spain developed her colonies, bringing to them the institutions and activities of the Spanish homeland, basic colonial record types remained similar, if not identical, to those in Spain itself. Both uniformity of government control as well as uniformity of religion produced records that from any colony, or even from Spain, differ only in small details. This is especially true for New Spain, the largest and most successful of the Spanish colonies.

CATHOLIC CHURCH RECORDS

The colonies continued the Catholic Church's policy of dividing ecclesiastical affairs into two categories, that of the organized church under direction of the local bishop and religious orders operating under direction of their superiors. In most cases the frontier missions were organized by members of a religious order, generally Jesuits or Franciscans. See figure 10-1 for a map showing the various areas controlled by Franciscans, Jesuits, and Augustinians during the colonial period.

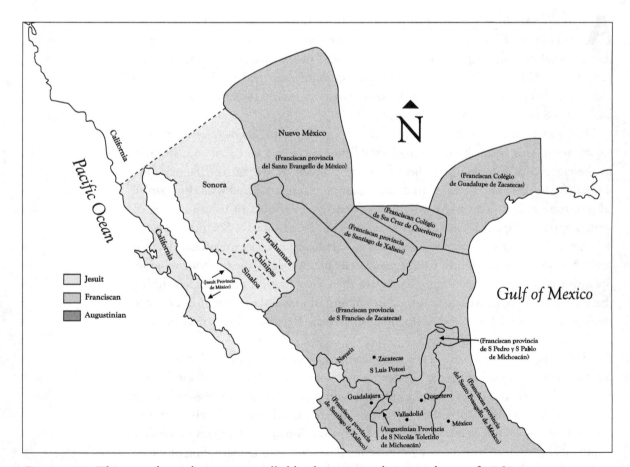

Figure 10-1: This map shows the areas controlled by the various religious orders as of 1767.

Catholic Church records are still the most important source for genealogical research during the three hundred years of the colonial period. The only major difference you will find in colonial Mexico is that many of the sacramental registers on the frontier were written in mission churches or military chaplaincies that would later become parish churches as the population grew. Whether generated by monks or friars in missions, military chaplains in *presidio* churches, or secular priests presiding over organized parish churches, sacramental registers are nearly identical. The records of the sacraments of baptisms, confirmations, marriages, and deaths found in nearly every mission or parish, are discussed in detail in chapter 4, "Parish Records."

VOCABULARY

Presidio—a military fortress.

Catholic Church Diocesan Records

As colonization continued and more Spanish civilians moved into an area, secular parishes (meaning those not of the religious order) were established under the direction of the nearest bishop, with each bishopric and the geographical area over which the bishop served known as a diocese. As evidenced in figure 10-2, a map showing the dioceses of the colonial period, there were considerably fewer of these dioceses during the colonial period. The Church dioceses (bishoprics) generated a variety of administrative and canon law documents as did the colleges, or central

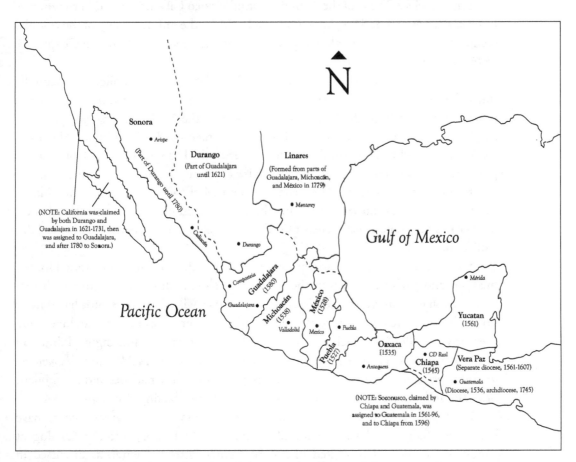

Figure 10-2: This map shows the colonial dioceses of Mexico and their years of creation.

headquarters, of the various religious orders. Each college or diocese will have personnel records of the monks or secular priests who served within that jurisdiction, generally providing the birth place and parentage of the individual cleric. Records such as marriage dispensations, ordinations of priests, censuses of communicants, tithing payment records, and records of bishop's visits may be found in the diocesan archives for the particular diocese to which a parish belonged when the record would have been generated (see figure 10-3).

Marriage dispensations, discussed in chapter 4, "Parish Records," and chapter 6, "Beyond the Parish: Church and Government Records," can prove particularly valuable to family historians. An excellent discussion of colonial marriage dispensation records can be found in *Index to the Marriage Investigations of the Diocese of Guadalajara, Provinces of Coahuila, Nuevo Leon, Nuevo Santander, Texas, Volume 1: 1653–1750*, which contains marriage dispensations for the state of Texas and related states in Mexico for the period of 1653 to 1750. Those from the states of Guadalajara and Zacatecas appear in *Sagrada Mitra de Guadalajara, Antiguo Obispado de la Nuevo Galicia, Expedientes de la Serie de Matrimonios, Extractos Siglos XVII–XVIII* by Maria Luz Montejano Hilton.

Those of Durango can be found using the CD index prepared by the Rio Grande Historical Society. Those of the Archidiocese of Mexico City are housed in the *Archivo General de la Nación* and are indexed in ARGENA II, the online catalog of the colonial section of that archive. A further discussion of diocesan records is found in Chapter 11 of *Finding Your Hispanic Roots*.

Diocesan records are both extensive and available to the public. For example, the archdiocese of Durango, begun in 1606, has an archival collection of 1,120,000 pages—3 percent from the 1600s, 32 percent from the 1700s, and 59 percent from the 1800s. The entire collection has been microfilmed by the Rio Grande Historical Collections, held at New Mexico State University in Las Cruces. Jack Colligan has published two volumes transcribing New Mexico dispensations in the collection.[2]

Records of the dioceses of Guadalajara and Michoacan have been microfilmed by the Genealogical Society of Utah. The few remaining records from the diocese of Hermosillo, Sonora have been filmed as part of the University of Arizona Film Collection #811.

Sacramental (baptism, marriage, and death) records can usually be located for the missions and parish churches in the current parish church or diocese to which that parish belongs. Numerous exceptions exist, of course, where parish records have ended up in diocesan archives, religious order archives, other parishes, state archives, and even private collections, such as that of Yale University or the Huntington Library in California. The best source for finding these is Lyman D. Platt's *Mexico: Guia general, divisiones eclesiasticas*. For each diocese Platt gives a list of the parishes and the modern province and colonial jurisdictions to which each parish belongs (see figure 10-4).

Furthermore, researchers will find that most colonial era parish records have been microfilmed and can be found in the Family History Library Catalog at FamilySearch.org and consulted in a local Family History Center, as discussed in chapter 4, "Parish Records."

Figure 10-3: Records such as this census of confession and communion are valuable resources.

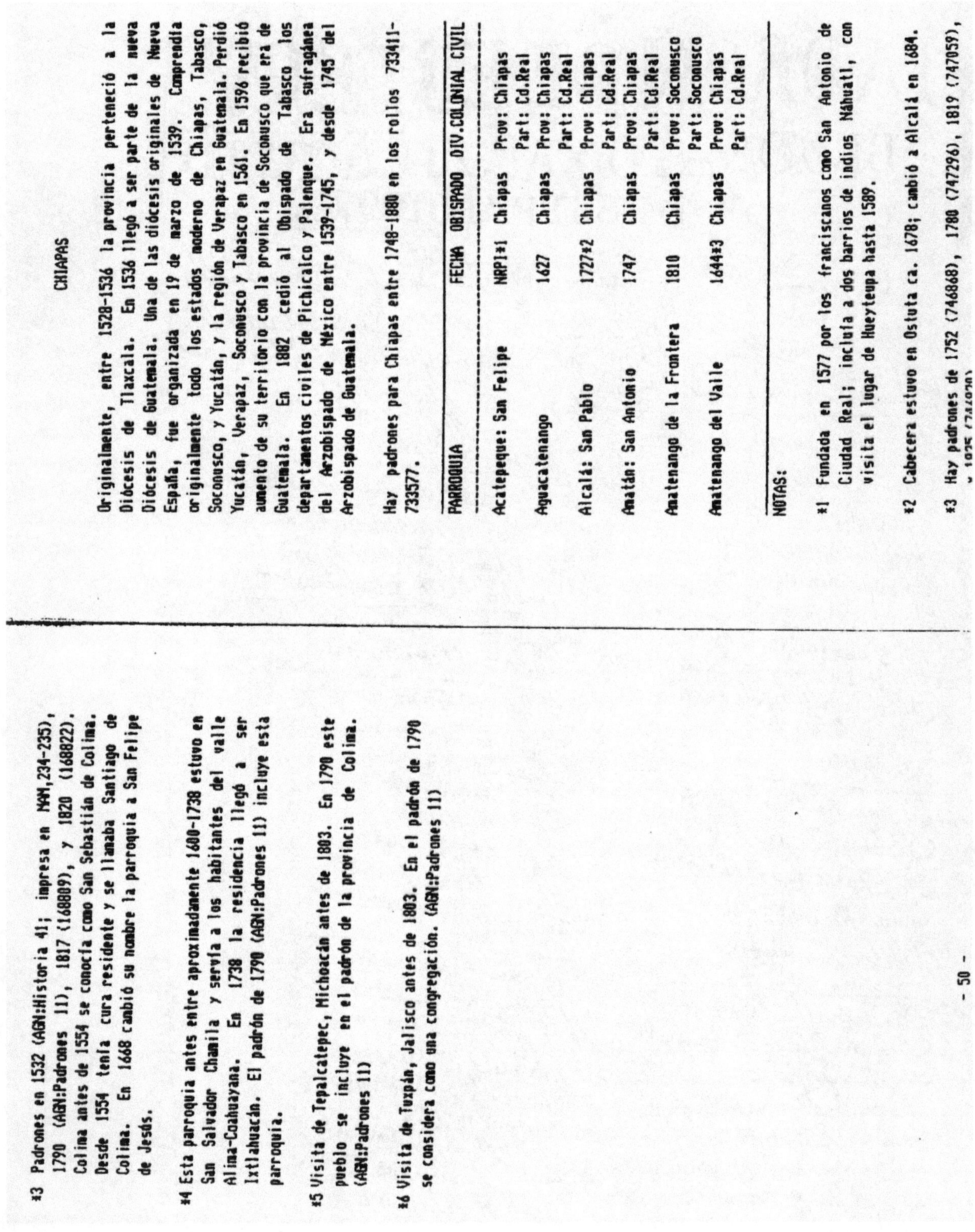

CHIAPAS

Originalmente, entre 1528-1536 la provincia perteneció a la Diócesis de Tlaxcala. En 1536 llegó a ser parte de la nueva Diócesis de Guatemala. Una de las diócesis originales de Nueva España, fue organizada en 19 de marzo de 1539. Comprendía originalmente todo los estados moderno de Chiapas, Tabasco, Soconusco, y Yucatán, y la región de Verapaz en Guatemala. Perdió Yucatán, Verapaz, Soconusco y Tabasco en 1561. En 1596 recibió aumento de su territorio con la provincia de Soconusco que era de Guatemala. En 1882 cedió al Obispado de Tabasco los departamentos civiles de Pichicalco y Palenque. Era sufragánea del Arzobispado de México entre 1539-1745, y desde 1745 del Arzobispado de Guatemala.

Hay padrones para Chiapas entre 1748-1880 en los rollos 733411-733577.

PARROQUIA	FECHA	OBISPADO	DIV.COLONIAL CIVIL
Acatepeque: San Felipe	NRPI#1	Chiapas	Prov: Chiapas Part: Cd.Real
Aguacatenango	1627	Chiapas	Prov: Chiapas Part: Cd.Real
Alcalá: San Pablo	1727#2	Chiapas	Prov: Chiapas Part: Cd.Real
Amatán: San Antonio	1747	Chiapas	Prov: Chiapas Part: Cd.Real
Amatenango de la Frontera	1810	Chiapas	Prov: Soconusco Part: Soconusco
Amatenango del Valle	1644#3	Chiapas	Prov: Chiapas Part: Cd.Real

NOTAS:

#1 Fundada en 1577 por los franciscanos como San Antonio de Ciudad Real; incluía a dos barrios de indios Náhuatl, con visita el lugar de Hueyteupa hasta 1589.

#2 Cabecera estuvo en Ostuta ca. 1678; cambió a Alcalá en 1684.

#3 Hay padrones de 1752 (746868), 1780 (747296), 1819 (747059),

#3 Padrones en 1532 (AGN:Historia 41; impresa en MAM,234-235), 1790 (AGN:Padrones 11), 1817 (168809), y 1820 (168822). Colima antes de 1554 se conocía como San Sebastián de Colima. Desde 1554 tenía cura residente y se llamaba Santiago de Colima. En 1668 cambió su nombre la parroquia a San Felipe de Jesús.

#4 Esta parroquia antes entre aproximadamente 1600-1738 estuvo en San Salvador Chamila y servía a los habitantes del valle Alima-Coahuayana. En 1738 la residencia llegó a ser Ixtlahuacán. El padrón de 1790 (AGN:Padrones 11) incluye esta parroquia.

#5 Visita de Tepalcatepec, Michoacán antes de 1803. En 1790 este pueblo se incluye en el padrón de la provincia de Colima. (AGN:Padrones 11)

#6 Visita de Tuxpán, Jalisco antes de 1803. En el padrón de 1790 se considera como una congregación. (AGN:Padrones 11)

Figure 10-4: Lyman D. Platt's Mexico : guia general, divisiones eclesiasticas, *provides information on parish and province jurisdictions.*

USING GOVERNMENT RECORDS

Spanish Colonial Institutions

An understanding of how Spain governed the American colonies will help you better understand the records generated. From the initial financing of the voyage of Columbus by Queen Isabel of Spain, the discovery and colonization of the Americas was a commercial venture. By the time of Columbus's second voyage, the Spanish government was sufficiently concerned about the commercial aspect of his undertaking that treasury (Hacienda) representatives were sent to accompany him, and a system was set up to govern any future commerce with the colonies. In 1503, the Spanish government established the *Casa de la Contratacion de las Indias*, which, from then until the end of the eighteenth century, governed all commercial transactions between Spain and her colonies. This body, established at Seville, remained there until the eighteenth century when, due to the silting of the Guadalquivir river and the port becoming inaccessible, the *Casa de la Contratación* was moved to Cadiz.

In 1519, the *Real y Supremo Consejo de las Indias* was organized in Madrid to control all governmental affairs and represent the crown in the American colonies. As colonial government expanded, the various colonies were divided up into *virreinatos* and *provincias*. The *virreinatos* were presided over by a *virrey*, who literally represented the king in those colonies. New Spain was the oldest and largest, with a legislative/judicial council known as the *audiencia* that advised the *virrey* in Mexico City and had both secondary and original jurisdictions and certain legislative powers. The *virreinato de Nueva España* was further divided into *provincias* in which a governor and council held the administrative, legislative, and judicial functions concurrently.

Larger towns or districts were governed by the *alcalde* or *corregidor*. Like all the other officials discussed above, these local officers were appointed by the crown through the Council of the Indies. Magdaleno's *Títulos de Indias* lists those appointed to such positions by the Spanish kings and provides the information to order files relating to those appointments. Each town also had a governing council called the *cabildo*, composed of a number of councilors as well as local magistrates, law enforcement officers, and royal treasury representatives. Between 1764 and 1790, the Spanish crown reorganized colonial government around larger, centralized units called *intendencias*, as shown in figure 10-5.

VOCABULARY

Virreinatos—a viceroyalty.

Provincias—a province.

Virrey—viceroy.

Audiencia—the regional high court.

Corregidor—magistrate.

Cabildo—municipal or town council.

Intendencias—territorial division under the direction of the *Intendente* (superintendent).

For more information, see appendix A, "Glossary."

Figure 10-5: This map shows the intendencias in Mexico in 1788.

All of these colonial divisions were directly supervised by the *Real Consejo de las Indias* in Madrid, which handled governmental affairs directly or delegated many of the activities relating to commercial transactions to the *Casa de la Contratacion de las Indias* in Seville. Records of all of these, as well as many local colonial records, are found in the Archivo General de las Indias in Seville. If a court case arose on a local level, it could be appealed to the *audiencia* in Mexico City, and from there to the *virrey* or directly to the *Consejo de las Indias* in Madrid. Ultimately, any matter could be appealed to the *Consejo de Castilla*, or to the king himself. This appellate procedure applied to administrative and executive, as well as judicial, matters.

Various overviews of Spanish colonial institutions in Mexico are found in Haring's *Spanish Empire* and Barnes's *Guide to Northern New Spain*.

Finding the Place and Other Geographical Questions in the Colonial Period

When questions come up about colonial Mexican geography, refer to one of the three books written about the geography of Colonial Mexico by Peter Gerhard.
- *The North Frontier of New Spain*
- *The Geography of New Spain*
- *The Southeast Frontier of New Spain*

For each of the major areas of Mexico, Gerhard first offers a detailed discussion, complete with historical maps of the area from its founding until 1821—with particular emphasis on geographical changes—of both government and church. He then gives a similar detailed description of the geography and history of each locality including a map like that in figure 10-6 and general maps like those in figures 10-2 and 10-5. His endnotes offer references to other places to go, including census records for the area. The index at the end of the book allows you to take a reference to a place that you may find in a record and locate the place. His work is so detailed that short lived place names and obscure towns regularly appear.

Censuses

As the reforms of King Charles III (1759–88) extended into the administration of the Spanish colonies, the Council of Indies initiated a series of empire-wide census projects. A page from the 1777 census for Saltillo, Coahuila, in figure 10-7, shows the detail they can contain.

The idea of keeping censuses was not a new one. Before this time, some governors in specific provinces and even local officials had ordered censuses prepared. Catholic bishops ordered censuses of those who took communion, and military leaders required censuses of men prepared to give militia service. *Census Records for Latin America and the Hispanic United States* by Lyman D. Platt identifies many of these censuses by specific locality. However, always watch as you search in municipal, state, and diocesan archival collections for censuses he does not identify.

Spanish censuses are considerably better in detail than their English language counterparts, normally identifying the head of household by name and surname,

Nueva Galicia

communicants in the secular parish (it still included Los Angeles), and 923 in the Franciscan doctrina, but otherwise made no racial breakdown. That of 1770 had 15,662 persons over two years of age in both parishes, omitting Los Angeles and Agostadero.[6] The 1772 padrón showed 2,657 families with 11,515 adults and 3,921 párvulos, a total of 15,436, but it also omitted those places which were in the parish of Asientos. A map submitted with the 1772 padrón noted that there were 3,117 families with 18,062 people, including some living in the jurisdiction of S Luis Potosí. Parish records of Sierra de Pinos and Ojuelos gave a total of 24,785 communicants in 1797. According to the *Matrícula*, in 1801 there were 1,753 Indian and 1,496 Negro and mulatto family heads in the subdelegación.[7] Still another "census" dated 1828 showed only 12,277 persons in the area:

8,070 at Pinos, 4,207 at Ahualulco,[8] and none at Los Angeles (Lemoine, 1964, pp. 320-321).

Sources

I have already cited the documents from which most of the above information was gleaned. There are records of three episcopal visits from 1668 to 1681.[9] I have seen but not examined a padrón of 1766.[10] The alcalde mayor's report of 1772 was accompanied by a magnificent map of the jurisdiction.[11] Testimony of a bishop's inspection in 1797 contains much about the cofradías, and also has a map.[12] The subdelegado's report to the Consulado de Vera Cruz in 1804 has much economic information (Florescano and Gil, 1976b, pp. 100-101).

Acosta Gómez (1978) has compiled a most valuable compendium with the aid of the parochial archives here.

24 Sombrerete

The southwestern part of this area is a series of high valleys in the Pacific drainage, separated by outlying ranges (up to 3,000 m) of the Sierra

Madre; northeast of the continental divide are headwaters of the Aguanaval, which flows into the Laguna basin. The climate is cool and dry (500-600 mm annual rainfall). The region is now in northwestern Zacatecas state.

The people here at contact were Zacateco-speaking Chichimecs.

Spaniards explored the area in 1552, and miners settled at S Martín *ca* 1555. Other reales (Sombrerete, Chalchihuites, etc.) were founded within the next few years, but they were besieged by hostile Indians until after 1590 (Bakewell, 1971, pp. 23-24).

Government

At first subject to Zacatecas, the mines of S Martín had a resident alcalde mayor by 1559 (Mecham, 1927, pp. 86, 91). His jurisdiction included Sombrerete, Nieves (q.v.), and Avino, although the latter was transferred to Nueva Vizcaya sometime after 1640.[1] He also claimed Nombre de Dios until that region became part

Figure 10-6: Peter Gerhard's books include geographical information and maps about each major area in Mexico during the colonial era.

along with occupation, material status, and age, and then providing a list of all other household members by name, frequently with their age and relationship to the household head (see figure 10-7). Some censuses were taken to enumerate specific categories of individuals, such as all resident aliens. A page from the abstract of such a census, from San Antonio, Texas, for the year 1795 from the book *Residents of Texas 1782–1836*, appears in figure 10-8.

CIVIL LEGAL DOCUMENTS

Notarial Records

As the Spanish colonies moved beyond the initial frontier stage, legal documents were recorded by *escribanos*. As previously discussed in chapter 7, "Beyond the Parish: Notarial Records," a summary of the kind of documents appearing in a notary archive indicates a wealth of information for the family historian, which only increases in variety during the colonial period: wills, adoptions, emancipations, sales of rural and urban land, construction of buildings, proof of purity of blood, records of nobility, transfers of titles, dowries, rescue of captives, sales of slaves, marriage contracts, sales of cloth, sales of horses, printing of books, apprenticeship records, contracts with professionals, land titles, executions, inventories of decedents' estates, guardianship estates, mining claims, powers of attorneys, and many others.

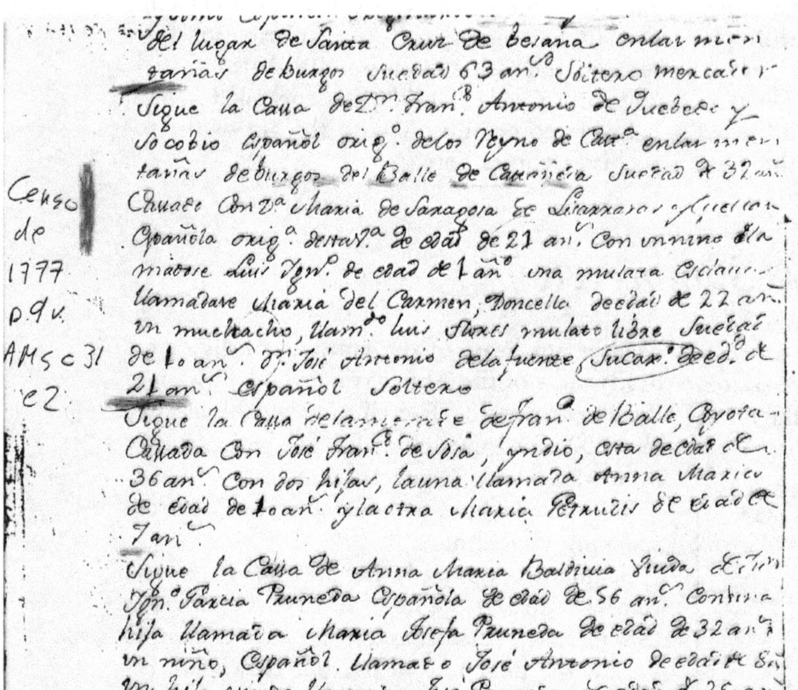

Except in Mexico City, where they are housed in the Colegio de Notarios, most notarial records are found in municipal archives, especially of colonial capitals. While the majority of the municipal archives do not have colonial records, most of the largest cities have excellent colonial collections. The many Mexican states such as Tamaulipas, Nuevo

Figure 10-7: Mexican colonial censuses usually give more information than their English counterparts.

```
Bexar Archives--University of Texas Archives, Austin, Texas.

Census of Nacogdoches, B. FERNANDEZ, December 25, 1795.

Province of Texas, Year of 1795,  Village of Our Lady of the Pilar
of Nacogdoches.

Census that includes the number of souls that live in this village
on this date, formed by the Lt. Commandant D. Fernando HERNANDES.


     Ministers, the Rev. Fathers Fray Bernardino VALLEJO and
Fr. Pedro PORTUGAL; their servants, one Spaniard born in San
Antonio de Bexar, his name Joaquin Montes de OCA, his age 44
yrs; and the other Tomas TUYU, Indian of Campeche and age of
20 yrs.                                                               4

     Don Cristoval Ilario de CORDOVA, widower, native of Los
Adaes, his age 68 yrs.                                                1

     Nicolas MORA, Spaniard, widower, native of Los Adaes, his
age 58 yrs; has one brother, his age 27 yrs; one son of 11 yrs.,
one daughter of 17 yrs., and one female negro slave, her age 30
yrs.                                                                  5

     Teresa MORA, Spaniard, widow, native of Los Adaes, her age
41 yrs; has five sons, of 16, 13, 12, 7 and 6 yrs., and two
daughters of 14 and 10 yrs.                                           8

     Jose SANCHES, Spaniard, married, native of Los Adaes, his
age 30 yrs; his occupation farmer; his wife Josefa YBARBO,
Spaniard, native of this village, her age 16 yrs.                     2

     Martin MENDES, Mulatto, married, native of Camargo, his age
26 yrs; occupation farmer, his wife Marian Andrea CHIRINO, half-
caste, native of Los Adaes, her age 42 yrs; has one daughter, a
widow of age of 24 yrs., and one grand-daughter, her age three
yrs.                                                                  4

     Francisco VILLALPANDO, Indian, married, native of New Mexico,
his age 41 yrs; his occupation trader to the Quichas, his wife
Getrudis ROSALES, Mulatto, native of Los Adaes, her age 27 yrs;
has one little boy that he reared of 5 yrs., and one sister of 17
yrs.                                                                  4
```

Figure 10-8: Some census records have been abstracted and indexed.

Leon, Coahuila, Sonora, Guanajuato, Zacatecas, Puebla, and Baja California all have state archives with colonial era records, including notarial records.[3] Others such as Chihuahua and Sonora have separate notarial archives with relevant materials.[4]

Lawsuits

Petitions or lawsuits filed as part of the governmental apparatus frequently appear in collections of civil legal documents retained in colonial archives. In some cases, these were lawsuits in the sense that they involved a dispute between two civil parties. In others, they were petitions requesting governmental approval or the granting of privileges, somewhat similar to probate or guardianship petitions in today's courts.

VOCABULARY

Petición—petition or application filed with a court or other governmental or ecclesiastical entity.

Demanda—demand, claim.

Hoja de servicios—service record.

Padrón—list or census of the residents or inhabitants of a village or parish.

For more information, see appendix A, "Glossary."

Generally, those labeled *petición* were of the type requesting governmental service or approval. A *demanda* was a claim—usually against a third party—relating to a contract or other dispute, the initial document in a litigation action. Similarly, a *diligencia* represents the final order or response of the responsible person to one of the above. Because the municipal *alcalde* was the primary local judge, most of these lawsuits are found in large municipal archives.

MILITARY RECORDS

Colonial military records helpful in doing family history fall into three categories: administrative records of the local *presidio* or fort; *hojas de servicio*; and *padrónes*. Administrative records are generally reports by military commanders and notices of transfers, purchases of supplies, and other routine activities.

Hojas de servicio form a significant part of military records. A service record relates to a specific individual, usually an officer of the rank of sergeant or above, giving his name, rank, place of origin, age, and, in some cases, his parents' names. The document will then set forth the time periods in which he served in particular places and/or ranks he achieved, and give a written summary of his service, highlighting important campaigns and locations where he has served. Figure 10-9 shows the military service record for Jose de Zuñiga.

Census records of military personnel are, in reality, a class of administrative records, generally containing a list of officers and soldiers serving in a *presidio* at a particular date, with the name and rank of each individual. Many times, however, they include lists of families of the soldiers also residing in the *presidio*. In such cases, relationships to the individual soldiers as well as ages are frequently given. Figure 10-10 shows the first page of a military census report for the *presidio* of San Buenaventura, Chihuahua, Mexico, dated 1 March 1818.

RACE IN COLONIAL TIMES

Race was an important social denominator in colonial Mexico. Racial designations were detailed and often complex, as set forth in the sidebar, "Racial Mixtures of Colonial Mexico." They appear in nearly all records as a way to identify people. One must note, however, that these were generally based more on physical observation and one's social position than on one's genealogy. Often a person will appear with a different racial designation at different times in his life. In many parishes there were separate parish books for *españoles, indios*, and *negros* (see the sidebar "Racial Mixtures of Colonial Mexico and figure 10-11).

Figure 10-9: Military service records can give excellent information about ancestors who were officers.

Figure 10-10: Military census records help place ancestors in a specific place and time.

RACIAL MIXTURES OF COLONIAL MEXICO

In parish and other records during the colonial period racial designations are generally given. Parish records were even separated into two books, one for españoles and the other for castas. Casta means 1) caste; 2) lineage; or 3) each one of the closed classes in which a society is divided. Several different "blood mixtures," as defined herein, could be included in the concept of casta. In many cases the caste distinctions were social rather than literal. They may also be the determinations the priest made based on skin color or living conditions, rather than knowledge of the racial composition of the child. There are many documented examples where the same man changes racial designation, even reaching the point of being designated español as his economic and social status improves.

albino—1) blood mixture: Spanish and Morisco; 2) albino.

cambujo/ja—blood mixture: Indian (1 part), negro (1 part), and Chinese (2 parts).

cambur/ra—blood mixture: Spanish (1 part), Indian (2 parts) and negro (1 part).

castizo—of a good caste.

chino/a—1) Chinese; 2) used for various racial mixtures: indio, mestizo, and mulato; 3) peasant girl, maid.

cimarron/na—blood mixture: Spanish (1 part), Indian (1 part), and negro (2 parts).

coyote—blood mixture: Spanish (4 parts), Indian (3 parts), and negro (1 part).

criollo/a—1) Creole; 2) Latin-American colonial born of European parents.

cuarteado—blood mixture: Spanish (2 parts), Indian (1 part) and negro (1 part); the offspring of a mestizo and a mulata.

cuarteron—blood mixture: Spanish (3 parts) and mulata (1 part); at times called morisco.

cuatrero—blood mixture: Spanish (1 part) and Indian (3 parts); the offspring of a mestizo and an Indian.

español/a—1) white or of pure Spanish blood; or 2) individual born of Spanish parents in peninsular Spain.

español criollo—Spanish creole; an individual born of Spanish parents within the Spanish colonies.

indio/dia—Indian; a person living with the Indians who adopts their customs, a social designation.

ladino/a—1) blood mixture: Spanish (3 parts) and Indian (1 part); 2) a name given to those Indians who speak Spanish.

lobo/ba—blood mixture: Indian (1 part) and negro (3 parts).

mestizo/za—1) a person born of parents of different races, usually Spanish and Indian; 2) crossbreed or half breed.

moreno/na—blood mixture: Spanish (2 parts), Indian (1 part), and negro (1 part); offspring of Spaniard and Zambaiga.

morisco/ca—Moorish; baptized Moors who lived in Spain or Mexico; Mexico, blood mixture: Spanish and mulato.

negro/ra—black or dark-skinned; native of various tribes of Africa.

negro fino—blood mixture: Spaniard (1 part) and negro (3 parts); offspring of mulato and negro.

pardo/da—blood mixture: Spaniard (1 part), Indian (2 parts), and negro (1 part).

zambaigo—blood mixture: negro (1 part), Indian (1 part); sometimes in Mexico Chinese (1 part) Indian (1 part).

LOCATING OTHER COLONIAL RECORDS OF GENEALOGICAL VALUE

Describing the location of all of the varied materials available for the Spanish colonial period with an accompanying bibliography of guidebooks, inventories, indexes, and published transcripts is far beyond the scope of this book. Rather, a description of the archives, libraries, and microfilm collections where a majority of those records may be found, as well as useful Internet sites appears in the remainder of this chapter.

Archives in Spain

The archives of Spain are rich in material about the colonial period in Mexico. That treasure house has been mined for decades and excellent guides, indexes, and inventories have been prepared, some to collections in the archives generally, others aimed specifically at the Americas and even at regions in the United States and Mexico. Computerized access to the archives is available at <www.aer.es>. The three described in this chapter are the most important both in the quality and quantity of their collections relating to the Mexican colonial period, but literally hundreds of other libraries and archives in Spain have collections with materials relating to Mexico:[5]

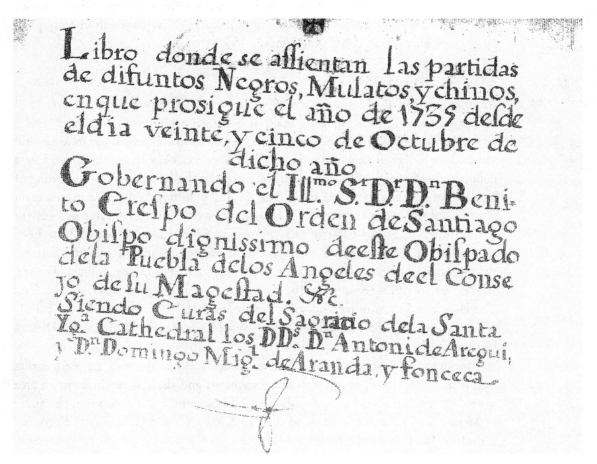

Figure 10-11: This image is the title page of a parish death register for negros *and mulattoes.*

BOOKS ABOUT THE MEXICAN COLONIAL PERIOD

Weber, David J. *The Spanish Frontier in North America.* New Haven: Yale University Press, 1992.

———— *The Mexican Frontier, 1821-1846, The American Southwest Under Mexico.* Albuquerque: University of N.M. Press, 1982.

Naylor, Thomas H., and Polzer, Charles W. *Northern New Spain. A Research Guide.* Tucson: The University of Arizona Press, 1981.

- *Archivo General de Indias,* Seville, Spain, is the primary archive for Spanish colonial documents, with governmental, judicial, commercial, and military records for all of the American colonies found there. Local government reports, passenger lists, censuses, and a multitude of other records, often intimately local in nature, are among the documents contained in the archive. Of particular interest are the various subsections relating to New Spain in the *Gobierno, Justicia,* and *Contratación* sections.[6]

- *Archivo General de Simancas,* Valladolid, Spain, is the oldest national archives in Europe. Although all of the sections relating entirely and specifically to the administration of the colonies were sent to Seville in 1790 to create the *Archivo General de Indias,* many records relating to the Americas remain that were integrated in collections covering all the functions of Spanish government.[7] Notably among those are *Títulos de Indias,* describing appointments to numerous government positions in what is now the United States, and *Hojas de Sevicio Militar en América,* which includes military officers' personnel sheets from posts throughout Mexico.[8]

- *Archivo General de Segovia,* Segovia, Spain, is Spain's premier military archive and it contains material about military operations in the New World. Of particular interest is the fully indexed section dealing with officers' service files, which includes those relating to the many who served in military posts in what is now the United States.[9]

Archives in Mexico

Archivo General de la Nación contains censuses, correspondence, reports, and diaries concerning political and financial administration, military affairs, ecclesiastical affairs, relations with the Indians, explorations, expeditions, mining, and much more. Originating as the archives of the Viceroy of New Spain, this is the richest collection of Spanish colonial materials concerning the United States, consisting of 115 record groups containing more than 41,000 volumes.[10] For more information visit the website of this archives at <www.agn.gob.mx>. This site contains an excellent online index to ninety-eight of the colonial sections, many of which have been microfilmed and can be consulted in the United States. See appendix E, "Researching the Archivo General de la Nación from the United States," for a chart showing where various AGN sections can be consulted in the United States on microfilm. The largest and most universally available are the 121,740 films held by the Family History Library in Salt Lake City, which can be ordered to local Family History Centers.

Mexican state archives primarily have material about the national period that begins in 1824, but there are sufficient exceptions and the state archives in an area should be checked for colonial records as well. See appendix D, "Archives of the States of Mexico," and chapter 6, "Beyond the Parish: Church and Government Records," for information on these archives.

Libraries and Archives in the United States

Universities and other libraries and archives in the United States have collected large amounts of materials relating to the Mexican colonial periods. Many are copies or transcripts of those found in foreign archives, as well as originals acquired by Anglo-American document collectors in the past. As a researcher moves beyond the basics of parish and census research, the catalogs for these collections should be consulted. In each case a website is provided to gain more information about these collections and many offer catalogs, indexes, and even digital documents.

Recognizing the importance of accessing colonial Mexican documents from the United States, appendix E, "Researching the Archivo General de la Nación from the United States," identifies the major collections of such documents and where they may be found in microfilm format and/or indexed.

- *Family History Library*, Salt Lake City, Utah, the world's largest collection of microfilms of original documents of genealogical value, has microfilms of many of the records described elsewhere in this chapter. Anyone researching Mexican colonial records should check to see what is available here, as most can be sent to a local Family History Center nearby for minimal cost. For an overview of major collections from national, state, and municipal archives see appendix E. Remember, however, that most of the best colonial records for Mexico are local census and parish records. To find those go again to FamilySearch.org under Family History Library Catalog. Check for any record source mentioned under "Place Search," using first the town, then the county, and then the state, for records for the colonial period. If all else fails, try a creative search using keywords.
- *University of Texas, El Paso* has more than 160 microfilm sets relating to Mexico, including copies purchased from other microfilming sources, such as the University of Texas at Austin, the National Archives, and so on. For details go to <http://libraryweb.utep.edu/special/special.cfm>.
- *University of Texas, Austin* has two very large collections containing Mexican materials: Nettie Lee Benson Latin American Collections <www.lib.utexas.edu/benson> and the Center for American History's Research and Collections Division <www.lib.utexas.edu/benson>.
- *University of California, Berkeley,* has the Bancroft Collection, which provides original and secondary materials in a variety of formats to support research in the history of the American West, Mexico, and Central America, with greatest emphasis on California and Mexico from the period of European exploration and settlement onward. For details go to <http://bancroft.berkeley.edu/collections/bancroft.html>.
- *The Documentary Relations of the Southwest (DRSW),* housed at Arizona State Museum at the University of Arizona in Tucson, holds an extensive collection of microfilm relating to the Southwest. Look online at <www.statemuseum.arizona.edu/oer/master_index_help.shtml> to access the *Master Bibliography and Indexes* containing over seventeen thousand records describing an

estimated total of five hundred thousand pages of primary documents dealing with the greater Southwest from 1520 to 1820, which corresponds to the Spanish colonial era. These documents cover an extensive geographical area bounded by the 22nd to the 38th parallel of north latitude, and the 92nd to the 123rd meridian of west longitude, approximating the colonial frontiers of northern New Spain. Culled from a total of thirty-one archives in Europe and the Americas, the indexed documents include significant materials from the following archives: Archivo Histórico del Hidalgo de Parral, Chihuahua; Archivo General de Indias (AGI-Sevilla); Archivo General de la Nación (AGN-Mexico City) including the entire Ramo Provincias Internas of Mexico City's Archivo General de la Nación; Archivo Histórico de Hacienda (AHH-Mexico City); Spanish Archives of New Mexico; the Béxar Archives of San Antonio up to the year 1790; and fifteen smaller archives. See appendix E for details on where to find filmed copies of records indexed by this program.

- *Yale University*, New Haven, Connecticut, has the Latin American Collection of the Yale University Library, the oldest Latin American manuscript collection in the United States, as well as approximately 435,000 printed volumes, plus newspapers and microfilms. Go to <www.library.yale.edu/latinamerica> for more detail.

- *Tulane University, New Orleans, Louisiana,* has the Latin American Collection, which includes an extensive manuscript collection rich in Mexican materials. At this time the index to the collection is only available through a card file index. Go to <www.tulane.edu> for more information.

NOTES

1. Peter Gerhard, *The North Frontier of New Spain* (Norman, Ok.: University of Oklahoma Press, 1982), 24–25; <http://teaching.arts.usyd.edu.au/history/hsty3080/3rdYr3080/Louisiana/louisiana_after_the_purchase>.

2. Rick Hendricks, ed., and John B. Colligan, comp., *New Mexico Prenuptial Investigations from the Archivos Historicos Del Arzobispado De Durango, 1760-1799* (Las Cruces, NM, 1997).

3. Go to <www.coahuila.gob.mx/sgob/ied/> for detailed information.

4. See Rodriguez Ochoa, Patricia, *Guía general de los archivos estatales y municipales de México* (Mexico, D.F.: Sistema Nacional de Archivos, 1988).

5. Dirección General de Archivos y Bibliotecas, *Guía de fuentes Para la historia de Ibero-América conservados en España*, 2 vols. (Madrid, 1966); José Tulela, *Los Manuscritos de América en las Bibliotecas de España* (Madrid: Ediciones Cultura Hispánica, 1954); Lawrence H. Feldman, *Anglo-Americans in Spanish Archives* (Baltimore: Genealogical Publishing Co., 1991); Lino Gomez Canedo, *Los archivos de la historia de América, período colonial española*, 2 vols. (Instituto Panamericano de Geografía e Historia, Comisión de Historia. Publicación Num. 225, Mexico City: Commissión de Historia, 1961).

6. Cristóbal Bermuda Plata, *El Archivo General de Indias de Sevilla: sede del americanismo* (Madrid: 1951); Charles E. Chapman. *Catalogue of Materials in the Archivo General de las Indias for the History of the Pacific Coast and the American Southwest* (University of California, Publications in History, vol. 8. Arthur H. Clark Co.: Glendale, California, 1927); Charles E. Chapman, *Catalogue of Material in the Archivo General de Indias for the History of the Pacific Coast and the American Southwest* (University of California, Publications in History, vol. 8. Berkeley: University of California Press, 1919); *Indice de documentos de Nueva España: existentes en el Archivo de Indias de Sevilla* (México, D.F.: Secretaria de Relaciones Exteriores, 1925-1931); Purificación Medina Encina, *Documentos Relativos a la Independencia de Norteamérica Existentes en Archivos Españoles. Vol. I: Archivo General de Indias, sección de gobierno, años 1752–1822* (Madrid: Ministerio de Asuntos Exteriores, Dirección General de Relaciones Culturas, 1976).

7. Plaza Bores, *Angel de la Archivo General de Simancas: Guía del Investigador*, (Madrid: Dirección General de Archivos y Bibliotecas, Patronato Nacional de Archivos Históricos, 1962).

8. Ricardo Magdaleno, *Catálogo XX del Archivo General de Simancas, Títulos de Indias* (Patronato Nacional de Archivos Históricos: Valladolid, 1954); Archivo de Simancas, *Secretaria de Guerra, Hojas de Servicios de América* (Patronato Nacional de Archivos Históricos: Valladolid, 1958).

9. *Guía de archivos militares españoles* (Madrid: Ministerio de Defensa, 1995); Federico Heredero Roura and Vicente Cadenas y Vicent, *Archivo General Militar de Segovia: Indice de Expedientes Personales*, 9 vols. (Ediciones Hidalguía: Madrid 1959 –1963).

10. Archivo General de la Nación, *Guía General* (México, D.F.: Difusión y Publicaciones del Archivio General de la Nación, 1991).

GLOSSARY

abuelastro/a—step-grandparent, parent of the stepfather or of the stepmother.

abuelo/a—1) grandparent; 2) ancestor; forefather; 3) old person.

acta—1) official act; 2) recording of an official act.

adelantado—1) colonial title used for the following: governor of a frontier province, supreme justice of the kingdom, captain general in times of war; 2) a discoverer, founder; 3) pacifier of Indian lands.

administración—administration.

adulterio—adultery, violation of the marriage vows.

adviento—Advent, the four weeks preceding Christmas.

afinidad—relation by marriage.

albacea—executor of a will.

albino—1) blood mixture: Spanish and **Morisco**; 2) albino.

alcalde—1) mayor; 2) magistrate; 3) official to whom mayor delegates his powers in a certain section of a city.

alcalde mayor—In colonial New Spain, the crown appointed mayor of a town that was not a provincial capital.

aldea—village, hamlet.

alferez—1) ensign; 2) army officer lower than lieutenant; 3) in Bolivia and Peru a municipal office in the Indian villages.

alma—1) soul; 2) person.

almoneda—1) public auction; 2) clearance sale.

alteza—an honorary title given to the kings, princes, and officials of the high court (**audiencia**) and to some of the royal councils; your highness.

amonestación matrimonial—proclamation published during three successive Sundays before marriages; banns.

amparo—1) the act of protection of an Indian by the Spaniard, specifically teaching him a trade, bringing him up; duty of the **encomendero** or **patron**.

anima—1) soul; 2) those spirits consigned to purgatory; 3) in the plural **animas** sometimes refers to the death mass, or the tolling of the bells to summon people to pray for a recently deceased person.

ante—1) before, in front of, in the presence of; 2) in view of, with regard to.

antiguo/gua—old.

apartamiento—judicial act or declaration by which one removes oneself from a legal action or right.

apodo—nickname, sobriquet.

apostólico—apostolic.

appellido—surname, family name, last name.

aprendizage—apprenticeship.

aprendizo/za—apprentice, beginner.

archivo—1) archive, place where records are kept, office; 2) a file.

arrendamiento—rent, letting, lease.

arroba—1) weight measure equivalent to twenty-five lbs. of sixteen oz. each; 2) liquid measurement equivalent to about three gallons; 3) the fourth part of a quintal.

artículo—article.

arzobispado—1) archbishopric; 2) ecclesiastical territory under the jurisdiction of an archbishop.

arzobispo—archbishop (the bishop of a metropolitan church to which other bishops are subordinate).

asiento—1) seat on a tribunal or council; 2) contract or obligation made to provide money or goods for the army.

audiencia—1) regional high court; 2) civil tribunal that dealt with the civil and criminal actions of last resort. (In the absence of a colonial viceroy this high court became the executive branch that represented the king.)

ausente—1) absent; 2) absentee, missing person.

ausente sin licencia—(military) absent without leave.

auto—1) judicial sentence; 2) warrant; 3) edict; 4) various legal documents both judicial and administrative but not wills nor inventories.

autos de bienes de difuntos—processing of assets of the deceased.

auto de fe—a public procedure in which those accused by the Inquisition were sentenced.

bachiller—1) graduate of the equivalent of junior college in the U.S.; 2) holder of a bachelor's degree, baccalaureate; 3) applied to priests who have graduated from the seminary.

bautizar—to baptize, to christen.

bisabuelo/la—great-grandparent.

bisnieto/ta—great-grandchild.

braza—length measure; length formed by having both arms of a person open and extended, which commonly is taken to be six feet of width.

bula—papal bull or proclamation.

caballería—1) military cavalry; 2) knightly order, knights, e.g **la caballeria de Santiago**, (the Knights of Santiago), knighthood, rank and privileges of a knight; 3) land measure (in Spain about 95 acres, in Cuba 33, in Puerto Rico 194, in Mexico 106.)

caballero—1) nobleman; 2) knight; 3) member of military order.

cabeza—head.

cabildo—1) municipal or town council; 2) chapter of a cathedral or collegiate church.

cabildo abierto—meetings of the town council and the citizens of the town.

cacicazo—the territory governed by and/or the authority of a **Cacique**.

Cacique—1) the chief or ruler of some Indian tribes; 2) local ruler.

cambio—1) change, alteration; 2) interchange, exchange; 3) (law) exchange of posts by two holders of government jobs or ecclesiastical benefices.

cambujo/ja—blood mixture: Indian (1 part), **negro** (1 part), and Chinese (2 parts).

camburo/ra—blood mixture: Spanish (1 part), Indian (2 parts) and **negro** (1 part); term used on parish registers of Mexico.

cantón—jurisdiction of government between municipality and state used in Mexico in the late nineteenth and early twentieth century.

capellán—a priest who has a chaplaincy or says mass in a private chapel and who is paid by a trust fund or private individual to administer the affairs of said fund or individual.

capellanía—1) benefice or foundation subject to certain obligations; 2) lay foundation without ecclesiastical intervention.

capital—1) assets; 2) principal of a trust fund.

Capitán General—supreme commander of a military region.

capitanía general—1) captaincy general; 2) territorial demarcation governed by a Captain General during the colonial era.

Casa de la Contratación de las Indias—Spanish governmental entity housed in Seville that was charged with handling the economic and commercial affairs of the American colonies, 1503–1790.

casa solar—ancestral home, manor house.

casado/da—married to.

casamiento—marriage; wedding.

casta—1) caste; 2) lineage; 3) each one of the closed classes into which a society is divided. (See the different "blood mixture" definitions herein.) In many cases the caste distinctions are social rather than literal.

castizo—of a good caste.

catedral/catedra—episcopal church of a diocese or archdiocese; cathedral.

cedula—1) royal decree; 2) document, manuscript.

cedula personal/documento nacional—identity card; identification papers.

cementerio—1) cemetery; 2) a place in the countryside where Christian Indians, slaves, and other poor persons are buried; 3) a churchyard burial ground that is behind, at the side of, or sometimes in front of the church, as well as places within the churches: in the floor, the walls, and special crypts, etc.; 4) civil burial grounds which date from the beginning of civil registration within each country.

censo—1) census of population; 2) official register of citizens having the right to vote; 3) head-tax, tribute, tax; 4) annual stipend paid formerly by some churches to their prelates; 5) (law) living pledge, contract whereby an estate is pledged to payment of an annuity as interest on a loan without transfer of title.

certificación—certification, attestation.

certificado (de nacimiento, de casamiento, de defunción)—1) certificate (of birth, of marriage, of death); 2) registered mail.

chino/a—1) Chinese; 2) term used for various racial mixtures: **indio, mestizo** and mulato; 3) peasant girl, maid.

cimarron/na—in Mexico and Guatemala, blood mixture: Spanish (1 part), Indian (1 part), and **negro** (2 parts).

ciudad—city.

ciudadano—citizen, a title given to all persons who appeared before the civil register.

clase—1) class, type, kind; 2) (military) non-commissioned officers.

clérigo—1) clergyman; 2) those who have been received into a sacred order (in military orders this is distinguished from **caballero**).

cobdicilio—codicil.

cofradía—1) congregation or brotherhood of religious individuals; 2) guild; 3) trade union.

colector—collector of taxes, or of collection for the church.

colegiata—collegiate church.

colegio notarial—notarial college.

colonial—1) time period beginning at the Spanish conquest and ending with the wars of independence, or approximately 1519–1821; 2) of or relating to that time period; 3) relating to a colony.

comadre—1) midwife; 2) godmother.

comandancia general—commanding general.

comandante—1) military commander; 2) commander of a **presidio**.

compañía—1) a legal association or society of several persons united for a single purpose, commercial, social, or ecclesiastical; 2) military unit.

comparecer—to appear officially before someone, such as a judge, civil register secretary, or notary.

compraventa—contract of purchase and sale.

compromiso—1) pledge, commitment, promise; 2) engagement (to be married); 3) (law) compromise, arbitration, agreement.

comunidad—1) community, particularly a religious group; 2) village, commune, community.

concejo/concejil—council.

concierto—1) agreement, contract; 2) arrangement, settlement.

concuñado/da—spouse of one's own spouse's brother or sister.

confirmación—1) confirmation, affirmation, corroboration; 2) the religious sacrament of confirmation administered by the bishop.

congregación—1) congregation; 2) assembly; 3) religious brotherhood; 4) committee of cardinals, or of a religious order.

conocido—known.

conquistadores—Spanish conquerors of the New World in the sixteenth century.

consanguinidad—consanguinity; kinship; blood relationship; measured in degrees in Canon Law by counting from each person to the common ancestor.

consejero—counselor, advisor.

consejo—council.

Consejo de Castilla or **Real**—Council of Castille, Royal Council, Supreme administrative body in Spain.

Consejo de Indias—Royal council that governed the colonies.

consentimiento—consent, compliance, acquiescence.

consorte de—1) spouse; 2) partner, associate.

constar—to be recorded or registered.

contratación—1) making a contract; 2) trade; 3) **Casa de la Contratación de las Indias**, Spanish governmental entity located in Seville that was charged with handling the economic and commercial affairs of the American colonies, 1503–1790.

contrato—contract; agreement enforceable by law.

contrayente—contracting party, such as in a marriage.

contribución—tax.

convenio—agreement, covenant, pact.

convento—convent.

conyuge—spouse, consort; (pl.) married couple.

copia literal—literal or word-for-word copy.

corregidor—magistrate, an administrator of a city or district.

corriente—current, present (week, month, year).

cosa—1) thing, something; 2) affair, business.

coyote—blood mixture, Spanish (4 parts), Indian (3 parts), and **negro** (1 part) term used on parish registers of Mexico.

criollo/a—1) Creole; 2) Latin-American colonial born of European parents.

crisma—chrism, consecrated oil.

cuadra—1) stable; 2) city block.

Cuaresma—Lent, the forty weekdays before Easter beginning on Ash Wednesday; 2) collection of lent sermons.

cuarteado—blood mixture: Spanish (2 parts), Indian (1 part) and **negro** (1 part); the offspring of a **mestizo** and a **mulata**.

cuarteron—blood mixture: Spanish (3 parts) and **mulata** (1 part), at times called **morisco**.

cuartillo—dry measure equivalent to three celemín, or 1.156 liters.

cuate/ta—in Mexico, the word used for twins; the Spanish word is usually **mellizos**.

cuatrero—blood mixture: Spanish (1 part) and Indian (3 parts); the offspring of a **mestizo** and an Indian.

cuenta—account, bill, report.

cuerpo—1) body; 2) volume, book, body of laws, of writings, of people; 3) corps (diplomatic and military).

cuñado/a—brother-in-law, sister-in-law.

cura—parish priest, vicar.

curato—parish.

curia—administrative and judicial organization under the bishop.

dado—as long as; provided that; given that.

de los mismos—of the same (usually refers to previous wording, such as month and year).

de repente—suddenly.

declaración—declaration, statement; affidavit.

defensor—defense, counsel.

defunción—death.

demanda—demand; claim.

depósito—deposit; depository.

desconocido—unknown.

despachar—1) to finish or shorten at a section; 2) to resolve or determine the causes; 3) to send a person or thing.

dicho/cha—1) said, the above mentioned; 2) (law) declaration, statement made by witness.

difunto/ta—deceased, dead.

digo—I say (frequently used by scribes in records to correct errors as they wrote).

diligencia matrimonial—premarital investigation conducted by a parish priest.

diócesis—diocese (unit of Catholic Church presided over by a Bishop).

diputado—deputy.

directorio—directory.

dispensa matrimonial—exception to Canon Law regulation given by a bishop to a bride and groom to permit marriage (e.g., for being related within the 4th degree).

dista/distante/distancia—distance (from).

distrito—district.

doctrina—1) doctrine; 2) ritual; 3) a village of Indians that as yet has not been designated as a parish (**curato** or **parroquia**); a district under the direction of a priest expressly called to indoctrinate the Indians; 4) Mexican parish.

documento nacional de identidad—personal identity document issued by the civil government.

Don—title of respect prefixed to Christian names (prior to 1832 this usually referred to nobility or to political or ecclesiastical office holders).

Doña—1) lady, (see **Don**); 2) woman; 3) (Chile) gift, bequest; 4) (pl.) bridegroom's presents to the bride.

donación—donation, gift, grant.

dotación—endowment, dowry.

dote—dowry (that property which a woman takes into marriage).

ducado—the gold coin created by the Catholic Monarchs, originally equivalent to 375 maravedis de vellon, but whose value varied according to the weight of gold at the time.

ducado de plata—a silver **ducado**.

eclesiástico—ecclesiastical.

edad—age.

ejecutor/ra—executor.

emancipación—emancipation (the act of freeing from servitude).

embarcar—1) to pack, crate, bale; 2) to go aboard a vessel.

encomendero—one who had Indians assigned to him in an **encomienda** during the first centuries of the colonial era (see **amparo**).

encomienda—1) patronage; commandery; 2) dignity of military order to which a geographical territory and certain income therefrom was attached; 3) a village or territory of Indians that was under the jurisdiction of an **encomendero** who was charged with the supervision of their moral and civil education in exchange for a tribute collected from the Indian labor.

entierro—burial, funeral, interment.

episcopal—of the bishop.

escribanía—1)notary office; 2) court clerkship, office of court clerk; 3) writing desk.

escribano—1) notary; 2) court clerk; judge's secretary.

escritura—1) writing, handwriting; 2) document, e.g.: deed; instrument; contract, indenture).

español/la—1) In colonial records, an individual born of Spanish parents in peninsular Spain; 2) the Spanish language; 3) of or relating to Spain; 4) in colonial records, one who is white or of pure Spanish blood.

español criollo—Spanish creole, an individual born of Spanish parents within the Spanish colonies.

esposo/sa—spouse.

estado—1) status (e.g. marital status); 2) state, nation, country; government.

este—east.

exhumación—exhumation (removal of a corpse from its grave, niche or mausoleum).

expediente—1) the written proceeding of an particular action; 2) petition; 3) file.

expósito—abandoned, foundling child (frequently used as the surname for such children).

extracto del certificado—summary, or abstract of a certificate (not **literal copia**).

extrema unción—extreme unction; last rite (fifth of the Seven Sacraments) administered to a gravely ill person, usually just before death.

familia—1) family; 2) all persons of the same blood, such as uncles, cousins, nephews, etc.

familiar—1) pertaining to a family; 2) domestic; 3) servant of the clergy; 4) local representative or servant of the Inquisition.

fecha—date.

feligres/a—parishioner, person belonging to a given parish.

feligresia—1) parish; 2) district of a parish.

fianza—deposit, garantee, bond, bail.

fichas—index cards.

fichero—1) filing cabinet; 2) index-card system, filing-card system, card-catalog.

filiación—1) military register of a soldier; 2) parental ties between parents and children.

filial—1) relating to a son; 2) dependent institution.

folio—page of a book, notebook or bundle (see **legajo**).

fornicación—fornication; sexual union outside of the marriage contract.

gemelo/la—twin (word used to distinguish one of two or more children born at the same time).

gobernación—government, governing.

gobernador—governor, the supreme ruler of a province, department, city, or territory.

grado—degree, grade, rank.

gran—grand, great, large.

guardia—1) guard, body of soldiers; 2) keeper, custodian.

guia—1) guide; 2) advisor, instructor, trainer.

habitante—inhabitant.

hace ya dos años—two years ago.

hacienda—1) farmstead, estate, a rural establishment; 2) the treasury department.

herederos—heirs.

hermandad—brotherhood; confraternity; fraternity; sisterhood.

hermano/na—brother/sister, born of the same parents, or of the same father, or of the same mother.

hermanon/a carnal—brother/sister, born of the same parents.

hermano/na político/ca—brother-in-law/sister-in-law.

hidalgo/ga—noble; of noble blood, gentry (from **hijo de algo** literally "a son of something").

hijo/ja—child; son/daughter.

hijo/ja adoptivo/va—adopted child, a person that legally uses the name of another.

hijo/ja legitimo/a—legitimate child, a child born of a legal union.

hijo/ja natural—common-born child, a child born of unwed parents who could have been legally married if they had desired but chose not to, an illegitimate child.

hijo/ja político/ca—son-in-law/daughter-in-law.

hijodalgo—see **hidalgo**.

hijuela—1) document listing the assets that a person is to receive from a decedent's estate; 2) the assets to be received from a decedent's estate 3) little daughter, little girl.

hipoteca—mortgage, pledge.

historía—1) history; 2) story.

hoja—leaf, sheet of paper, page of book.

hoja de servicios—service record, document containing the personal and professional antecedents of government employees, used extensively in the military.

iglesia—church.

igual—equal.

impedimiento—1) obstacle, hindrance, obstruction; 2) impediment (in particular one of those imposed by Canon Law to prevent marriage by related persons, married persons, etc).

imponible—taxable.

incógnito/ta—unknown, unrecognized.

indemnidad—indemnity (security or protection against injury, damage, or loss).

Indias—Indies; the Americas, including the Caribbean, Mexico, and Central and South America.

índice—written index, list, catalog.

indio/dia—1) Indian; 2) a person living with the Indians who adopts their customs, a social designation.

infacie ecclesiae—Latin phrase meaning "before the church," (used in marriage documents to describe full church marriage).

información matrimonial—bundle of papers or an entry in a parish book that originates from pre-marriage proceedings, includes the publication of banns (**amonestaciones matrimoniales**), declarations by the contracting parties and witness, and at times a copy of the marriage ceremony, copies of baptismal records of bride and groom and consents of parents to the marriage or copies of their death records.

infrascrito/ta—1) written hereafter; 2) undersigned person.

inhumación—burial.

instancia—petition, request.

intendencia—1) superintendant; administration; 2) intendancy; territorial division under the direction of the **Intendente**. It had its origin in the Americas during the last quarter of the eighteenth century under the reign of Carlos III and it continued until the Independence Era.

intestado—intestate, without testament.

inventario—inventory; list.

inventario de bienes de difunto—inventory of a deceased person's assets.

investigador—1) investigating, researching; 2) investigator.

izquierda—left.

jornalero—day laborer.

juez—1) judge, juryman; 2) governor of Castile.

juramento—oath.

jurisdicción—1) jurisdiction; 2) boundary; 3) district.

juros—1) right of perpetual ownership, perpetual annuity; 2) pension.

justicia—justice, rightness, fairness, court (of justice), tribunal.

juzgado—local court.

ladino/a—1) blood mixture: Spanish (3 parts) and Indian (1 part); 2) a name given to those Indians who speak Spanish; 3) in Panama, a Christian **negro** who spoke Spanish; 4) in Costa Rica, a name indicating a social position, or a Spaniard with a small amount of Indian blood.

lasto—receipt given to a person who pays for someone else.

latifundia—large landed estate typical of Andalucia and some parts of Mexico.

legajo—bundle of loose papers that are usually tied together because they deal with a common subject, most common unit of filed papers in Spanish archives.

legítimo/ma—legitimate, lawful.

legua—1) league (three and half miles); 2) length (land measurement which varies depending on the nation, equivalent to approximately 5.572 m).

lengua—language, tongue.

liberación—exoneration, exemption from taxes, or obligations.

libertad—1) freedom, liberty; 2) privilege, right.

libra—1) weight measure, (commonly 16 oz., even though it can change depending on the place); 2) measurement by which some liquids, like olive oil, are sold (it is divided in four cuarterones, which is the same as sixteen oz. In the drugstores this measure has twelve oz.).

libramiento—1) deliverance; 2) warrant or order of payment.

libranza—draft; bill of exchange; money order.

libro de actos—minute book.

libros sacramentales—parish registers.

licencia—1) permission, authority; 2) leave, furlough.

licenciado—1) release; 2) licensed, authorized; 3) licentiate, holding a degree, often specifically a master's degree.

limite/limita—limit, boundary.

limpieza de sangre—1) purity of blood, a phrase used in the records of the Inquisition, civil fraternal orders, and some other governmental employment records indicating that a person and his ancestry were not contaminated with heretic religion nor the blood of Moors, Moriscos, Jews, or Africans; 2) records showing the purity of ancestry of the person applying for a position.

liquidación—1) liquidation, winding up; 2) liquidation of debts.

lobo/ba—blood mixture: Indian (1 part) and **negro** (3 parts).

lonja—public exchange, market.

lugar—1) village, hamlet; 2) place, spot, site.

madrastra—stepmother.

madre—mother.

madre política—mother-in-law; stepmother.

madrina—godmother; a woman who assists in one of the sacraments of baptism, marriage, etc. Many times the godmother is a near relative or family friend.

magistratura—judgeship.

mancipación—transfer of property.

mandas—bequests.

Mar del norte—the North Sea; the Atlantic and Caribbean Oceans in early colonial records.

Mar del sur—the South Sea: the Pacific Ocean.

margen—margin.

marido—husband.

marina—Navy.

marino—sailor.

marítima/mo—maritime.

marques—marquis (anciently, a lord over the lands situated on the frontiers of a kingdom; later, a noble title between that of count and duke).

más—more.

materno/na—maternal; pertaining to the mother's family.

matrícula—register, list, roster, roll census.

matrimonial—matrimonial; relating to marriage.

medio hermano/na—half-brother/sister; brother/sister only by father or mother.

mejora—1) special bequest, additional bequest; 2) development, improvement.

mellizo/za—twin; two children born of one pregnancy.

memoria—1) memory, recollection; 2) report; 3) study account.

menor—1) younger, youngest; 2) smaller, smallest.

menos—less.

merced—grant or privilege given by a monarch or lord to his vassals (these came to be associated with control over income-producing property).

meritos—1) merits; 2) accomplishments.

mestizo/za—1) a person born of parents of different races, usually Spanish, and Indian; 2) crossbreed.

militar—1) pertaining to the military or to war; 2) a person serving in the army.

mismo—1) the same; 2) as expressed; 3) equal.

monasterio—monastery.

moneda—1) public auction; 2) clearance sale.

moreno/na—blood mixture: Spanish (2 parts), Indian (1 part), and **negro** (1 part); offspring of a Spaniard and a **Zambaiga**.

morisco/ca—Moorish; those baptized Moors that lived in Spain and the colonies; Mexico, a blood mixture: Spanish and mulato.

mozo/za—1) single, unmarried, bachelor; 2) young man; 3) the younger, or junior.

muerte—death

mujer—1) woman; 2) wife.

municipal—of or relating to the **municipio**.

municipio—municipality; the territorial jurisdiction that includes the inhabitants governed by a town council.

murió—died, third person, past tense of **morirse**.

nacer—to be born.

nacimiento—birth.

nació—past tense of **nacer**, he/she was born.

natural—1) native of; born in a given locality; 2) born outside of the marriage contract.

naturaleza—1) nature; 2) nationality; 3) place of origin.

nave—1) ship; 2) nave, aisle.

necesidad—necessity; need.

negro/ra—black or dark-skinned; native of various tribes of Africa.

negro fino—blood mixture: Spaniard (1 part) and **negro** (3 parts); offspring of mulato and a **negro**.

nombramiento—appointment; election; nomination; commission.

nombre de pila—name; Christian name (e.g. name given at baptismal font).

nordeste—northeast.

noroeste—northwest.

norte—north.

notable—notable, noteworthy, outstanding.

notario—notary; authorized official for preparing and certifying public actions, contracts, deeds, bonds, wills, etc. Before 1869 those using this title were usually ecclesiastically appointed, and the civil notaries of that era were generally called **escribanos**.

nuera—daughter-in-law; wife of a son.

nuestro/ra—our; of ours; ours.

Nueva España—colonial Mexico.

Nueva Extremadura—the territory of Coahuila, Mexico.

Nueva Galicia—colonial Aguascalientes, Jalisco, and parts of Durango, Zacatecas, Nayarit, San Luis Potosi, and Coahuila, Mexico. Its capital was Guadalajara.

Nueva Navarra—the Californias in the early colonial period.

Nueva Vizcaya—separated form Nueva Galicia from 1573 to 1576; Sinaloa, Sonora, Durango, Chihuahua, and parts of Coahuila, Mexico. Its capital was Durango.

Nuevo Leon—Nuevo Leon, Mexico and its surrounding areas, including part of Tamaulipas.

Nuevo Santander—the northern part of colonial Colombia, the northeastern Mexican state of Tamaulipas, and the part of Texas south of the Nueces River during the period before 1848.

nupcias—nuptials; marriage; wedding.

obispado—bishopric, episcopate.

obispo—bishop (spiritual and ecclesiastical leader of a diocese).

óbito—death.

obituario—obituary (book wherein are registered deaths and burials; section of death notices in the newspapers).

obligación—1) obligation, responsibility, duty; 2) obligation, liability, bond.

obras pias—foundation or donation created or given for church work or for charitable works (literally, "pious works").

oeste—west.

oficialía—office or district of the civil register.

oficio—1) occupation; job; work; craft; trade; 2) office; post; position; 3) function; 4) written communication.

oidor—magistrate who, in the royal courts (**audiencia**), heard and sentenced disputes and lawsuits.

óleo—blessed oil used in the ceremonies of the Church.

originario—native of a given place.

oro—gold.

otorgar—to set forth, establish, offer, grant, stipulate or promise something (usually used when the notary is preparing the actual document).

otrosi—1) furthermore, besides, moreover; 2) (law) each additional petition after the principal one.

padrastro—stepfather.

padre—1) father; 2) (pl.) parents; 3) (pl.) ancestors.

padre político—father-in-law; stepfather.

padrino—godfather; a man who assists in one of the sacraments of baptism, marriage, etc. The godfather is usually a friend or relative.

padrón—list or census of the residents or inhabitants of a village or parish.

panteón—cemetery; funeral monument where the dead are buried.

pardo/da—blood mixture: Spanish (1 part), Indian (2 parts), and **negro** (1 part).

parecer—1) to appear, seem, look; 2) manner of viewing.

párroco—parish priest.

parroquia—1) parish, territory covered by the spiritual jurisdiction of a parish priest; 2) the church of the parish.

parte—1) part, fragment; 2) part, share, portion; 3) party to a transaction.

partición—1) division, partition, separation, especially a division of assets following death.

partido judicial—district, usually made up of several villages in a province, in which a judge exercises original jurisdiction over civil and criminal judicial matters (judicial district).

párvulo/la—a small child.

paterno/na—paternal; from the male line.

pedimiento—1) petition; 2) petition or claim presented to a judge and each separate case therein.

peninsular—peninsular; born in Spain or Portugal.

perdón—pardon; forgiveness; grace; reprieve.

permuta—1) an exchange (usually of two public or ecclesiastical offices or benefices); 2) interchange, barter.

peso—1) weight; 2) Spanish coin used in the colonies.

petición—petition or application filed with a court or other governmental or ecclesiastical entity.

pie—length measurement that was equivalent to twenty-eight cm. in Castille.

pieza de indias—one slave in good condition; various young slaves or women in poor condition.

plata—silver.

plaza—1) main square of a town; 2) space or place for a person with others of similar type; 3) office, position, employment.

plazo—1) term, period of time; 2) installment.

pleitos—lawsuit, suit, court or judicial action or proceedings.

población—population.

poder—1) power; strength; 2) power of attorney; 3) (pl.) authority.

político/ca—when applied to a term of blood relationship, it indicates a relationship by marriage (e.g. **padre político**, father-in-law).

por—1) by, for, through, along, over, by way of, via, around, about, in, at, by means of, with, in exchange for, in return for; 2) times, multiplied by.

posesión—1) possession (in all senses); 2) (pl.) possessions; property; estate.

postura—1) posture, position; attitude; 2) bid, offer; 3) agreement; 4) stake, wager, bet.

prelado—prelate, ecclesiastical dignitary; superior of a convent.

presente—present, current.

presidente—head or leader of the courts (**audiencias**), one of the titles of the viceroy president.

presidio—military fortress.

pretendiente—1) claimant, petitioner; 2) candidate; 3) suitor (for a woman's hand).

previsto—anticipated.

primo/ma—cousin; child of an uncle or aunt.

primo/ma carnal—first cousin; child of an uncle or aunt.

primo/ma hermano/na—first cousin; child of an uncle or aunt.

primogénito—firstborn.

privilegio—1) privilege, grant, concession; 2) exemption; 3) franchise, patent.

probanza—1) (law) proof, proving; 2) (law) proof, evidence.

proceso—1) process; 2) (law) trial, lawsuit, action.

prohijación—adoption of a child as one's own.

promesa—1) promise, offer; 2) vow, pledge.

prorrogación—extension or postponement for a specified period of time.

protesta—protest, protestation, declaration, affirmation.

protesto—declaration made before a notary to protect one's rights when a letter of exchange is not paid.

protocolo—book generated and preserved by the notary publics.

provincia—province, a territorial division representing different extensions of jurisdiction depending on the country.

Provincias Internas—Interior Provinces (that region of northern Mexico that included the states of Durango, Coahuila, Chihuahua, Nuevo Leon, Nuevo Mexico, Sonora, Tamaulipas, and Texas).

pueblo—1) town, village, population; 2) in the colonies, a geographical area under the administration of royal officials in contrast to the **encomienda** or **mission**, which were administered by private and ecclesiastical personnel respectively.

quinceñera—the celebration of a female's fifteenth birthday marking transition from childhood to womanhood.

rancho—ranch, often large enough to form a separate community with its own name and in some cases a small chapel.

ratificación—ratification; confirmation.

real—1) royal, of or pertaining to the Crown; 2) coin of value of 34 maravedíes, which were called of real de vellon. In some places it was understood as the silver real; 3) a mining town.

real audiencia—the supreme court or tribunal of the colonial Americas; the court of last resort. The court served as a representative of the king; its decisions were final and only the king could reverse them.

Real y supreme consejo de Indias—see **Consejo de Indias**.

rebisabuelo/a—great-great-grandparent.

rebisnieto/a—great-great-grandchild.

recepción—1) reception, receiving, receipt; 2) admission; 3) (law) examination of witnesses.

recibo—receipt, document acknowledging payment.

reclamación—1) claim, demand; 2) objection, protest, complaint; 3) (law) remonstration.

reconocimiento—1) recognition, admission, acknowledgment; 2) inspection, examination.

redención—1) redemption, salvation; 2) redemption of a pledge, mortgage, etc.

reducción—1) reduction; 2) a village of Indians converted to Christianity, usually directed by a religious order such as the Jesuits.

regimento—military unit headed by a colonel.

registro—1) register, record, record book; 2) registration, registry; 3) examination, inspection, search; 4) entry, record; register.

reglamento—regulation, bylaws.

reina—queen.

reinado—reign.

reino—kingdom; realm.

religioso/sa—1) religious; 2) one who has taken the vows of an order (i.e., monk, priest, or nun).

renta—1) revenue; income; 2) rent; 3) annuity; 4) government bonds, public debt.

renunciación/renuncia—1) renunciation; 2) resignation; 3) (law) waiver, disclaimer.

repartimiento—1) distribution of lands after reconquest; 2) the assessment of work assignments and the subsequent distribution of those to be assigned to their work stations in the mines, haciendas, public works, etc. In many cases this was an involuntary servitude, especially by Indians in the colonies.

repudiación—repudiation.

requerimiento—1) request, requisition, demand, summons; 2) (law) injunction.

resguardo—1) protection, shelter; 2) security, voucher; 3) frontier customs guard.

residencia—review of a colonial official at the end of his term.

residente—resident.

retatarabuelo—great-great-great-grandfather.

revista—review, inspection of troops.

revocación—1) revocation, abrogation; 2) annulment; 3) (law) reversal.

rey—king.

riachuelo—stream.

rio—river.

sacramento—1) sacrament (e.g. baptism, marriage, etc.); 2) Sacrament, Eucharist.

sacristán—sacristan; sexton; the individual who took care of church property, including cemeteries

sala—1) parlor, hall, lounge, salon; 2) court, tribunal.

santo/ta—1) holy, saintly, hollowed, sacred, blessed; 2) saint.

secretaría—the office of secretary, secretariat.

secretario/ria—secretary.

segundo/da—second, secondary.

seguridad—1) safety, security; 2) certainty, assurance; 3) surety bond.

seguro/ra—1) safe, secure, steady; 2) insurance, insurance policy; 3) permit, warrant, license.

señalamiento—designation; appointment; indication (of place, time).

señorío—domain.

septentrion/al—northern, septentrional.

sepultura—1) interment, burial; 2) tomb, grave; 3) burial place, sepulchre.

servicio—1) service, serving; 2) voluntary donations given to king or state; 3) (pl.) emergency direct tax.

signatura—1) filing mark (to facilitate filing of documents), library number; 2) (ecc.) Roman Catholic court of justice and pardons.

sínodo—ancient name given to the ecclesiastical councils of a diocese.

situación/ situado/a—location.

sobrino/na—nephew/niece, child of a brother or sister, or of a cousin; the first are called first nephews/nieces (**sobrinos carnales**), and the others, second nephews/ nieces (**sobrinos segundos**) etc.

sobrino-bisnieto/ta—great-grandnephew/niece, relationship of an individual to his great-grand uncle (the brother of the great-grandfather).

sobrino-nieto/ta—grandnephew/niece, relationship of an individual to his grand uncle (the brother of the grandfather).

soldada—1) salary, wages; 2) soldier's pay.

soldadera—female soldier.

soldado—soldier.

soltero/ra—1) single, unmarried; 2) bachelor, unmarried woman.

subrogación—subrogation, substitution.

sudeste—southeast.

sudoeste—southwest.

suegro/a—parent-in-law.

sufragáneo—suffragan.

sur—south.

sustitución—substitution (usually an agreement for one man to fulfill the military service of another).

tarjeta—1) card (visiting, personal or invitation card); 2) index card, etc.; 3) heading; title (on a map).

tasación—appraisal; appraisement; valuation.

tasador—public appraiser.

tatarabuelo/la—great-great-grandparent.

tataranieto/ta—great-great-grandchild.

teniente—1) assistant, deputy, substitute; 2) (mil.) lieutenant.

tercero/ra—1) third; 2) (ecc.) tertiary; 3) third party.

término—1) term, word, expression; 2) end, finish, conclusion; 3) limit, boundary, landmar; 4) time limit, term, period, space of time; 5) district.

terrritoro/territorial—territory.

testador—testator (person who writes or dictates a will).

testamentario—executor (person who oversees distribution of decendents assets in accordance with last will and testament).

testamento abierto/nuncupativo—will that is dictated by a dying person before witnesses and in some cases the notary and is later recorded by the notary in his **protocolo**.

testamento cerrado—a will that is written in secret and then sealed before a notary and witnesses to be opened after the death of the testator.

testamento ológrafo—a holographic will, or a will that is written and signed in the hand of the testator.

testamento—will (a document in which one declares his last will and in which he disposes of his property and makes other arrangements for after his death).

tío—uncle, the brother of an individual's father or mother.

tío carnal—cousin of an individual's father or mother (in English, the equivalent of a first cousin, once removed).

tío-abuelo/la—granduncle; the brother/sister of an individual's grandparent.

tío-bisabuelo/la—great-granduncle/aunt; the brother/sister of the great-grandparent.

titulo—1) title, name, sobriquet; 2) caption, heading; 3) section (into which laws and regulations are divided); 4) (law) title, such as a title of nobility; 5) diploma.

traducción—translation.

transacción—1) transaction, negotiation; 2) settlement, agreement, compromise.

traspasos—transfers of property not involving a sale.

tributo—1) tribute, tax; 2) tribute, respect.

trinidad—trinity.

trueco—trade.

tutela—1) guardianship (the authority conferred by law to an individual to care for the fortune and at times the person of a minor); 2) the documents generated from the guardianship.

tutor—guardian.

universidad—university.

ut supra—Latin term meaning "as above."

vara—length measurement equivalent to 835 mm. and nine-tenths.

véase—look at.

vecindad—neighborhood; local area.

vecindario—1) persons taken together who reside in the same vicinity or neighborhood; 2) list or census of the **vecinas** residing in a town.

vecino/na—1) legal resident, citizen of a local town, village or city, usually owning a home and contributing to the local tax collections (by law this status was available only after residing for a fixed number of years in the town); 2) neighbor.

velación—1) vigil, watch; 2) (ecc.) veiling ceremony of bride and groom in nuptial mass.

velado/da—1) veiled; 2) having received the **velacion**.

venta—1) sale, selling.

vicario—vicar (the religious functionary who, as an assistant, takes full charge when his superior is gone), the functionary in charge of a parish at times.

vicario general—vicar general; the alternate bishop or assistant to the chief judge of the diocesan courts and head of the **curia** of the dioceses.

virreinato—viceroyalty; the territory governed by a viceroy.

virrey—viceroy; the personal representative of the king in colonial America.

viruela—1) smallpox; 2) pockmark.

visita—1) visit; call; inspection.

viudo/da—1) widowed; 2) widower; widow.

vuelto/ta—verso, reverse side.

yerno/na—son-in-law/daughter-in-law; the spouse of one's child.

zambaigo—blood mixture: **negro** (1 part), Indian (1 part); sometimes in Mexico Chinese (1 part), Indian (1 part).

TIMELINE OF MEXICAN HISTORY

Human habitation began in Mexico about twenty thousand years ago. Since that time there have been many native cultures in Mexico. Seven are considered to be the most influential, each developing in a different epoch of the history of ancient Mexico: the Olmecs, the Teotihuacans, the Toltecs, the Mayans, the Zapotecs, the Mixtecs, and the Aztecs. The pre-columbian age in which these civilizations flourished is divided into three periods

The Pre-Classic period, from 2,000 B.C. to 500 B.C., covers the time when the civilization of Mexico arose. Nomadic natives became settlers. Many advances in art and the sciences were made. Agricultural methods improved and the population increased. Rural villages became towns and ceremonial centers began growing in importance.

The Classic Period dated from 500 B.C. to A.D. 800, and was a time of great social change. Urban centers became more powerful than rural ones and outstanding advances in architecture were made. It was a true renaissance period for art and learning. In A.D. 350, the city-state of Teotihuacán, located on the central highland of Mexico, covered an area of approximately 22.5 sq km. and its population reached 200,000 inhabitants by the year (probably the largest city in the world at the time).

The Post-Classic Period dated from A.D. 800 to A.D. 1521, and it is notable because of the increasing emphasis on military rule. It was a time of great change for several important ceremonial centers and cities: some went into decline, some died, and others grew in power and influence.

In August, 1521, Tenochtitlán was conquered by the Spanish, under Hernán Cortés, marking the fall of the huge Aztec empire. The Spanish did not act alone, but with native allies such as the Tlaxcalans.

TIMELINE

1521–35	Hernán Cortés governed as Head of the Army.
1523	Friar Pedro de Gante founded the first school for the indigenous population, the School of San José, where languages and arts were taught.
1528	First bishop of Mexico appointed.
1530	The construction of the first cathedral of the American continent began in Mexico City.

1530–31	Rapid and brutal conquest of Nueva Galicia under Niño de Guzman. Guadalajara became the capital.
1535	Don Antonio de Mendoza was appointed the first viceroy of New Spain by Emperor Charles V. He was succeeded by sixty-three viceroys in the space of 284 years.
1536	First province of the Franciscan order established.
1538	Catholic bishopric of Michoacan created.
1539	The Royal Mint and the first printing house established in Mexico City.
1542	Efforts of Friar Bartolomé de las Casas culminated with the New Laws, which abolished slavery and recognized the human rights of indigenous peoples and their right to property.
1545–48	Typhus epidemic killed four hundred thousand.
1548	Creation of the bishopric of Guadalajara.
1548	Discovery of silver in Zacatecas begins the movement into the northern area.
1551	The first university of the American mainland was opened in Mexico City.
1563	Conquest of Nueva Vizcaya and founding of Durango as capital under Ibarra.
1598	Conquest of New Mexico under Juan de Oñate.
1621	Creation of the bishopric of Durango.
1736–38	Another Typhus epidemic ravished populations from central New Spain (Mexico) to California and Texas.
1767	Jesuits expelled from New Spain by order of King Carlos III.
1770–88	Division of entire country into *Intendencias*, which by 1788 numbered sixteen.
1776	Creation of the *Provincias Internas* and appointment of Teodoro de Croix as Comandante of the Provincias Internas gave power over the entire northern area to a single administrator independent of the viceroy in Mexico City. During the following years, until 1792 power gradually shifted back to the viceroy. From 1792 to 1811 power over the region was again separated from the viceroy.

1786–87	Decrees of King Carlos III ordered the creation of municipal cemeteries and the requirement of parental consent for marriages of persons under twenty-five.
1789–94	Juan Vicente de Güemes-Pacheco, Second Count of Revillagigedo, governed as viceroy and established the viceregal archives, which became the Archivo General de la Nación.
16 September 1810	The priest Miguel Hidalgo initiated a revolt against the Spanish rule that began the War of Independence, which ended in 1821 with the establishment of the first independent government.
1822	Agustín de Iturbide proclaimed Emperor of Mexico.
1824	Congress adopted a constitution instituting a Federal Republic under the first president of Mexico, Guadalupe Victoria. During his government, England and the United States of America recognized the country's independence, noble titles and slavery were abolished, and different measures were taken to develop a more democratic society.
1836	Texas declared its independence from Mexico.
1845–48	The United States instigated a war against Mexico in which Mexico was defeated and lost one third of its original territory: the modern states of California, Arizona, New Mexico, Texas, and parts of Colorado, Nevada, and Utah.
1859	President Benito Juárez issued the Laws of Reform which established the separation of the church and the state.
1859	Law passed establishing Civil Registration in Mexico.
1862	French Emperor Napoleon III intervened militarily in Mexico: an empire was established from 1864 to 1867, under the Austrian prince Maximilian of Hapsburg, who was ultimately executed.
5 May 1862	Mexican Army obtained victory in the Battle of Puebla against the French.
1867	Benito Juárez reestablished the Republic, and while in power died in 1872.
1872	Porfirio Díaz became president. He remained in power, directly or through those he designated until 1911. During his dictatorial rule, internal peace was established, economic development started, and foreign investment was encouraged

	with the aim of exploiting raw materials and promoting industrial development. However, the social unrest and the political opposition to the regime of Porfirio Díaz triggered the Mexican Revolution.
1911	Francisco I Madero elected as the new president but assassinated. With his assassination the Mexican Revolution started. Various factions lead by Emiliano Zapata in the south, Francisco Villa in the north, and others, took up arms against dictator Victoriano Huerta, who had ordered the murder of Madero and Vice President Pino Suarez.
1910–20	Nearly a million Mexicans crossed into the United States fleeing the political instability of the Mexican Revolution.
1917	Under the new leadership of Venustiano Carranza, the constitution was approved. It was one of the most advanced constitutions of its time due to its high social content.
1929	Former President General Plutarco Elías Calles created the National Revolutionary Party (PNR), which was restructured several times and became the Institutional Revolutionary Party (PRI) in 1946. The PRI controlled the government until the election of Vicente Fox in 2002.
1938	President of the Republic General Lázaro Cárdenas declared the expropriation of oil companies, and concessions ceased.
1942	Mexico entered the Second World War, against Germany, Italy, and Japan.
1945	Mexico signed the Charter of San Francisco, being one of the founding members of the United Nations.
1989	Revolutionary Democratic Party (PRD) was formed.
1994	Mexico signed the North American Free Trade Agreement (NAFTA) wth the United States and Canada. The former was accompanied by a wide program of structural reforms, privatizations, and deregulations.
2002	The election of Vicente Fox as president marked the end of control of the presidency by the PRI, which began in 1929.

RESEARCH FORMS

This appendix contains a variety of research forms and examples for you to use in your own research. First, you will find completed extract forms that correspond with the sidebars in chapter 3, "Civil Registration Records," and in chapter 4, "Parish Records." After these are blank extract forms that you can copy and use. Finally, there is a sample research log for you to use, either in your research, or as a template in designing your own. The research log is an valuable tool in keeping track of what research you have done so far.

Birth Record Extraction Form ☐ P ☒ RC Fecha de la búsqueda _11/6/06_ Persona que busca _____ ES

Parroquia _____ Diócesis _____ Pueblo _Actopan_ Provincia/Estado _____

Fecha de bautismo / Fecha de presentación [x] _10 Feb 1873_	Fecha de nacimiento _21 Feb 1873_		Hora	Libro folio cart. _vol. 1873, #3_	
Primer apellido y segundo apellido _Rodriguez_		Microfilm _0782190, ft. 2_	Archivo _A.R.C.E. - Vera Cruz_		
Nombre de pila _Tomasa Candelaria del Carmen_	M / F	Leg. / Ileg.	Comentarios sobre el matrimonio de los padres		
Padre _José Domínguez_		Natural de Vecino de		Edad	Raza
Madre _Marcelina Grajales (difunta)_		Natural de Vecino de		Edad	Raza
Abuelo paterno _Rafael Domínguez_		Natural de Vecino de		¿Difunto?	Raza
Abuela paterna _Filomena Lagunes_		Natural de Vecino de		¿Difunta?	Raza
Abuelo materno _Antonio Grajales_		Natural de Vecino de		¿Difunto?	Raza
Abuela materna _Micaela Rosado_		Natural de Vecino de		¿Difunta?	Raza
Padrinos					
Inscripciones marginales u otros comentarios					

*This extract form corresponds with the record in the sidebar, "An Example of a Civil Birth Record,"
on page 29.*

Marriage Record Extraction Form ☐ P ☒ RC Fecha de la búsqueda _10/18/0_ Persona que busca _PR_ ___ ES

Parroquia _____ Diócesis _____ Pueblo _Tlaxcala_ Provincia/Estado _Tlaxcala_

Fecha de casamiento 17 Ene 1879	Libro folio cart. vol. 1879, p. 3, #2	Microfilm 0773818, It.2	Archivo Tlaxcala C.R.	
Esposo: Nombre de pila y apellidos Vicente Razo	Edad y/o estado civil soltero / 30 años	Natural de Vecino de Vecino de este		Raza
Padre del esposo D. Laureano Razo		¿Defunto? Natural de Vecino de		Raza
Madre del esposo Doña Sipriana Gonzalez de Razo		¿Defunta? Natural de Vecino de		Raza
Esposa: Nombre de pila y apellidos D.a Manuela Rodriguez	Edad y/o estado civil soltera / 16 años	Natural de (circled) Tesuitlan Vecino de esta		Raza
Padre del esposa D. Eusebio Rodriguez		¿Defunto? Natural de Vecino de		Raza
Madre del esposa Doña Maria de la Luz Garcia		¿Defunta? Natural de Vecino de		Raza
Comentarios: ✷ prof.: zapatero				
→ Information contained in the acta de presentacion #1 dated 1 Jan 1879 same volume, p. 1v.				

This extract form corresponds with the record in the sidebar, "An Example of a Civil Marriage Record," on page 31.

Death Record Extraction Form ☐ P ☒ RC Fecha de la búsqueda _11/7/06_ Persona que busca _PR_ ___ ES

Parroquia _____ Diócesis _____ Pueblo _Tlaxcala_ Provincia/Estado _Tlaxcala_

Fecha de entierro	Fecha de defunción 29 Nov 1867	Libro folio cart. #26 vol. 1867-1869, p. 10	Microfilm It.1 773823	Archive R.C. de Tlaxcala
Nombres y apellidos del difunto/difunta D. Manuel de la Trinidad Bautista		Natural de Vecino de	Raza	Edad 66 años
Esposo/a de o (viudo/a de) Maria Ysabel		Esposo/a: Natural de Vecino de		
Hijo/a de		Padres: Naturales de Vecinos de		
¿Hizo testamento?	Fecha del testamento y ante quién se hizo			Causa de muerte idropecia
Hijos del difunto/a Antonio Bautista (see below)				Lugar de entierro
Comentarios Date of presentation at R.C. - 30 Nov 1867				
Death reported by son Antonio Bautista, "natural y vecino del pueblo de San Mateo Huescyocan."				

This extract form corresponds with the record in the sidebar, "An Example of a Civil Death Record," on page 33.

Birth Record Extraction Form ☒ P ☐ RC **Fecha de la búsqueda** 11/8/06 **Persona que busca** PR _____ ES

Parroquia San Nicolás **Diócesis** _____ **Pueblo** Actopán **Provincia/Estado** Hidalgo

Fecha de bautismo / Fecha de presentación [iv] 5 Ago 1603		Fecha de nacimiento		Hora	Libro folio cart. S/h vol. 1546-1652	
Primer apellido y segundo apellido			Microfilm 0614336, It.1	Archivo Archivo de la parroquia		
Nombre de pila Jacinta	M/F	Leg. / ileg.	Comentarios sobre el matrimonio de los padres			
Padre Anton Catalan		Natural de Vecino de			Edad	Raza
Madre Ysabel Guerrero		Natural de Vecino de			Edad	Raza
Abuelo paterno		Natural de Vecino de			¿Difunto?	Raza
Abuela paterna		Natural de Vecino de			¿Difunta?	Raza
Abuelo materno		Natural de Vecino de			¿Difunto?	Raza
Abuela materna		Natural de Vecino de			¿Difunta?	Raza
Padrinos Juo Lopez vellido y Ana Ma su muger, vecinos						
Inscripciones marginales u otros comentarios						

This extract form corresponds with the record in the sidebar, "An Example of a Parish Baptismal Record," on page 42.

Birth Record Extraction Form ☒ P ☐ RC **Fecha de la búsqueda** 11/8/06 **Persona que busca** PR _____ ES

Parroquia Sn Nicolás **Diócesis** _____ **Pueblo** Actopan **Provincia/Estado** Hidalgo

Fecha de bautismo / Fecha de presentación [ad] 5 Ago 1603		Fecha de nacimiento		Hora	Libro folio cart. vol. 1546-1652, S/h	
Primer apellido y segundo apellido			Microfilm 0614336, It.1	Archivo Archivo de la parroquia		
Nombre de pila Juo	M/F	Leg. / ileg.	Comentarios sobre el matrimonio de los padres			
Padre "hijo de la yglesia"		Natural de Vecino de			Edad	Raza meztizo
Madre		Natural de Vecino de			Edad	Raza
Abuelo paterno		Natural de Vecino de			¿Difunto?	Raza
Abuela paterna		Natural de Vecino de			¿Difunta?	Raza
Abuelo materno		Natural de Vecino de			¿Difunto?	Raza
Abuela materna		Natural de Vecino de			¿Difunta?	Raza
Padrinos Juo de foronda vezino deste real						
Inscripciones marginales u otros comentarios						

This extract form corresponds with the record in the sidebar, "An Example of a Parish Baptismal Record," on page 42.

Birth Record Extraction Form ☑ P ☐ RC   Fecha de la búsqueda _11/8/06_   Persona que busca _PK_   ES

Parroquia _____ Diócesis _____ Pueblo _Actopán_ Provincia/Estado _Hidalgo_

Fecha de bautismo / Fecha de presentación (x) _5 Aug 1603_		Fecha de nacimiento		Hora	Libro folio cart. _vol. 1546-1652, 8/0_	
Primer apellido y segundo apellido			Microfilm	Archivo		
Nombre de pila _Miguel_	M/F	Leg./ileg.	Comentarios sobre el matrimonio de los padres			
Padre _"hijo de la yglesia"_		Natural de Vecino de			Edad	Raza
Madre		Natural de Vecino de			Edad	Raza
Abuelo paterno		Natural de Vecino de			¿Difunto?	Raza
Abuela paterna		Natural de Vecino de			¿Difunta?	Raza
Abuelo materno		Natural de Vecino de			¿Difunto?	Raza
Abuela materna		Natural de Vecino de			¿Difunta?	Raza
Padrinos _alsonso de segura y mariana meztiza Estãtes enesterreal_						
Inscripciones marginales u otros comentarios						

This extract form corresponds with the record in the sidebar, "An Example of a Parish Baptismal Record," on page 42.

Marriage Record Extraction Form ☑ P ☐ RC   Fecha de la búsqueda _3/10/05_ Persona que busca _PK_   ES

Parroquia _Teocaltiche †_ Diócesis _____ Pueblo _Teocaltiche_ Provincia/Estado _Jalisco_

Fecha de casamiento _25 Dic 1874_	Libro folio cart. _vol. 29, p. 2v_	Microfilm _639764_	Archivo _Teocaltiche parish archive_	
Esposo: Nombre de pila y apellidos _Mateo Ramos_		Edad y/o estado civil _soltero / 20 años_	Natural de _[esposo y esposa]_ Vecino de _"originarios de_	Raza
Padre del esposo _Ambrocio Ramos_		¿Defunto?	Natural de _Buena Vista?"_ Vecino de	Raza
Madre del esposo _Norberta Santos_		¿Defunta?	Natural de Vecino de	Raza
Esposa: Nombre de pila y apellidos _Yrinea Olmos_		Edad y/o estado civil _doncella / 18 años_	Natural de Vecino de	Raza
Padre del esposa _Leocadio de Olmos_		¿Defunto?	Natural de Vecino de	Raza
Madre del esposa _Estefana Ortis_		¿Defunta?	Natural de Vecino de	Raza
Comentarios: _Padrinos: Seberiano Trujillo y Angela Trujillo_				
† Nuestra Señora de los Dolores				

This extract form corresponds with the record in the sidebar, "An Example of a Parish Marriage Record," on page 47.

Death Record Extraction Form ☒ P ☐ RC Fecha de la búsqueda _11/6/06_ Persona que busca _PR_ ___ ES

Parroquia _Sagrario_ Diócesis _Puebla_ ___ Pueblo _P de los Angeles_ Provincia/Estado _Puebla_ ___

Fecha de entierro	Fecha de defunción	Libro folio cart. _Vol. 3, p. 50_	Microfilm	Archive	
18 Ene 1677		_Def. 1673-1699_	_0227800_	_Sagrario Metropolitano_	
Nombres y apellidos del difunto/difunta		Natural de		Raza	Edad
Catharina Sisneros		(Vecino de) _esta ciudad_			
Esposo/a de o (viudo/a de)		Esposo/a: Natural de			
Gabriel Hernandez		Vecino de			
Hijo/a de		Padres: Naturales de			
		Vecinos de			
¿Hizo testamento?	Fecha del testamento y ante quién se hizo			Causa de muerte	
_no_ *					
Hijos del difunto/a				Lugar de entierro	

Comentarios
* _"por no tubo de que"_
"se enterro en esta sta iglesia cathedral"
recivio los Santos sacramentos

This extract form corresponds with the record in the sidebar, "An Example of a Parish Death Record," on page 48.

Birth Record Extraction Form   ☐ P ☐ RC **Fecha de la búsqueda** _____   **Persona que busca** _____ *ES*

Parroquia _____ **Diócesis** _____ **Pueblo** _____ **Provincia/Estado** _____

Fecha de bautismo / Fecha de presentación [RC]		Fecha de nacimiento		Hora	Libro folio cart.	
Primer apellido y segundo apellido			Microfilm	Archivo		
Nombre de pila		M / F	Leg. / ileg.	Comentarios sobre el matrimonio de los padres		
Padre			Natural de Vecino de		Edad	Raza
Madre			Natural de Vecino de		Edad	Raza
Abuelo paterno			Natural de Vecino de		¿Difunto?	Raza
Abuela paterna			Natural de Vecino de		¿Difunta?	Raza
Abuelo materno			Natural de Vecino de		¿Difunto?	Raza
Abuela materna			Natural de Vecino de		¿Difunta?	Raza
Padrinos						
Inscripciones marginales u otros comentarios						

Birth Record Extraction Form   ☐ P ☐ RC **Fecha de la búsqueda** _____   **Persona que busca** _____ *ES*

Parroquia _____ **Diócesis** _____ **Pueblo** _____ **Provincia/Estado** _____

Fecha de bautismo / Fecha de presentación [RC]		Fecha de nacimiento		Hora	Libro folio cart.	
Primer apellido y segundo apellido			Microfilm	Archivo		
Nombre de pila		M / F	Leg. / ileg.	Comentarios sobre el matrimonio de los padres		
Padre			Natural de Vecino de		Edad	Raza
Madre			Natural de Vecino de		Edad	Raza
Abuelo paterno			Natural de Vecino de		¿Difunto?	Raza
Abuela paterna			Natural de Vecino de		¿Difunta?	Raza
Abuelo materno			Natural de Vecino de		¿Difunto?	Raza
Abuela materna			Natural de Vecino de		¿Difunta?	Raza
Padrinos						
Inscripciones marginales u otros comentarios						

Marriage Record Extraction Form ☐ P ☐ RC Fecha de la búsqueda _____ Persona que busca _____ *ES*

Parroquia _____ **Diócesis** _____ **Pueblo** _____ **Provincia/Estado** _____

Fecha de casamiento		Libro folio cart.		Microfilm	Archivo	
Esposo: Nombre de pila y apellidos			Edad y/o estado civil		Natural de Vecino de	Raza
Padre del esposo				¿Defunto?	Natural de Vecino de	Raza
Madre del esposo				¿Defunta?	Natural de Vecino de	Raza
Esposa: Nombre de pila y apellidos			Edad y/o estado civil		Natural de Vecino de	Raza
Padre del esposa				¿Defunto?	Natural de Vecino de	Raza
Madre del esposa				¿Defunta?	Natural de Vecino de	Raza
Comentarios:						

Marriage Record Extraction Form ☐ P ☐ RC Fecha de la búsqueda _____ Persona que busca _____ *ES*

Parroquia _____ **Diócesis** _____ **Pueblo** _____ **Provincia/Estado** _____

Fecha de casamiento		Libro folio cart.		Microfilm	Archivo	
Esposo: Nombre de pila y apellidos			Edad y/o estado civil		Natural de Vecino de	Raza
Padre del esposo				¿Defunto?	Natural de Vecino de	Raza
Madre del esposo				¿Defunta?	Natural de Vecino de	Raza
Esposa: Nombre de pila y apellidos			Edad y/o estado civil		Natural de Vecino de	Raza
Padre del esposa				¿Defunto?	Natural de Vecino de	Raza
Madre del esposa				¿Defunta?	Natural de Vecino de	Raza
Comentarios:						

Death Record Extraction Form ☐ P ☐ RC Fecha de la búsqueda _____ Persona que busca _____ *ES*

Parroquia _____ **Diócesis** _____ **Pueblo** _____ **Provincia/Estado** _____

Fecha de entierro	Fecha de defunción	Libro folio cart.	Microfilm	Archive		
Nombres y apellidos del difunto/difunta		Natural de Vecino de			Raza	Edad
Esposo/a de o viudo/a de		Esposo/a: Natural de Vecino de				
Hijo/a de		Padres: Naturales de Vecinos de				
¿Hizo testamento?	Fecha del testamento y ante quién se hizo			Causa de muerte		
Hijos del difunto/a				Lugar de entierro		
Comentarios						

Death Record Extraction Form ☐ P ☐ RC Fecha de la búsqueda _____ Persona que busca _____ *ES*

Parroquia _____ **Diócesis** _____ **Pueblo** _____ **Provincia/Estado** _____

Fecha de entierro	Fecha de defunción	Libro folio cart.	Microfilm	Archive		
Nombres y apellidos del difunto/difunta		Natural de Vecino de			Raza	Edad
Esposo/a de o viudo/a de		Esposo/a: Natural de Vecino de				
Hijo/a de		Padres: Naturales de Vecinos de				
¿Hizo testamento?	Fecha del testamento y ante quién se hizo			Causa de muerte		
Hijos del difunto/a				Lugar de entierro		
Comentarios						

RESEARCH LOG

Date	Time	Record Searched*	Reason Searched	Comments

ARCHIVES OF THE STATES OF MEXICO

State	Archive Name	Address	Guides, Indexes, and Inventories
Aguascalientes	Archivo General del Estado de Aguascalientes	Jose Maria Chavez, 12 Aguascalientes, Ags.	inventories, guides, and card catalogs
Baja California	Archivo General del Estado de Baja California	Centro Civico, Palacio de Gobierno, Mexicali, Baja California	inventories
Baja California Sur	Archivo Historico del Estado de Baja California Sur Pablo L. Martinez	Navarro, entre Altamirano y Heroes de Independencia (unidad cultural), La Paz, Baja California Sur	inventories, catalogs
Campeche	Archivo General del Estado de Campeche	Calle 55, num. 23, Actas de Sesiones Campeche, Camp.	(restricted)
Coahuila	Archivo General del Gobierno del Estado de Coahuila	Ramos Arezpe, Saltillo, Coahuila	Indexes
Colima	Archivo General del Estado de Colima	Venustiano Carranza 180, Colima, Col.	inventories
Chiapas	Archivo General del Estado de Chiapas	5a. Norte Poniente 1410, Tuxtla, Gutierrez, Chiapas	inventories, card catalogs (restricted)
	Archivo Historico del Estado de Chiapas	Boulevar Angel Alvino Corzo, km 1087 s/n Tuxtla, Gutierrez, Chiapas	not given
Chihuahua	No state archive		
Distrito Federal	Archivo Historico del Exayuntamiento de la Ciudad de Mexico	Republica de Chile 8, esq. con Donceles Mexico, D.F.	guides, indexes, catalogs

State	Archive Name	Address	Guides, Indexes, and Inventories
Durango	Archivo Historico del Estado de Durango	Palacio de Gobierno (planta baja), Durango, Dgo.	inventories, guides, microfilms
Guanajuato	Archivo Historico del Estado de Guanajuato	Cantarranas 9, Guanajuato, Gto.	inventories, catalogs
Guerrero	Archivo General del Estado de Guerrero	Palacio de Gobierno (Sotano), Chilpancingo, Guerrero	inventories (restricted)
Hidalgo	Archivo General del Estado de Hidalgo	Hidalgo	inventories
Jalisco	Archivo Historico del Estado de Jalisco	Edificio "A," entrada sureste, Avenida Prolongacion Alcalde 1350, Guadalajara, Jalisco	card catalogs, guides, bulletins, catalog
Estado de Mexico	Archivo General del Poder Ejecutivo del Estado de Mexico	Francico Guerra esq. con Jose Maria Luis Mora ISSEMYM "San Juan de la Cruz," Toluca, Estado de Mexico	inventories, card catalogs, catalogs
Michoacán	No state archive		
Morelos	Archivo General del Estado de Morelos	Jardin Los Heroes (sotano del Palacio de Gobierno), Cuernavaca, Morelos	inventories, card catalogs
Nayarit	No state archive		
Nuevo Leon	Archivo General del Estado de Nuevo Leon	Juan 1, Ramirez y Zaragoza, Monterrey, Nuevo Leon	inventories, catalogs, card catalogs
Oaxaca	Archivo General del Estado de Oaxaca	Santos Degollado 400, Oaxaca, Oax.	inventories, catalogs, guides
Puebla	No state archive		
Querétaro	Archivo General del Estado de Querétaro	Madero num. 70 (Centro), Queretaro, Qro.	inventories, catalogs
Quintana Roo	Archivo General del Estado de Quintana Roo	Francisco Mayo num. 343, Chetumal, Q.R.	inventories

State	Archive Name	Address	Guides, Indexes, and Inventories
San Luis Potosí	Archivo Historico del Estado de San Luis Potosí	Arista num. 400, esq. con Independencia San Luis Potosi, SLP	inventories, catalogs, card catalogs
Sinaloa	Archivo Historico del Estado de Sinaloa	Palacio de Gobierno Culiacan, Sinaloa	inventories
	Archivo General de Notarias del Estado de Sinaloa	Madero Ote., num. 370, Culiacan, Sinaloa	inventories
Sonora	Archivo General del Estado de Sonora	Obregon num. 58, planta baja, Hermosillo, Sonora	card catalogs, catalogs, guides
Tabasco	Archivo General del Estado de Tabasco	Nicolas Bravo y Rovirosa Villahermosa, Tabasco	inventories, pamphlets, catalogs
Tamaulipas	Archivo General del Estado de Tamaulipas	Palacio de Gobierno Ciudad Victoria, Tamaulipas	inventories
	Archivo General del Poder Legislativo del Estado de Tamaulipas	Palacio de Gobierno Ciudad Victoria, Tamaulipas	inventories
Tlaxcala	Archivo General e Historico del Estado de Tlaxcala	Avenida Juarez 16, Tlaxcala, Tlaxcala	Not given
Veracruz	Archivo General del Estado de Veracruz	Biblioteca Central, Universidad Veracruzana, Zona Universitaria, Xalapa, Veracruz	inventories, card catalogs
Yucatan	Archivo General del Gobierno del Estado de Yucatan	Calle 65 por 60, Palacio de Gobierno Merida, Yucatan	inventories, guides, published catalogs
Zacatecas	Archivo Historico del Estado de Zacatecas	Exconvento de Guadalupe, Guadalupe, Zacatecas	inventories

RESEARCHING IN THE ARCHIVO GENERAL DE LA NACIÓN FROM THE UNITED STATES

Collection	FHL Film #	Internet Index	Published Indexes (see numbered notes at end of table)
Abasto y Panaderías		ARGENA	
Acordada		ARGENA	
Aguardiente de Caña		ARGENA	1, 2
Alcabalas		ARGENA	
Alcaldes Mayores		ARGENA	3
Alhóndigas		ARGENA	
Almacenes Reales		ARGENA	4
Archivo Histórico de Hacienda		ARGENA	5, 6
Arzobispos y Obispos		ARGENA	
Ayuntamientos		ARGENA	
Bandos		ARGENA	
Bienes de Comunidad		ARGENA	7, 8
Bienes de Difuntos	725338+ (10 rolls)	ARGENA	9

Collection	FHL Film #	Internet Index	Published Indexes (see numbered notes at end of table)
Bienes Nacionales		ARGENA	10
Bulas de la Santa Cruzada		ARGENA	
Caja Matriz Californias, 1582–1842	1857189+ (50 rolls)	ARGENA DRSW (partial)	
Caminos y Calzados		ARGENA	
Capellanías	1520908+ (118 rolls), 1563780+ (5 rolls)	ARGENA	
Cárceles y Presidios		ARGENA	
Casa de Moneda		ARGENA	
Censos		ARGENA	
Civil			
Clero Regular y Secular		ARGENA	12
Cofradías y Archicofradías		ARGENA	13
Colegios		ARGENA	14
Comisos		ARGENA	
Concurso de Calvo		ARGENA	
Concurso de Cotilla		ARGENA	
Concurso de Peñaloza		ARGENA	
Congregaciones		ARGENA	
Consolidación		ARGENA	
Consulado		ARGENA	
Correos			

Collection	FHL Film #	Internet Index	Published Indexes (see numbered notes at end of table)
Correspondencia de Diversas Autoridades		ARGENA	
Correspondencia de Virreyes, 1664–1820	1700907+ (129 rolls)	ARGENA	
Criminal		ARGENA	
Cultos Religiosos		ARGENA	
Derechos Parroquiales		ARGENA	
Desagüe		ARGENA	15
Diezmos		ARGENA	
Donativos y Préstamos		ARGENA	
Edictos de Inquisición		ARGENA	16
Epidemias		ARGENA	
Escribanos		ARGENA	
Expolios		ARGENA	
Factorías		ARGENA	
Filiaciones de Tucson, 1797–1817	1162420 Item 13		
Filipinas		ARGENA	17, 18
Fonseca y Urrutia			
Gallos		ARGENA	
General de Parte		ARGENA DRSW (partial)	
Historia, 1522–1822	1857411+ (81 rolls)	DSRW (partial)	19, 20
Historia: Notas Diplomáticas		ARGENA	
Hospital del Jesús, 1531–1860	1856649+ (540 rolls)	DRSW (partial)	

Collection	FHL Film #	Internet Index	Published Indexes (see numbered notes at end of table)
Hospitales		ARGENA	
Iglesias		ARGENA	
Impresos Oficiales			
Indiferente de Guerra		ARGENA	
Indios, 1574–1821	1857316+ (43 rolls)	ARGENA	
Industria y Comercio		ARGENA	
Infidencias		ARGENA	
Inquisición		ARGENA DRSW (partial)	21
Intendencias		ARGENA	
Intestados, 1704–1898	1507357+ (208 rolls)	ARGENA	
Jesuitas		ARGENA DRSW (partial)	
Cuentas			
Judicial		ARGENA	
Lotería		ARGENA	
Marina		ARGENA	
Matrimonios		ARGENA	
Media Anata		ARGENA	
Mercados		ARGENA	
Mercedes		ARGENA	22
Minería		ARGENA	
Misiones	1521015+ (13 rolls)	ARGENA DRSW (partial)	
Montepíos		ARGENA	
Obras Pías		ARGENA	
Obras Públicas		ARGENA	
Oficio de Hurtado		ARGENA	
Oficio de Soria		ARGENA	

Collection	FHL Film #	Internet Index	Published Indexes (see numbered notes at end of table)
Oficios Vendibles		ARGENA	
Operaciones de Guerra			
Ordenanzas		ARGENA	
Padrones	1520343+ (39 rolls)	ARGENA	23
Parcialidades		ARGENA	
Peajes			
Pensiones		ARGENA	
Policía y Empedrados			
Pólizas			
Pólvora		ARGENA	
Propios y Arbitrios		ARGENA	
Protomedicato		ARGENA	
Provincias Internas		DRSW ARGENA	24
Pulques		ARGENA	
Real Acuerdo		ARGENA	
Real Audiencia		ARGENA	
Real Caja			
Real Fisco de la Inquisición		ARGENA	
Real Hacienda			
Real Junta		ARGENA	25
Reales Cedulas		ARGENA	26, 27
Reales Ordenes			
Registro de Fianzas, Depósitos, y Obligaciones		ARGENA	
Renta del Tobaco			

Collection	FHL Film #	Internet Index	Published Indexes (see numbered notes at end of table)
Ríos y Acequias		ARGENA	
Salinas		ARGENA	
Subdelegados			
Tobaco		ARGENA	
Templos y Conventos			
Tempora-lidades		ARGENA	28
Tierras	1563722+ (2057 rolls)	ARGENA	29
Títulos y Despachos de Guerra		ARGENA	30
Tribunal de Cuentas			
Tributos		ARGENA	
Universidad			
Vínculos y Mayorazgos		ARGENA	
Colección del Instituto de Estudios y Documentos Históricos, AC			
Colección de Documentos para la Historia de México		ARGENA	

PUBLISHED INDEXES

1. Patricia Luna Marez, *Guía del ramo de aguardiente de caña en el Archivo General de la Nación* ([Mexico]: Biblioteca Nacional de Antropologia e Historia, 1980).

2. Guillermina Ramírez Montes, *Ramo aguardiente de caña* (Mexico, D.F.: Dirección de Difusión y Publicaciones del Archivo General de la Nación, 1980).

3. María Elena Bribiesca Sumano, Elisa Cruz Domínguez, and Silvia Ojeda Jiménez, *Indice del ramo alcaldes mayores* (Mexico, D.F.: Archivo General de la Nación, 1980).

4. Patricia Luna Marez, *Guía del ramo de almacenes reales en el Archivo General de la Nación* ([Mexico]: Biblioteca Nacional de Antropología e Historia I.N.A.H., 1980).

5. Esperanza Rodríguez de Lebrija, *Guia Documental del Archivo Histórico de Hacienda*, 3 vol.s. (Mexico, D.F.: Archivo General de la Nación, 1981). FHL book 972 B4a no. 61.

6. Esperanza Rodríguez de Lebrija, Indice analítico de la guía del Archivo Histórico de Hacienda (Mexico, D.F.: Archivo General de la Nación, 1976). FHL fiche 6030618.

7. Alberto López Guerrero, *Indice del ramo bienes de comunidad* (Mexico, D.F.: Archivo General de la Nación, 1979).

8. Miguel Angel Fernández Delgado and Gerardo Blas, *Indice de la encuesta de bienes de comunidad hecha en 1704 que se encuentra en el Archivo General de la Nación: Indios,* vol. 97, 421 folios (Mexico: El Colegio de Mexico, Centro de Estudios Históricos, 1999).

9. Claudio Jiménez Vizcarra, *Indice del Archivo del Juzgado General de Bienes de Difuntos de la Nueva Galicia, siglos XVI y XVII* (Mexico, D.F.: Instituto Nacional de Antropología e Historia, 1978).

10. Jorge I Rubio Mañé, *Indice del archivo de cartas de bienes nacionales* (Mexico) Microform 7 reels.

11. Beatriz Arteaga Garza and Roberto Villaseñor Espinosa, *Indice del ramo de Californias*, 2 vol.s. (Mexico, D.F.: Archivo General de la Nación, 1977). FHL book 972 B4a no. 3.

12. Archivo General de la Nación (Mexico), *Indice del ramo clero regular y secular* (Mexico: Departamento de Publicaciones del Archivo General de la Nación, 1978).

13. Enrique B. Gonzalez Ponce, *Catalogo del ramo de cofradias y archicofradías* (Mexico, D.F.: Archivo General de la Nación, 1977). FHL book 972 B4a no. 4.

14. Archivo General de la Nación (Mexico), *Indice del ramo colegios* (Mexico: Archivo General de la Nación, 1977).

15. Manuel Carrera Stampa, *Guía del ramo de desagüe*, 2nd ed. (Mexico: Archivo General de la Nación, 1981).

16. María Teresa Esquivel Otea, *Indice del ramo edictos de la Santa y general inquisición* (Mexico: Departamento de Publicaciones del Archivo General de la Nación, 1978).

17. Archivo General de la Nación (Mexico), *Indice del ramo Filipinas* (Mexico: Archivo General de la Nación, 1977).

18. Archivo General de la Nación (Mexico), *Guía del ramo Filipinas,* 2nd ed. (Mexico: Departamento de Publicaciones del Archivo General de la Nación, 1980).

19. Celia Medina Mondragón, *Ramo historia* (Mexico: Archivo General de la Nación, 1981).

20. Guillermina Ramírez Montes, *Catálogos de documentos de arte, Archivo General de la Nación, Mexico: ramo, historia* (Mexico: Universidad Nacional Autónoma de Mexico: Instituto de Investigaciones Estéticas, 1998).

21. Adriana Rodríguez Delgado, *Catálogo de mujeres del ramo inquisición del Archivo General de la Nación,* 1st ed. (Mexico, D.F. : Instituto Nacional de Antropología e Historia, 2000).

22. Mario Colin, *Indice de documentos relativos a los pueblos del estado de Mexico: Ramo de Mercedes del Archivo General de la Nacion* (Toluca, Mexico: Biblioteca Enciclopédica del Estado de Mexico, 1967). FHL book 972.52 R2cm.

23. Archivo General de la Nación (Mexico), *Indice de padrones de Mexico,* FHL book 972 X22m.

24. Archivo General de la Nación (Mexico), *Indice del ramo de provincias internas,* 2 vol.s (Mexico, D.F.: Archivo General de la Nación, 1900). FHL book 972 A3ma.

25. María Elena Bribiesca Sumano and Efraín Vera Núñez, *Indice del ramo de real Junta* (Mexico, D.F.: Departamento de Publicaciones del Archivo General de la Nación, 1980).

26. Secretaría del Virreinato Real Audiencia, *Catalogo de cedulas reales* (Salt Lake: Filmed by the Genealogical Society of Utah, 1989). FHL Films 1521118+, 7 films total.

27. Archivo General de la Nación (Mexico), *Indice del ramo de reales cedulas* (Mexico: Secretaria de Gobernación, Archivo General de la Nación, 1967). FHL book 972 A3me.

28. Archivo General de la Nación (Mexico), *Indice del ramo de Temporalidades* (Mexico, D.F.: El Archivo, [197--?]). FHL book 972 A5, FHL Film 1149545 Item 6.

29. Enrique Méndez Martínez, *Indice de documentos relativos a los pueblos del estado de Puebla: Ramo Tterras del Archivo General de la Nación* (Mexico: SEP, Instituto Nacional de Antropología e Historia, 1979). FHL book 972.48 R2.

30. Maria Elena Bribiesco Sumano, *Guia del ramo titulos y despachos de guerra* (Mexico: Archivo General de la Nación, 1977). FHL book 972 B4a no. 9.

INTERNET SITES FOR MEXICAN GENEALOGY

GENERAL HISPANIC GENEALOGY WEBSITES

- **www.alsgenealogy.com**—A starting point for Hispanic genealogy
- **www.elanillo.com**—Hispanic genealogy ring
- **www.cyndislist.com/hispanic.htm**—Hispanic, Central and South America, and West Indies index
- **www.hispanicgenealogy.com**—Hispanic Genealogy Center
- **www.rootsweb.com/~bwo**—Books We Own (a look-up resource for international genealogical research)
- **www.lasculturas.com/lib/libGenealogy.php**—Excellent list of Hispanic genealogy links
- **www.hispanicgs.com**—The Hispanic Genealogical Society Web page
- **www.members.aol.com/shhar**—Society for Hispanic Historical and Ancestral Research
- **www.genealogia-es.com**—Spain GenWeb project
- **www.cubagenweb.org**—While emphasizing Cuba this sites references many general materials about Spanish genealogy

GENERAL ARCHIVES AND HISTORY WEBSITES

- **www.hartford-hwp.com/archives/index.html**—World History Archives
- **www1.lanic.utexas.edu/la/region/library**—Links to libraries and archives in Latin America
- **www.uidaho.edu/special-collections/latam.html**—A list of repositories of primary sources
- **www.bne.es/**—National Library in Madrid, Spain
- **www.lanic.utexas.edu/project/tavera/espana/indias/indias.html**—Archivo General de Indias (general description and inventory, not an official website)
- **www.lanic.utexas.edu/project/tavera/espana/simancas.html**—Archivo General de Simancas (general description and inventory, but not an official website)
- **www.lanic.utexas.edu/project/tavera/espana/nacional.html**—Archivo Historico Nacional (general description and inventory, not an official website)
- **www.aer.es**—Official Spanish national archives site with excellent index to collections in the National Archives of Spain

MEXICAN AND MEXICAN AMERICAN WEBSITES

- **www1.lanic.utexas.edu/la/Mexico**—Links to websites of Mexican archives
- **www.rootsweb.com/~mexwgw**—Mexican GenWeb project
- **www.whowhere.lycos.com/wwphone/world.html**—General information about Mexico, including an online phone book
- **http://members.aol.com/tejasjj/baptism.html**—Index to the Baptismal Registers of Revilla 1751–1803
- **www.geocities.com/Heartland/Prairie/6728**—History and genealogy of Nuevo Leon
- **www.rootsweb.com/~mextam**—History of Tamualipas including chronology and founding families
- **http://archives.nmsu.edu/rghc/contents/contents.html**—Rio Grande Historical Collection at New Mexico State University at Las Cruces; has extensive New Mexico, Chihuahua, and Durango, materials including the microfilms of and index to the Archivo Historico del Arzobispado de Durango
- **www.lib.panam.edu/info/speccoll/lrgv.html**—Rio Grande Valley Historical Collection
- **www.catolicos.com/diocesismexico.htm**—Links to Catholic archdioceses and dioceses websites
- **http://maxpages.com/ourlostfamily**—Research addresses, phone numbers and fees for ordering birth, marriage, and death records from the Mexican Civil Register State Archives and other genealogical information
- **http://members.tripod.com/~GaryFelix/index1.htm**—Historical and surname information about colonial Mexico
- **http://genealogypro.com/directories/Mexico.html**—Hire professional genealogists for Mexican research
- **http://genforum.genealogy.com/mexico**—Queries regarding Mexican research
- **http://members.aol.com/mrosado007/mxstarc.htm**—Mexican State Archives addresses
- **www.genealogy.com/00000379.html?Welcome=1035493984**—Mexican genealogy how-to guide
- **www.infowest.com/personal/l/lplatt**—Purchase surname histories and other books from the Institute of Genealogy and History for Latin America
- **http://members.aol.com/mrosado007/mxcivreg.htm**—Addresses of Mexican civil registrars
- **www.vsalgs.org/stnemgenealogy**—History and genealogy of south Texas and northeast Mexico

BIBLIOGRAPHY

Archivo de Simancas. *Secretaria de guerra, hojas de servicios de América*. Valladolid : Patronato Nacional de Archivos Historicos, 1958.

Bravo Ugarte, José. *Diócesis y obispos de la Iglesia Méxicana (1519–1965)*. México: México, Editorial Jus, 1965.

"Bibliografía del Notariado en España." In *Estudios históricos y documentos de los archivos de Protocolos*, 195–98 Barcelona: Colegio Notarial de Barcelona, 1974.

Bowman, Peter Boyd. *Indice geobiográfico de más de 56 mil pobladores de la América hispana*, 2 vols. Mexico: Fondo de Cultura Económica, 1985. Volume one includes 1493 through 1519, while volume two includes 1520 through 1539.

Chavez, Angelico. *Archives of the Archdiocese of Santa Fe, 1678–1900*. Publications of the Academy of the American Franciscan History, Bibliographical Series, vol. 3. Washington, D.C.: Academy of American Franciscan History, 1957.

Church of Jesus Christ of Latter-day Saints. *Resource Papers, Series H. Major Genealogical Record Sources in Mexico. PRGS0717 (English) and PRGS0717SP (Spanish)*.

———. "Latin American and Iberian Family and Local History." *World Conference On Records*. Vol. 9. Salt Lake City, UT, 1980.

Coleccion diplomatica de varios papeles antiguos y modernos sobre dispensas matrimoniales. Imprenta de Ibarra: Madrid, 1809. (FHL#0908241).

Covington, Paula H., ed. *Latin America and the Caribbean: A Critical Guide to Research Sources*. Series: Bibliographies and Indexes in Latin America and Caribbean Studies, No. 2. 1992.

Etchegaray, Ignacio Narro and Martha Durón Jiménez, *Diccionario biográfico de Saltillo*. Saltillo: Archivo Municipal de Saltillo, 1995.

Galindo Mendoza, A., M. Sp. S. *Parroquias y vicarias fijas de la iglesia Méxicana*. Tijuana, B.C.: Vicario Apostolico de Tijuana, B.C., 1961.

Galindo Mendoza, P. Alfredo, M. Sp. S. *Apuntes geográficos y estadísticos de la Iglesia Católica en México*. México, D.F.: Administración de la Revista "la Cruz," 1945.

Garcia-Carraffa, Alberto. *Enciclopedia heráldica y genealógica Hispano-Americana*, 88 vols. Madrid: Garcia-Carraffa, 1920–67.

Garcia de Miranda, Enriqueta and Zaida Falcon de Gyves. *Nuevo atlas porrua de la Republica Mexicana*. Mexico, D.F. : Editorial Porrua, 1980.

Gazetteer of México, Volumes I & II. 3rd ed. Washington, D.C.: Defense Mapping Agency, 1992.

Gerhard, Peter. *A Guide to the Historical Geography of New Spain*. Cambridge [U.K]: Cambridge University Press, 1972.

———. *The North Frontier of New Spain.* Norman, OK: University of Oklahoma Press, 1982.

———. *The Southeast Frontier of New Spain.* Norman, OK: University of Oklahoma Press, 1993.

Gomez Canedo, Lino. *Los archivos de la historia de America, periodo colonial espanola.* 2 vols. Instituto Panamericano de Geografia e Historia, Comision de Historia. Publicacion Num. 225. Mexico City: Commission de Historia, 1961.

Gonzalez Salas, Carlos, and Fidel Zorilla. *Diccionario biográfico de Tamaulipas* (Ciudad Victoria: Universidad de Tamaulipas, 1984).

Greenleaf, Richard E., and Michael C. Meyer. *Research in Mexican Hispanic Topics, Methodology, Sources, and a Practical Guide to Field Research.* Lincoln: University of Nebraska Press, 1973. One of the best guides for Mexican and borderlands research.

Guerra, Raul J. "How to Use and Understand Diocesan Marriage Investigations and Records of Colonial Mexico." In *1992 Buscando Nuestras Raices Seminar: Intermediate and Advanced Strategies.* Huntington Beach, CA: Society for Hispanic Historic and Ancestral Research, 1992.

Guerra, Raul J, Nadine M. Vasquez, and Baldomero Vela, Jr. *Index to the Marriage Investigations of the Diocese of Guadalajara, Provinces of Coahuila, Nuevo Leon, Nuevo Santander, Texas, 1653–1750.* Edinburgh, TX: University of Texas at Pan America, 1989.

———. *Index to the Marriage Investigations of the Diocese of Guadalajara, Provinces of Coahuila, Nuevo Leon, Nuevo Santander, Texas, 1750– 1776.* Edinburgh, TX: University of Texas at Pan America, date unknown.

Guía de fuentes para la historia de Ibero-América conservados en España. 2 vols. Madrid: Direccion General de Archivos y Bibliotecas, 1966.

Hansen, Holly T. *The Directory of North American Railroads, Associations, Societies, Archives, Libraries, Museums and Their Collections.* Published by the author, 1999.

Herrera Huerta, Juan Manuel, and Vincente San Vicente Tello. *Archivo General de la Nacion, Mexico, guia general.* Mexico, D.F.: Archivo General de la Nacion, 1990.

Herrero Mediavila, Victor, and Lolita Rosa Aguayo Hayle. *Indice biográfico de España, Portugal e Ibero-América.* New York: K.G. Sur, 1990.

Iglesia Católica. *Directorio eclesiástico de la República Mexicana.* ed. Piñeyro Jorge Durán. México: La Arquidiócesis, 1985.

Lane, (Sister) M. Claude. *Catholic Archives of Texas: History and Preliminary Inventory.* Houston: Sacred Heart Dominican College, 1961.

Lo Buglio, Rudecinda. "The Archives of Northwestern Mexico." In *Latin American and Iberian Family and Local History.* Vol. 9, *World Conference on Records.* Salt Lake City: Genealogical Society of Utah, 1980.

Magdaleno, Ricardo. *Catálogo XX del Archivo General de Simancas, títulos de Indias.* Valladolid: Patronato Nacional de Archivos Historicos, 1954.

Millares Carlo, Agustín. *Tratado de paleografia española.* 3 vols. Madrid: Espasa-Calpe, S. A.: 1983.

Mogrobejo, Endica de. *Diccionario hispanoamericano de heráldica, onomástica y genealogía/por Endika de Mogrobejo, con la colaboración de Aitziber, Irantzu y Garikoitz de Mogrobejo-Zabala.* Bilbao, Vizcaya: Editorial Mogrobejo-Zabala, 1995–2001.

Muñoz de San Pedro, Miguel. *Reflejos de siete siglos de vida estremeña en cien documentos notariales.* Cáceres, 1962).

Neagles, James. *U.S. Military Records.* Orem, UT: Ancestry, 1984.

Naylor, Thomas H., and Charles W. Polzer. *Northern New Spain: A Research Guide.* Tucson, Arizona: The University of Arizona Press, 1981.

Nuevo atlas porrua de la Republica Mexicana. Mexico, D.F.: Editorial Porrua, 1980.

Pérez Fernández del Castillo, Bernardo. *Derecho Notarial.* 2nd ed. Mexico, D.F.: Editorial Porrua S.A., 1983.

Platt, Lyman D. *Una guía genealógico-histórico de Latinoamérica.* Salt Lake City: Acoma, 1977.

———. *Latin American Census Records.* Baltimore: Genealogical Publishing Company, 1998.

———. *Hispanic Surnames.* Baltimore: Genealogical Publishing Company, 1997

———. *Serie de Investigaciones Genealógicas del IGHL.* Salt Lake City: Instituto Genealógico Histórico Latinoamericano, 1991. Volume 2. *Mexico, Guía General: Divisiones Políticas.* Volume 3. *Mexico, Guía General: Divisiones eclesiásticas.* Volume 4. *Mexico, Guía de Investigaciones Genealógicas.*

———. *A Genealogical Historical Guide to Latin America.* Detroit: Gale Publishing Co, 1978.

Putney-Beers, Henry. *Spanish and Mexican Records of the American Southwest.* Tuscon: University of Arizona Press, 1979.

Querexteta, Jaime de. *Diccionario onomástico y heráldico vasco.* Bilbao: La Gran Enciclopedia Vasca, 1970–1975.

Robinson, David J. *Finding Aids to the Microfilmed Manuscript Collection of the Genealogical Society of Utah: Preliminary Survey of the Mexican Collection.* Salt Lake City: University of Utah Press, 1978.

———. *Finding Aids to the Microfilmed Manuscript Collection of the Genealogical Society of Utah: Research Inventory of the Mexican Collection of Colonial Parish Records.* Salt Lake City: University of Utah Press, 1980.

Rodriguez Ochoa, Patricia. *Guia general de los archivos estatales y municipales de Mexico.* Mexico, D.F.: Sistema Nacional de Archivos, 1988.

Romero, José A., S.J., and Juan Alvarez Mejía, S.J. *Directorio de la Iglesia en Mexico.* México, D.F., La Buena, 1952.

Rio Grande Historical Collections. *Los Archivos Históricos del Arzobispado de Durango, Mexico.* Las Cruces, New Mexico: New Mexico State University Library, 2003. CD-Rom.

Ryskamp, George R. *Tracing Your Hispanic Heritage.* Riverside, California: Hispanic Family Research, 1984.

———. *Finding Your Hispanic Roots.* Baltimore: Genealogical Publishing Company, 1997.

Ugarte, José Bravo. *Diócesis y Obispos de la Iglesia Mexicana (1519–1965), Colección Mexico Heroico,* no. 39. Mexico: Editorial Jus, 1965.

Veyna, Angelina F. "It Is My Last Wish That . . . A Look at Colonial Nuevo Mexicanas Through Their Testaments," in *Building With Our Hands: New Directions in Chicana Studies,* ed. Adela de la Torre and Beatriz M. Pesquera. Berkeley: University of California Press, 1993. 91–108.

Vollmar, Edward R., S.J. *The Catholic Church in America: An Historical Bibliography.* New Brunswick, NJ: Scarecrow Press, 1956.

INDEX

M

maps
> of dioceses
>> boundaries (1972), 57
>> colonial, 127
> of Mexico
>> 1767, 126
>> 1788, 131
>> 1824, 58
>> modern, 10

marriage, impediments to, 44

marriage records
> civil registration, 28, 30–32
> of dispensation, 81
> example of, 31
> extraction forms for, 177
> parish, 43–47

mass (Catholic), as referred to in records, 51

memorial card, example of, 5

Mexican Vital Records Index, 53

Mexico
> archives, list of, 181–83
> colonial
>> geography of, 132
>> races in, 138
> history of, timeline, 165–68
> maps of
>> 1767, 126
>> 1788, 131
>> 1824, 58
>> modern, 10
> political divisions of, 55–56

Mexico: Guia general, divisiones eclesiasticas, 128

microfilm
> of border crossing records, 110, 112, 113, 116–17
> of civil registration records, 13–17
> of diocese records, 60
> of parish records, 13–17
> ordering from Family History Library, 15–16

migration periods, ix–x

military records
> colonial, 136
> as home source, 5
> of service (U.S.), 119, 121
> WWI draft registration (U.S.), 119–20

Montejano Hilton, Maria Luz, 128

municipal archives, 72–74

N

national archives, 74–75

naturalization records
> as home source, 2
> in United States, 119–20

New Mexico border crossing records, 113

newspapers, as home source, 7

North Frontier of New Spain, The, 132

notarial records
> colonial, 134–36
> locating, 94–96
> organization of, 88–91
> overview of, 87–88
> types of, 95
> wills, 92–93

Nuevo atlas Porrúa de la república mexicana, 62

O

occupational records, as home source, 7

ordinations to the priesthood (records), 81–82

P

parish records
> of baptisms, 41–43
> census, 82
> of confirmations, 43
> of deaths, 46, 48–50
> finding with International Genealogical Index, 50
> format of, 38–39
> information found in, 52
> of marriages, 43–47
> on microfilm, 13–17
> reading, 37–38
> in United States, 121–22

passport, example of, 4

pension records, railroad (U.S.), 121

photographs, as home source, 2

Platt, Lyman D., 58, 67, 81, 102, 128, 132

priesthood ordinations (records), 81–82

protocols, 88–91

published indexes, 191–92

R

race, in colonial Mexico, 136, 138

railroad pension records (U.S.), 121

ABOUT THE AUTHORS

GEORGE R. RYSKAMP

George R. Ryskamp, J.D., AG, teaches Latin American and southern European family history and the use of American legal documents and concepts in family history at Brigham Young University, where he also serves as director of the Center for Family History and Genealogy and the Immigrant Ancestor Project. He is a fellow of the Utah Genealogical Association, a Miembro Académico of the Academia Americana de Genealogía, and a corresponding member of the Academia Real Matritense de Genealogía y Heráldica.

PEGGY H. RYSKAMP

Peggy H. Ryskamp has done Hispanic family history in the United States and on numerous trips to Spain and Mexico for more than twenty years. Coauthor of *A Student's Guide to Mexican-American Genealogy*, a speaker at local and national conferences, and former coeditor of the *Genealogical Journal*, she juggles client work and writing.